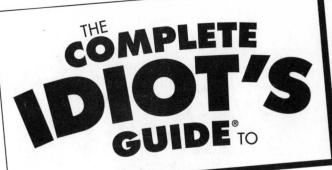

THE COMPLETE IDIOT'S GUIDE® TO

Financial Aid for College

Second Edition

by David Rye, M.B.A.

ALPHA

A member of Penguin Group (USA) Inc.

To my best friend and wife, Marcia, who made sure I was fed and watered while I wrote this book. You dealt with my episodes of stress and frustration throughout the process and I love you more than ever for all the support you gave me.

ALPHA BOOKS

Published by the Penguin Group

Penguin Group (USA) Inc., 375 Hudson Street, New York, New York 10014, USA

Penguin Group (Canada), 90 Eglinton Avenue East, Suite 700, Toronto, Ontario M4P 2Y3, Canada (a division of Pearson Penguin Canada Inc.)

Penguin Books Ltd., 80 Strand, London WC2R 0RL, England

Penguin Ireland, 25 St. Stephen's Green, Dublin 2, Ireland (a division of Penguin Books Ltd.)

Penguin Group (Australia), 250 Camberwell Road, Camberwell, Victoria 3124, Australia (a division of Pearson Australia Group Pty. Ltd.)

Penguin Books India Pvt. Ltd., 11 Community Centre, Panchsheel Park, New Delhi—110 017, India

Penguin Group (NZ), 67 Apollo Drive, Rosedale, North Shore, Auckland 1311, New Zealand (a division of Pearson New Zealand Ltd.)

Penguin Books (South Africa) (Pty.) Ltd., 24 Sturdee Avenue, Rosebank, Johannesburg 2196, South Africa

Penguin Books Ltd., Registered Offices: 80 Strand, London WC2R 0RL, England

Copyright © 2008 by David Rye, M.B.A.

International Standard Book Number: 978-1-59257-746-0
Library of Congress Catalog Card Number: 2007935867

10   09   08   8   7   6   5   4   3   2   1

Interpretation of the printing code: The rightmost number of the first series of numbers is the year of the book's printing; the rightmost number of the second series of numbers is the number of the book's printing. For example, a printing code of 08-1 shows that the first printing occurred in 2008.

Printed in the United States of America

Note: This publication contains the opinions and ideas of its author. It is intended to provide helpful and informative material on the subject matter covered. It is sold with the understanding that the author and publisher are not engaged in rendering professional services in the book. If the reader requires personal assistance or advice, a competent professional should be consulted.

The author and publisher specifically disclaim any responsibility for any liability, loss, or risk, personal or otherwise, which is incurred as a consequence, directly or indirectly, of the use and application of any of the contents of this book.

Most Alpha books are available at special quantity discounts for bulk purchases for sales promotions, premiums, fund-raising, or educational use. Special books, or book excerpts, can also be created to fit specific needs.

For details, write: Special Markets, Alpha Books, 375 Hudson Street, New York, NY 10014.

Publisher: *Marie Butler-Knight*
Editorial Director: *Mike Sanders*
Managing Editor: *Billy Fields*
Acquisitions Editor: *Michele Wells*
Development Editor: *Julie Bess*
Senior Production Editor: *Janette Lynn*

Copy Editor: *Amy Lepore*
Cartoonist: *Shannon Wheeler*
Cover Designer: *Kurt Owens*
Book Designer: *Trina Wurst*
Indexer: *Joan Green*
Layout: *Chad Dressler*

Contents at a Glance

Contents

Appendixes

Forewords

David Rye invites you to participate in the college financial aid application process. Quite frankly, you're an idiot if you don't. Millions of Americans do it annually, and so can you with a little help. In this insightful and practical book, David Rye illuminates what it takes to apply for and get the financial aid your kid needs for college. The book is filled with how-to examples and solid advice to avoid the pitfalls that are inherent in applying for financial aid. It begins by introducing you to what financial aid is all about and shows you how you can get in on the action, even if you don't think you qualify.

You'll learn how to estimate the amount of money you'll need for your kid's college education so that you'll know how much aid to apply for. And it doesn't end there. The author shows you where you can go and how to apply for literally thousands of college scholarships. The information you'll need to make it all happen is conveniently listed in the back of the book in a comprehensive directory and state-by-state listings of financial aid offices and agencies. This is the only book you'll need to learn how to apply for financial aid.

Dr. T. K. Nelson

Dr. Tim Nelson is a successful two-time entrepreneur, speaker, and student aid consultant. He is currently president of Western Publications.

The rapid increases in college tuition costs and a corresponding increase in student borrowing have created an $85 billion per year student loan industry that has transformed many college financial aid offices into businesslike operations designed to maximize a university's net revenue. Private student loans totaled some $17.3 billion in 2005–2006 and have grown at an annual average rate of 27 percent in the past five years, according to the College Board. They represented 20 percent of all educational borrowing in 2005–2006, compared with 4 percent a decade earlier.

Fully 55 percent of students receive some financial aid, at an average value of more than $6,000 a year. Most of the free money handed out to students is in the form of grants, which are awarded on the basis of need. The federal government doled out 4.8 million Pell Grants worth an average of $2,400 in 2006. And schools, mostly private colleges, dispense about $20 billion in aid, most of which was need-based.

A growing number of states and schools are also offering merit scholarships. Typically, these programs require that students maintain a B average. Many service and community groups, corporations, and foundations also hand out checks to students who, say, win an essay contest. Websites like www.fastweb.monster.com are good places to start searching for these opportunities.

The subsidized Stafford federal loan is available only to students who qualify as needy. Others can apply for an unsubsidized Stafford, which, unlike its subsidized cousin, starts accruing interest charges right away. But it has low variable interest rates. Students who need to borrow more than Stafford allows ($2,625 for freshmen, more for older students) should apply for a federally backed Perkins loan, which had a fixed interest rate of 5 percent in 2007. Parents with good credit can borrow from the federally insured PLUS program.

"Schools have incentives to partner with a loan provider in exactly the same way that a baseball stadium has an incentive to partner with either Coke or Pepsi," says Rick Hess of Education Policy Studies at the American Enterprise Institute. Deals can yield lower interest rates, eliminate fees, and offer more responsive customer service. In exchange, companies listed as preferred lenders reap the lion's share of a school's private loan business. The relationships between schools and lenders are under scrutiny and so is the role of college financial aid officers. Students and parents may assume that a college's financial aid officer may be biased toward their college, and might also have financial interests in the companies that provide private loans.

To apply for federal aid, families must fill out the Free Application for Federal Student Aid (www.fafsa.ed.gov). Many private colleges also require the similar Profile (profileonline.collegeboard.com). The information sources for this section are in the April 19, 2004 and April 23, 2007 editions of *U.S. News & World Report*.

So although it will cost lots of money to go to college (no surprise), with some time and effort you can find the necessary financial help. Plus, here's the kicker: even if you come out of college thousands of dollars in debt, it pays off in the long run.

So how do you get the $$$ you need? First, it takes time and effort. For many, the research and paperwork can be daunting and discouraging. You'll have to investigate a wide range of opportunities, collect and organize your family's financial data, maybe write an essay or two, and perhaps be interviewed. But always remember that the payoff is worth it. You will literally be well rewarded for your troubles. And *The Complete Idiot's Guide to Financial Aid for College, Second Edition*, will be a significant help. It offers clear instructions, state-by-state guidelines, insider tips, and steady reassurance. It even teaches you how to negotiate for a better financial aid package than the one you are offered.

Don't let the scarcity of funds in your own bank account deny you the opportunity for a better life. Your college career depends on finding the money you need—and with time and effort you will.

Good luck!

Marian Edelman Borden

Author of *Unbelievably Good Deals and Great Adventures That You Absolutely Can't Get Unless You're a Student* (Contemporary Books, 2001).

Introduction

Each year, colleges and universities routinely deliver the painful news of yet another tuition increase. At $35,000–$42,000, the average cost of a public institution is soaring. You'll pay at least $80,000 or more if your kid wants to go to a private institution. How are you going to pay for that education? Are you willing to bite the bullet and take drastic financial steps like selling your house to come up with the money you'll need to ensure your child's future? Fortunately, there are a number of alternative ways to fund your kid's education so that you won't have to jeopardize your own financial well-being.

This book explains it all in easy-to-understand terms. We show you not only how to plan for college expenses, but how to apply for grants, scholarships, and low-interest loans to pay for them. In this unique and comprehensive guide, you'll learn how to do everything that's required to get the money you need. We've even included the necessary forms. In addition, we'll show you how to …

◆ Pick colleges that offer the best financial aid packages.

◆ Plan ahead to improve your chances of receiving financial aid.

◆ Negotiate to get the best financial aid offer that you can.

◆ Take advantage of the tax laws to build a college savings plan.

◆ Find the best low-interest financial aid loan programs.

◆ Get your kids involved in the process so they'll appreciate college that much more.

The Complete Idiot's Guide to Financial Aid for College, Second Edition, takes you through the process step by step with lots of examples and explanations along the way; we want to get you the financial aid you deserve. You'll be amazed at how easy it is if you follow our advice. We encourage you to keep your son or daughter involved in the process from start to finish. In the end, your kids will have a better appreciation of what their college education is going to cost, and they'll study a lot harder to earn their degrees.

How to Use This Book

The chapters are laid out to guide you sequentially through the college financial aid application process. Treat each chapter as you would a stepping-stone. Read Chapter 1 and complete what it tells you to do, and then go on to the next steps in the subsequent chapters. The book is divided into five parts.

In **Part 1, "The Lowdown on Financial Aid,"** you'll learn what college financial aid is and about the different types of financial aid programs you can apply for. You'll also find the answers to many of the questions you have about funding your kid's college education.

Where does your kid want to go to college? In **Part 2, "Planning Is Everything,"** we'll show you how to get the most bang for your buck. In the process, you'll discover how to determine the amount of money to apply for when you estimate the cost of sending your kid to the college of his or her choice. We'll also show you how to get your kid involved in the application process right from the beginning so that he or she will have an appreciation of what it costs to go to college these days.

In **Part 3, "Seek and You Shall Find—Money,"** we show you how to first determine what financial aid is out there before you go looking for sources. We start off with federal aid programs and move on to state, corporate, and community aid sources. You'll also learn how to apply for low-cost educational loans and how to save money on taxes.

Filling out the college financial aid application forms is about as much fun as filling out your tax return forms. In **Part 4, "From Applications to Offers,"** we make it as painless as possible by giving you an overview of what's in a financial aid package and showing you how to properly fill out the forms. You'll also learn about financial aid offers, how to negotiate and appeal them, and what options you have if your application is rejected.

The chapters in **Part 5, "Okay, You're Accepted and You Have Aid: Now What?"** guide you through the ins and outs of finding additional financial aid—and having fun while doing it! For students, there's a wealth of advice on how to cut college expenses where it doesn't hurt so that they can have more to spend on the important stuff.

Watch for Road Signs

In addition to all the information and explanations we offer throughout this book, we include road signs to make it even easier and more interesting to learn about the financial aid process. There are four types of road signs to watch for. Each provides useful information in the form of short asides designed to help you focus on important ideas that deserve a little more attention. Here's what they look like:

Action Plan

Here we direct you to specific steps you may want to include in your financial aid action plan.

 Use the ideas in this Help box to simplify the task of applying for financial aid and to increase your chances of getting it.

Getting Started

This box gives you another perspective on the principles and practices covered in a chapter, and it defines less-familiar financial aid terms. By providing you with an example or some background, the Getting Started box helps you focus on the bigger picture.

 Warning

Mistakes are always possible when applying for financial aid. The Warning box alerts you to what might go wrong and how to minimize errors so that your application won't be turned down.

How to Use Our Directory of General Financial Aid Resources

Successfully qualifying for financial aid for your kid's college education is easier than you think. By the time you finish reading this book, you'll know everything you need to know to make it happen. And because we've included a comprehensive directory and a listing of state financial aid resources (alphabetical by state) in the back of the book, you won't have to waste your time trying to find additional financial aid reference books or websites to complete the process. The directory is full of information about how to contact federal and private financial aid sources; where to find aid for veterans, women, and minorities; which forms to fill out; and much more. In the appendix that follows, you can find all the important state offices and agencies listed by state. We wish you the best of luck in your quest for college financial aid!

Acknowledgments

To all the friends I made while writing this book, thanks for helping me along the way: Jim and Roey Fitzpatrick, Reta and Dan Rye, Maida Naden, Dale Mosier, Tim Nelson, Doug Hoagland, Kristi Rye, Kori and Dan Bowers, Marcia Miller, and Jack Washburn.

Special Thanks to the Technical Reviewer

The Complete Idiot's Guide to Financial Aid for College, Second Edition, was reviewed by an expert who double-checked the accuracy of what you'll learn here to help us ensure that this book gives you everything you need to know about college financial aid. Special thanks are extended to Alan Gerstle.

Trademarks

All terms mentioned in this book that are known to be or are suspected of being trademarks or service marks have been appropriately capitalized. Alpha Books and Penguin Group (USA) Inc. cannot attest to the accuracy of this information. Use of a term in this book should not be regarded as affecting the validity of any trademark or service mark.

Part 1

The Lowdown on Financial Aid

Paying for college can be a bummer, but don't let "sticker shock" stop your kids from attending the schools that are right for them. These chapters give you an overview of what financial aid is all about and get you started on seeking the scholarships, loans, grants, and tuition money you need.

What's Financial Aid All About?

In This Chapter

◆ Discovering what the financial aid process is all about

◆ Learning what types of financial aid are available to you

◆ Identifying scholarship assistance companies that make fraudulent claims

Financing education is not a pleasant topic. Most parents probably wish that it weren't a consideration at all. Unfortunately, each year many students face limited choices because of the lack of financial planning for college. In order to best prepare for the future, families need to understand what it costs to go to college and what financial aid is available to them.

Financial aid makes up the difference between what a family can afford and what it will cost to send a son or daughter (or both!) to the college of their choice. The belief is that students who can't afford the full cost of education should still have the chance to go. In the past, financial aid was synonymous with grants and scholarships, also known as "gift aid." Today, education loans are the main source of financial aid. The recent shift in financial aid, from grants to loans, has raised much confusion and concern.

College graduates may be required to pay off the cost of their education for many years after graduation. Unfortunately, there doesn't seem to be much hope for change in the near future. It isn't just students who have been forced to borrow. Parents are also borrowing money to meet their share of the cost.

Where's the Money Coming From?

Families trying to finance rising college costs have many questions. What about financial aid? Is there money for everyone? If not, who will receive whatever assistance is available? If a family isn't eligible for much financial aid, what kinds of planning will help meet the rising costs of higher education? As you can see, it's important that families develop a financial plan for college costs.

More and more students are unable to attend the college of their choice because their families haven't planned for financing their college costs. Perhaps you had the foresight to set up a special college education savings account when your kids were young. Maybe you didn't! Who else can help you pay college expenses? Fortunately, there are lots of other sources of education funds out there.

Uncle Sam's Contribution

Uncle Sam is the largest source of need-based aid. Most of the aid is made available through the U.S. Department of Education. Since the federal government is the largest source of student aid, it pays to know all you can about its major programs. The Department of Education provides aid primarily through grant programs in which students are awarded "free" money to apply toward tuition or federally subsidized low-interest loans.

The Federal Aid Umbrella

In recent years, the federal government has increased the amount of available loan money but decreased the amount of money for grants. The need to increase spending on educational programs across the board is one of the few programs politicians of both parties can agree on. Since the sources of federal funds are constantly changing, get the latest copy of *The Student's Guide: Federal Financial Aid Programs* by calling 1-800-4-FEDAID (1-800-433-3243). It's free and lists all current federal financial aid programs. Also be aware that eligibility for various types of federal aid can change from year to year. Just because you didn't qualify for a program last year doesn't mean you won't make the cut this year.

State Coffers

State funds for financial aid vary widely between the states, and there are often restrictions. To qualify, you typically have to be a resident of the state. States go through annual cycles of generosity and stinginess depending on how well their financial year is going. So it's impossible to predict how much aid you might be able to get from year to year. Check the newspapers for new legislation that might affect funding in the state or states where your potential college choices are located.

Hidden College Funds

School aid, which is often called institutional aid, can come directly from a state college in the form of need-based or non–need-based dollars. Any amount of financial assistance provided to you by a college will depend on the individual school's policies. This money includes everything from *merit scholarships* for athletic, academic, or special achievement to scholarships earmarked for specific fields of study, such as nursing.

In the last few years, hundreds of millions of dollars in endowments have been flowing into colleges. Some of this endowment money has been earmarked for scholarships.

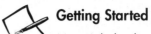

Getting Started

Merit scholarships are awarded to students based on their individual merit rather than their financial need. Merit could be based on academic achievement, athletic capabilities, or a range of other distinctions that are considered important to the institution.

Private Sources

Private sources of financial aid come from community associations, businesses, interest groups, and other organizations. Funds from these sources generally come in the form of scholarships or loans. Be prepared to do some legwork to find private source money. However, it can be well worth your while. Many employers help put students through college by participating in *cooperative education programs*, in which students alternate school semesters with work semesters. Not only does this provide your kids with a chance to build their professional skills, it also helps finance their education. Most of the employers that participate in cooperative education programs offer students flexible work hours to accommodate their class schedules.

Types of Financial Aid

Financial aid consists of three kinds of assistance: grants and scholarships, work-study loan programs, and student loans. Grants and scholarships are only a small part of the available funds. *Work-study programs* give students the chance to earn money working part-time while they're in school. There are a number of government-sponsored, low-interest loans to consider, and these are covered in Chapter 15. Most financial aid comes in the form of student loans.

> **Getting Started**
>
> In **cooperative education programs,** students alternate semesters of work and study. **Work-study programs** provide part-time jobs for undergraduate and graduate students with financial need, allowing them to earn money to help pay education expenses. They are also known as federal work-study (FWS) programs because they are sponsored by the federal government, which makes them different from co-op programs. Co-op work-study programs are usually sponsored by private organizations.

Grants Are Great

Grants do not have to be repaid and are need based. Pell Grants are need-based grants of up to $2,340 funded by the federal government and are available only to undergraduate students. Supplemental Education Opportunity Grants are campus-based federal grants that are based on financial need and provide awards up to $4,000 per year.

Make sure you read Chapter 9, which provides details on how to apply for grants. Grants are a special form of scholarship. Chapter 11, deals specifically with how and where to apply for scholarships.

Scholarships Are Everywhere

Some students receive merit scholarships for outstanding achievement, athletic skill, special talents, or their academic record. Such scholarships are awarded without regard to a family's ability to pay. The idea is that outstanding accomplishments, inside and outside the classroom, deserve recognition. However, less than 5 percent of all financial aid is in the form of merit scholarships.

> **Getting Started** _____
>
> What's the difference between grants, scholarships, and loans? Loans have to be repaid, whereas grants and scholarships do not. Grants are usually awarded on the basis of need. Scholarships are usually awarded to students who demonstrate or show potential for distinction, either academically or in a specific skill such as music or athletics.

Athletic Scholarships

Colleges offer athletic scholarships to attract certain students to play for specific teams. Many parents and students are unrealistic about the availability of these well-publicized awards. Athletic scholarships are quite rare, and only unusually gifted athletes receive them. Unfortunately, coaches in high school and athletic leagues often raise unrealistic expectations about the availability of athletic scholarships.

Merit Scholarships

Scholarships are generally given to students with a mix of talents. A student with unique skills in a specific area, such as music, might find a college interested in recruiting him or her through a merit-based scholarship that recognizes the academic credentials as well as the personal qualifications of the student. Although there are fewer academic scholarships than athletic ones, the number of academic scholarships has been steadily increasing over the last five years. The bottom line is that any scholarship is tough to win. In reality, all colleges look at the "total you" when they consider you for a scholarship. Can you make it academically? Do you have demonstrated leadership qualifications? Do you have special skills (athletic or musical, for example) that you can apply while you attend college?

> **Action Plan** _____
>
> Check out the scholarship search at www.collegeview.com to locate possible scholarship opportunities. Also see the "Scholarships, Grants, and Fellowships" section in Appendix B.

Low-Interest Loans

Federal student loans are one way to pay for college. Although the loans must be repaid with interest, they have deferment options and favorable terms for repayment, which typically does not start until after graduation. These loans generally have low interest rates and are not based on your credit history.

Federal Direct Loan Program

Many schools are now participating in the Federal Direct Loan Program. In this program, schools rather than banks act as the lending institutions and the federal government supplies the funds. Some students prefer the Federal Direct Loan Program to the traditional Federal Family Education Loan Program (FFELP) because it seems to simplify the process and speed up the disbursement of funds.

Family Education Loans

The majority of federal student loans are funded through the FFELP. This program differs from the Federal Direct Loan Program in that the school is not the lender; rather, private lenders, such as banks, credit unions, and other financial institutions, supply and manage the loan funds. The federal government guarantees the loans against default to help keep the interest rates down.

HELP!

Stafford Loan rates, amounts, and terms are constantly changing and are linked to the prime rate. You can learn more about Stafford Loans through their website at www.staffordloan.com. For the latest information on these and other loans, check the loan websites listed in the "Loan Programs" section of Appendix B.

Stafford Loans

Subsidized and unsubsidized Stafford Loans are available through both the FFELP and the Federal Direct Loan Program. Eligibility for a subsidized Stafford Loan is based on financial need. The federal government pays the interest accrued on such loans until a student graduates. An unsubsidized Stafford Loan is not based on financial need, and the student is responsible for paying interest from the date of origination. For both types of loans, the annual amounts vary. For dependent students, the amounts that can be borrowed each year range from $2,625 to $5,500, depending on how many years the student has been in school. For independent students, the annual borrowing amounts range from $6,625 to $10,500.

Parent Loans

Parent Loans for Undergraduate Students (PLUS) are available through the FFELP and Federal Direct Loan Program. Parents can borrow up to the total amount of their student's education costs, minus any financial aid that the student has received. These loans require a credit check.

Perkins Loans

Federal Perkins Loans are campus-based loans that offer a low interest rate and are available to undergraduate and graduate students who have great financial need. The school acts as the lender but uses partial funds from the federal government to cover the loan. Undergraduate students can borrow up to $4,000 annually; graduate students can borrow up to $6,000 annually.

Work-Study Programs

Work-study programs are campus-based programs in which federal dollars are distributed through colleges to eligible students who are assigned part-time jobs. To qualify for the program, students must be able to demonstrate a need for financial aid and be enrolled at least part-time in an undergraduate or graduate program. Most of the employment is on the college campus, although some campuses arrange for off-campus jobs through community service programs. The pay is at least minimum wage and often higher.

This need-based federal program lets students earn money that gets paid directly to them while in school. These jobs are sometimes related to the student's field of study so that he or she will be getting some practical experience. Some schools do not allow freshmen to participate in work-study programs. Talk to the school's financial aid officer about opportunities that might be available. The typical commitment to work-study jobs is 10 to 15 hours per week.

Service-Learning Programs

Service learning combines service to the community with student learning in a way that improves both the student and the community, according to the National and Community Service Trust Act of 1993.

Getting Started

Service-learning programs were designed to help foster civic responsibility.

Service learning is a method whereby students learn and develop through active participation in thoughtfully organized service that is conducted in, and meets the needs of, communities close to where a college is located. It's coordinated with an elementary school, secondary school, institution of higher education, or a community service program. Service learning is integrated into and enhances either the academic curriculum of the students who are enrolled or the education components of the community service program in which they are participants. Such programs, which provide structured time for students to reflect on their service experiences, can foster learning, even though the learning may not be directly related to their academic work.

The Connection Between Community and College

Service learning is part of the academic curriculum in a college. In community organizations, youth develop practical skills, self-esteem, and a sense of civic responsibility. Examples of service-learning projects include preserving native plants, designing neighborhood playgrounds, teaching younger children to read, testing the local water quality, creating wheelchair ramps, preparing food for the homeless, developing urban community gardens, starting school recycling programs, and much more.

Why Service Programs Are Important

A national study of Learn and Serve America programs suggests that effective service-learning programs improve academic grades, increase attendance in school, and develop personal and social responsibility. Whether the goal is academic improvement, personal development, or both, students learn critical thinking, communication, teamwork, civic responsibility, mathematical reasoning, problem solving, public speaking, vocational skills, computer skills, scientific methodology, and research and analytical skills.

Tips on Applying for Financial Aid

Is there any way to "beat the system" when applying for financial aid? Can families rearrange their finances so that they can receive more financial assistance? There are two things to remember before these questions can be answered.

First, you should always be honest and accurate when applying for financial aid. There are severe penalties if dishonesty is discovered.

Second, the federal government often changes the rules and regulations that determine how financial aid is awarded. Today's savvy financial aid strategy may be obsolete next year.

Don't be dishonest or manipulate your income and assets in an attempt to secure more money. Instead, structure your entire college financial-planning process to maximize your resources, keep debt levels manageable, and meet college expenses in a rational and comprehensive way.

Before you apply for financial aid, however, there are certain peculiarities of the current formula for financial aid and need analysis that you should understand. The tips in the following sections will help you get your fair share of the action.

The Federal Formula

The current federal formula expects students to contribute 35 percent of their assets each year to meet their college costs. That same formula requires that parents contribute only 5.6 percent of their assets to meet their kids' college expenses. For example, if your family has assets of $10,000, it's better to have them in the parents' names rather than in the kids'. As parents, you would have to contribute 5.6 percent, or $560, under the current need-analysis formula. Your student would be expected to contribute $3,500, or 35 percent, toward meeting school bills.

Consider Using Your Home

Home equity loans allow parents to borrow against the value of their house to pay for their kids' college education. Parents can take out a second mortgage and establish a line of credit based on the equity they've built up in their house. Unlike the interest on other consumer loans, the interest on home equity loans is tax-deductible.

Although financing college costs with home equity loans would not work for everyone, it's an effective college-financing plan for homeowners.

Some parents use the funds from a home equity loan to prepay four years of college costs to save on tuition increases.

Watch Your Assets

Investigate ways of reducing your income and assets, including investing in retirement accounts and life insurance policies.

Delay taking any profits from investments or real estate holdings; that way, they won't be included as part of the family's income for the year preceding college enrollment.

Timing is important. Because financial aid awards are based on the previous tax year—in other words, the year *before* the college year—make sure that you shift any income and assets in advance of the college year.

Your Expected Contribution

A family's contribution is reduced by the number of family members in college at the same time. If two kids are simultaneously enrolled, the expected family contribution is reduced by almost 50 percent for each one. The same is true if two parents are simultaneously enrolled in higher education courses.

Watch for Fraud

When school is about to start, advertised offers for "guaranteed" scholarships, grants, and loans may look very attractive to college-bound students who didn't apply or qualify for financial aid. However, many civic organizations—for example, the Better Business Bureau (BBB)—warns students to be cautious of unethical scholarship companies.

Some scholarship companies promise a "guaranteed match" of students to sources of funding, regardless of the students' academic qualifications, scholastic credentials, or family economic status. Their advertisements and sales pitches assert that there are millions of dollars in unclaimed scholarship money waiting to be tapped. However, in the BBB's experience, many of these promises prove empty, and few if any students receive funds. In exchange for an upfront fee, which can range from $50 to several hundred dollars, these scholarship companies only supply lists of possible scholarship sources.

Here are some points to keep in mind if you're considering getting help from a scholarship company:

- ◆ Even though the company making the offer may claim that scholarships are "guaranteed," only the sources actually granting the funds can guarantee approval.

- ◆ Unethical scholarship companies do not assist students in obtaining loans and do not screen applicants. After buying the lists from the firm, the student is responsible for researching and contacting each organization listed as a possible funding source.

◆ Many ads by these companies offer a "money back guarantee" to students who do not receive any scholarship funds. Students who are unsuccessful in obtaining funds may find that refunds are difficult, if not impossible, to obtain. In many cases, companies require that students prove through documentation that they were turned down by every source on the list.

If students do decide to seek the help of a scholarship service company, the Better Business Bureau recommends that they first check the service's references. Reference checks can be made through high school guidance offices, reference sections of libraries, or the financial aid office of the college the student is planning to attend.

The Least You Need to Know

◆ Financial aid is available to millions of American families. Don't make the mistake of assuming you don't qualify. You won't know until you apply!

◆ There are literally thousands of financial aid sources out there for the people who are willing to search for them. You may even find a pot of gold at the end of the rainbow!

◆ If you research financial aid possibilities and do some advance planning, you won't have to overburden yourself with debt to send your kids to college.

◆ Beware of scholarship service companies that guarantee scholarship funds.

Staking Out Your Financial Aid Claim

In This Chapter

- ◆ Discovering what the eligibility requirements are for financial aid

- ◆ Learning how the application process works and why it's important to apply even if you think you don't qualify

- ◆ Exploring financial aid myths and misconceptions

- ◆ Learning how to calculate what college will cost and how much you can expect to pay

- ◆ Dispelling financing myths

A survey published in *Business Week* found that a huge majority of parents who are paying tuition bills say the current financial aid system doesn't meet the needs of the beleaguered average American family. To be honest with you, I believe that it never will because, quite simply, the cost of going to college now and in the future is outstripping the funding that's available for college aid. In this chapter, I show you techniques you can employ to enhance your chances of getting a larger piece of the action.

Eliminate Frustration: Do Your Research

Now that Cheri Rye's second child is in college, Cheri is somewhat of a professional at applying for financial aid. And, as is the case for many parents who face the fact that college expenses are more than their budgets allow, Cheri's learning curve was a steep one. Even though she had ready access to a wealth of information about financial aid from books, magazine articles, websites, and high school financial aid experts, anxiety was her biggest obstacle.

When she looked at the cost of tuition in relation to her income, paying for tuition seemed a terrifying prospect, particularly because the idea that her children wouldn't go to college was not an option. "The first time I filled out the aid forms for my daughter Lisa, I was physically sick," she recalls. "I was told that if you make a mistake you get rejected by the system and go to the end of the line."

Well, Cheri knows better now, and her distress is history. Her daughter Lisa is half-way through her undergraduate degree at a good college. So when she began seeking financial aid for her daughter Jennifer, Cheri was somewhat less apprehensive. By the time Jennifer was securely enrolled in college, Cheri was on a first-name basis with the college's financial aid administrator.

> **Warning**
>
> If you don't get to know your financial aid administrator (FAA) or officer, you're in trouble. The help of the FAA will be essential if questions arise when you're filing for aid. FAAs can also point you to numerous financial sources that you hadn't thought of.

Ronald Shunk probably has heard all there is to hear about the frustration and confusion surrounding financial aid from a parent's perspective. For 10 years, he answered parents' questions on *USA Today*'s Financial Aid Hotline, and he is currently Director of Financial Aid at Gettysburg College in Gettysburg, Pennsylvania. "What impresses me is that many callers into my hotline don't have even a fundamental understanding of financial aid and don't know where to begin."

With all the information about financial aid available, why do parents panic the first, and even the second, time around?

Cheri's experience and that of other parents who have been through the process indicate some common concerns. Ronald explains, "It's because most of them don't take the time to understand the application process before they apply. When they make a mistake and their application gets rejected, they get frustrated and blame everybody but themselves."

Who Gets the Money?

Generally, all college financial assistance is based on "need." Financial aid services used by colleges and universities have a standard formula to determine whether you and your children qualify for various forms of assistance. All institutions granting assistance are required by federal law to use the formula.

This formula uses a family's income, assets, and expenses to calculate the *expected family contribution (EFC)*. In theory, the expected family contribution remains constant from school to school. The individual institutions then subtract this number from the cost of attending their institution in order to come up with an estimate of "need." The amount of "need" will vary depending on that institution's cost of attendance.

In determining a family's need, the standard formula takes into account more than just a family's annual income. Equity in the home, the value of a family-owned business, savings, stock holdings, and other assets that may be potential sources of funding for education are factored in as well. The formula also considers whether other siblings are in college, requiring the family's support.

Getting Started

The **expected family contribution (EFC)** is the amount of money the student and his or her family are expected to contribute toward the student's cost of college attendance, as calculated by a federally mandated formula. Very clearly, the objective of college financial aid programs is to ensure that the limited amount of financial aid available is reserved for those who truly need it.

Do You Need the Money?

Many colleges, including some of the most selective, are opposed to merit-based assistance. These colleges give only need-based assistance and feel that only students who demonstrate need deserve assistance.

Their concern is that merit awards reduce the money available to help those who really need it. To determine your kid's eligibility for need-based aid, the expected family contribution is subtracted from the total cost of attending the college. The difference is the family's need for assistance. Therefore, the need increases as

HELP!

For more information about educational and living expenses at college, check out the college cost projector at www.finaid.org.

the total cost goes up. The total cost varies from one college to another. For example, private colleges are nearly always more expensive than public institutions.

What's Considered Total Cost?

Total cost includes tuition and fees as well as other associated expenses, such as the cost of books and other supplies. If a student plans to live on campus, room and board will be considered, and allowance is made for traveling home at least once during the school year. If the student will be commuting, transportation is included. In other words, the amount is the total cost of attending college for one year.

More Expensive May Be Cheaper

More expensive colleges tend to have more money available, so the "sticker price" at any college may be very misleading. Students should explore every college that interests them on the assumption that they will receive financial aid if they need it.

> ⚠ **Warning**
>
> Students should always apply to a financial "safety" school, a less expensive alternative such as a state college or university where the costs tend to be lower. At the same time, students should still be encouraged to apply to the college of their choice, even if it costs more.

But they should keep in mind that while the college's financial aid office will attempt to meet the total "need for assistance," there's no guarantee that the college will be able to do so.

Colleges that can provide assistance to meet the full need of each student are the exception. Some colleges meet the need of as many students as possible, whereas others meet a portion of the need of all students. In either case, there's no guarantee that a student's needs will be met.

Misconceptions About Need

One common misconception is that having savings or assets will automatically exclude a family from financial aid. Many parents assume that aid won't be offered until all savings and assets have been exhausted. This is simply not true. Some parents assume that owning a home or having significant savings makes them ineligible. Having home equity and money in the bank does not mean that students will not qualify for assistance. In fact, home equity isn't even considered by some colleges when determining eligibility.

What You're Expected to Pay

What you'll be expected to pay, or your EFC, is a combination of what you and your student will be expected to contribute toward a college education. The parents' contribution is based on the number of family members in college, and it allows for living expenses. This allowance is conservative and reflects a minimum budget for any family. As a result, it is rare to find a family that can meet its expected contribution from current income. Most families meet this expense through a combination of savings, current income, and loans.

Income is the major factor in establishing a family's contribution. Assets and savings are also considered, but no more than 6 percent of parents' assets are included in any given year. Parents should be honest about their ages because the 6 percent maximum assessment would be lower for older parents who are closer to retirement. There are three general family income categories that are considered in determining your EFC, or what you are expected to pay.

Low-Income Families

Families with incomes under $25,000 are eligible for assistance. Families should communicate this to their children so that they do not assume they cannot afford college. As an example for their children, parents might consider putting spare change in a coffee can labeled "college fund." The amount saved may not make a dent in the total cost of college, but it sends a powerful message about the importance of education.

HELP! Use a financial aid calculator to help you determine your eligibility. There are several calculators available on the web. Check Appendix B for helpful sites in the "Financial Aid Resources" or "Financial Planning" sections.

Middle-Income Families

Middle-income families should understand where they stand in relation to others applying for financial aid. Income alone can be deceiving. Family size, number of children in college, unusual expenses, and savings and other assets will also be considered. Currently the "statistical" middle class consists of the 3 out of 5 families with incomes between $25,000 and $70,000.

Middle-income families usually qualify for financial assistance, but they will also be expected to make a significant EFC. This may require a number of sacrifices and a possible change in lifestyle. Going out to eat may become a rare luxury, and these families should probably get accustomed to driving the same car for a while.

Wealthy Families

Families with incomes above $70,000 make up one-fifth of the population in the United States. According to the government, high-income families should be in the best position to contribute toward their children's education, but even they may struggle to meet college costs. If you're in a high-income category or believe you will be when your kids reach college age, you should begin long-term college financial planning as early as possible.

Is Your Kid Eligible?

Although the process of determining a student's eligibility for federal student aid is basically the same for all applicants, there is some flexibility. For instance, if your FAA believes that, based on the documentation you provided, it's appropriate to change the student's status from dependent to independent, he or she can do so.

In some cases, your FAA may consider circumstances that might affect the amount of your EFC and may adjust your "cost of attendance" or the information used to calculate your EFC accordingly.

These circumstances could include a family's unusual medical or dental expenses, or tuition expenses for children attending a private elementary or secondary school. Also, an adjustment may be made if you, your spouse, or either of your parents (if applicable) has been recently unemployed. If conditions such as these apply to you or your family, contact your FAA.

Check with your FAA if you feel you are subject to any other special circumstances that might affect the amount of your expected contribution. But remember, there have to be very good reasons for the FAA to make any adjustments, and you'll have to provide adequate proof to support those adjustments. Also, remember that the FAA's decision is final and cannot be appealed to the U.S. Department of Education.

To quickly determine whether you qualify for federal financial aid, follow these easy steps:

1. Take 5 percent of the value of your total family assets, including home equity, savings, and investments, and add this figure to your adjusted gross income from last year's tax return.

2. Divide that result by the anticipated annual college expense.

3. If the result is 6 percent or less, you could qualify for financial aid.

4. If the final number is higher, you may have a difficult time convincing financial aid officers of your need.

Note: No matter what you predict your chances to be, you should still go through the application process. Many different factors enter into the final outcome. Public and private institutions alike offer varying amounts of aid, and you may be pleasantly surprised. If you do not receive aid from your chosen institution, there are other alternatives.

Action Plan

You can calculate your expected family contribution by using several of the websites listed in Appendix B under "Federal Financial Aid."

Stepping Into the Application Process

No doubt about it, the financial aid process can leave you bewildered. I've put together a brief summary that will be helpful as you explore the world of federal aid. Later chapters will get into more detail about how to apply for college aid, but for right now, the following are the basic steps in applying for aid.

Warning

Don't hang back waiting to be admitted to a college before filing your financial aid request forms. Too many students make this mistake. For any college you're even thinking about attending, submit your application as soon as possible, even if it's before you're allowed to apply for financial aid. If you think that it should be financial aid money first and application second, you may find yourself in last place. Colleges will first review financial aid requests received from students whose applications have already been accepted.

Step 1: Complete the Application

To get the process started, you and your parents must fill out and submit a Free Application for Federal Student Aid (FAFSA) sometime between January 1 and March 1 to qualify for funds starting in September of the coming school year. This means you will need to include information from your parents' tax return (last year's return) to complete the form. If they wait until the April 15 cutoff date to complete and file their return, it will be too late for you to apply for financial aid. The FAFSA form is available through your high school, from the financial aid office of the college, or on the Internet. You can review a copy of the FAFSA on the Internet at www.fafsa.us.

Step 2: Evaluate the Student Aid Report

You'll receive your Student Aid Report (SAR) four to six weeks after submitting the FAFSA. The SAR indicates whether you are eligible for a Pell Grant, and it outlines your expected family contribution (EFC). The EFC is determined by subtracting parent and student contributions from the cost of attendance (COA) at the college of your choice. Remember, the EFC varies depending on several factors, including your family's income, assets, size, and whether the student is a dependent or independent. It also varies according to the COA, since the COA is different for each college.

Action Plan

Prioritize your efforts by beginning with the federal government. But don't forget to explore Appendix C for state financial assistance programs, and use the websites you'll find in Appendix B to locate other sources.

Step 3: Receive and Consider Offers

Next you will get an award letter from the college you've applied to or are currently attending. This letter will outline how much financial aid you are eligible for. If you receive a rejection letter, don't give up. Chapters 20 and 21 show you how to compare and negotiate the best offer possible even if initially your school has denied you aid.

Dispelling Financial Aid Myths

Everything you've heard about what it's going to take to pay for your kid's college education is driving you crazy. Before you let that happen, make sure you can separate the facts from the most common myths.

> **Millions of scholarship dollars go unclaimed.** False! The idea that private scholarship dollars go unclaimed is unfounded. This is what professional scholarship search services would like you to believe because they want you to pay for their services. You can do your own search for scholarships.

> **Your family's income is too high to qualify.** False! Income is only one of the criteria on which financial aid is based. If the school's costs exceed your family's means, you may qualify for some form of financial aid. Remember, there are some scholarships that are based on merit and not family income.

Don't consider high-tuition colleges. False! As a general rule, the higher the total school costs, the easier it is to demonstrate eligibility for financial aid. Also, the stated costs at a school can be deceiving. Aid is often available to offset some of the higher costs. If you're truly interested in attending a school with high tuition, you should apply to the school and wait to see the financial aid award letter before you make a decision. You may get a favorable response.

Financial aid funds are dwindling. False! A recent statistic published by the Department of Education's National Center for Educational Statistics showed that there has been a 59.3 percent increase in financial aid from 1990 to 2003, using as a constant 2003 dollars. It is true, however, that loans and work-study are now a larger percentage of the total financial aid award than they used to be.

With some of the myths out of the way, you're now ready to tackle the process of financing your kid's education. Paying for school isn't much fun to think about, but it is something you need to do. There are lots of resources available to help you afford school, but to tap into them, you have to know they exist!

 Warning

The fees charged by a consultant may vary widely, depending on the type of assistance provided. Remember, most of the information and assistance offered by a consultant should be available free of charge from a college financial aid office.

Do You Need Help?

An increasing number of school counselors, instructors, and administrators familiar with the complex world of financial aid for education offer their expertise to students, parents, and guardians, for a fee. These private educational consultants can help a client choose the best possible colleges, given the student's academic abilities and interests, and assist in applying for, and obtaining, financial aid.

Although it certainly is not necessary to have this kind of professional advice, and consultants cannot guarantee the availability of funds, in some cases it can make researching and considering options much easier. The time to consider hiring an educational consultant is early in the student's junior year of high school. Ask the school guidance counselor for recommendations on private consultants in your area. Set up meetings with the prospective consultants. Examine and check out their credentials with local academic references. But only hire one if you feel confident that he or she has your best interests at heart.

Other Sources of Money

Other sources of financial aid include corporations, businesses, professional associations, philanthropic organizations, credit unions, labor unions, religious organizations, fraternities and sororities, and civic organizations. As the college years approach, students and parents need to be alert to announcements for financial support offered by these organizations.

No one knows a student's educational progress or potential better than the student's teachers and counselors. High school counselors can help you research sources of aid and complete college applications and financial aid forms. Keep in contact with them. Guidance counselors can help explore various available choices.

Maintain communication with these professionals in order to keep current. In addition, counselors can help identify the most appropriate possibilities for individual students. With years of experience in counseling many different students, guidance professionals have a unique perspective.

Admissions Counselors

College admissions counselors can also provide help. Just keep in mind that there are thousands of two- and four-year colleges and universities and trade, technical, and career schools with different requirements, expectations, and policies. So advice from a counselor at one college may not apply to others.

Special-Programs Operatives

There are a variety of special programs that serve disadvantaged students, including Upward Bound and Talent Search, among many others. Often hosted by colleges, these programs are a wonderful source of support for students and families. They often help students preserve educational options. If there is no college nearby or if your local college does not sponsor such a program, check with the nearest Educational Opportunity Center for further information. Libraries have books on financial aid available from private, state, and federal sources. Employers may offer employee tuition benefits and assistance for family members. Several million dollars in employee education benefits go unused each year.

> ⚠ **Warning**
>
> The College Board website (www.collegeboard.org) has loads of useful resources for the college-bound student and many links to the College Board's online services.

Financial Aid Officers

Since funds are limited, college financial aid administrators or officers are usually quite eager to help families in early financial planning. These professionals have information on a variety of aid packages you may be eligible for. Consider attending a local financial aid night at the high school. Keep your eye out for other programs on financial aid and planning. Each state has an agency that administers state scholarships and other forms of financial aid. In recent years, these agencies have become involved in a variety of outreach programs to families.

Don't forget that financial aid procedures and policies do change. State financial aid offices can provide you with information about the types of financial aid they offer. You can find financial aid offices and other state agencies listed by state in Appendix C. It's very important for families to have the most current information. What is true today may not be true tomorrow. Stay informed!

In conclusion, it's important for all families to have a good sense of what their expected contribution might be. Taking the time to secure a realistic estimate of college costs will help you plan more effectively.

The Least You Need to Know

- Just about everybody is eligible for some form of financial aid. At this point, you should have a general idea of the amount of aid you can qualify for and where to begin looking for it.

- You should be familiar with the four basic steps of applying and qualifying for college financial aid.

- The myths about financial aid are just that: myths. Now that you know the facts, you can take a realistic approach to searching for the aid you need.

Answers to All Your Financial Aid Questions

In This Chapter

◆ Exposing many of the myths that have plagued the financial aid process

◆ Understanding why the confidential information you disclose on a form won't be shared with others

◆ Learning the basics of getting started

◆ Finding out where to get additional information you need

"A friend of a friend of a friend of mine told me … about financial aid." That's how the myths that surround financial aid get started. This chapter helps to expose these myths by answering the most common questions that parents and students ask about financial aid. It also addresses the most common questions about how to get started in the financial aid process. Where appropriate, I'll point you to other places in this book where you can find more information about a topic.

Why Does College Cost So Much?

Parents who went to college 30 years ago and are now putting their own children through college are shocked when they compare today's fees to what they paid. And when other parents who didn't have a college experience learn the current price of a college education for their kids, they, too, are shocked and automatically assume that they can't possibly get enough aid to get their kids through school.

Action Plan

Just about anybody can get some form of financial aid. You just have to be willing to properly complete the necessary forms, provide the required documentation to support your application, and follow up on the process.

Although the cost of college today is indeed stunning, the reality is that *all* families are eligible for *some* level of federal assistance, and many state-funded institutions offer state financial aid.

Additionally, colleges are responding to the competition to attract good students, so there is more merit-based aid available now.

"Institutions have dramatically increased their financial aid budgets, and there is a much higher proportion of financial aid than 10 years ago," asserts Robert Baum, author of the bestseller *Logic*.

How Much Money Goes into Financial Aid Annually?

Unfortunately, too many students feel they are denied their chance to go to college simply because they can't afford the rising costs of higher education. Many students and parents do not know that more than $35 billion in financial aid is available each year. You have to start by filling out a few simple forms, which are covered in Part 3 of this book, "Seek and You Shall Find—Money."

If I Apply, Will Strangers Pry into My Personal Business?

The financial aid process feels intrusive. People are used to paying income taxes because they do it every year and know what's expected. But applying for financial aid is, for most people, a new experience. With pages and pages of instructions and applications to fill out, financial aid forms are intimidating.

In addition, people are disinclined to share so much of their personal financial profiles with people they don't know. To the first-timer, the forms seem worse than they are. However, when you start filling them out, you'll find they're not as complicated as you might have anticipated, nor is the information requested more than what's commonly requested by the IRS. In Chapter 19, we show you how to fill out the main federal aid form, the Free Application for Federal Student Aid (FAFSA).

Isn't Asking for Financial Aid the Same as Asking for Welfare?

Many people are embarrassed to ask for assistance because it means they aren't making six-figure incomes. Often parents hesitate to ask difficult questions about financial aid and don't want to bring up the subject of their personal income to financial aid staff. They don't feel comfortable soliciting guidance about their money from strangers.

Don't hesitate to seek out high school counselors and financial aid officers who can give you the information you need. Financial aid officers are very service- and people-oriented. They're aware of the need to educate qualified students and their parents about how to get financial aid. That's their job! Competition for top students is tight, so it's also in the best interest of colleges to attract top-ranked students with appropriate financial aid packages.

Does Each College Have a Different Financial Aid System?

All colleges operate on different systems. Talk to the representatives at the financial aid office for each of the colleges where your child will apply. They're the best sources of information in terms of what is available and what their policies are. Find out how each institution allocates aid and what criteria are used to award it. Then get the appropriate forms from each institution, fill them out, and send them in. Many applications are available through your student's high school guidance counselor's office. To make this process go smoothly, make sure you review all of the material in Chapter 4. It will give you a better idea of what questions to ask the guidance counselor and the financial aid people working for the colleges your child is thinking about attending.

How Can I Get the Most out of the System?

Parents can easily become overwhelmed because of the perceived volume of facts and figures that are required in seeking financial aid. Many rely on hearsay and secondhand knowledge to educate themselves about the process of paying for college. However, there are abundant helpful resources out there, especially for parents and families with access to the Internet. Parents can research not only government and university resources for aid, but also private sources of scholarships and grants.

How Do I Know If I'm Eligible for Financial Aid?

You won't know if you're eligible unless you apply. Most students qualify for some kind of financial assistance. Here are the basic qualifications a student needs in order to qualify for financial aid:

> **Action Plan**
>
> Students: In addition to exploring the information available on the Internet, contact your high school counselor or the financial aid department at the college your child plans to attend. These sources can provide you with invaluable information.

- Demonstrate financial need, or merit for some scholarships

- Have a high school diploma or a General Education Development (GED) certificate

- Be enrolled in an eligible degree or certificate program and be making satisfactory progress

- Be a U.S. citizen or eligible noncitizen

- Have a valid Social Security number

- Register with the Selective Service, if applicable

Is My Kid Eligible for Special Aid?

Find out if your child is eligible for merit-based aid. Merit-based financial awards are based on students' scores on standardized tests such as the SAT and high school grades, as well as on how they have spent their free time during high school.

Exemplary academic and extracurricular performance increases a student's chances of qualifying for merit-based financial aid. To become eligible for these scholarships, your child must strive to excel in a variety of school activities, so make sure his or her honors and awards are recorded in school files.

Merit-Based Scholarship Myths

There's a rumor that only students with high academic achievement win merit-based scholarships. The truth is that scholarships are awarded to students with all sorts of talents and interests. In fact, many of the best scholarships are awarded to students who devote their time to such diverse pursuits as music, art, community service, writing, and foreign languages, to name a few. Many of these scholarships are based not on students' grades but rather on their accomplishments in such areas.

Many scholarships that *do* take students' grade point averages into consideration do it to create a cutoff point in order to limit the number of applicants. If you make the grade-point cut, the judges turn their attention to what a student has accomplished outside school hours.

Every scholarship contest is judged differently, and anywhere from one judge to dozens of judges can be responsible for evaluating entries.

Athletic Scholarships

Just as the letter grades on your transcript aren't necessarily a prerequisite—and if so, certainly aren't the only one—for winning scholarships, varsity letters earned on the playing field don't make the great impact people think they do.

Although a few merit-based contests are targeted at athletes who excel on and off the field, in the vast majority of scholarship contests, athletic prowess is just one element of a student's record, equivalent to having a skill in any other field.

Extracurricular Activities

Are we saying that the student who has the most extracurricular activities generally wins? As is the case in many other aspects of life, winning scholarships is about quality, not quantity.

Some people think that, to win a scholarship, you must have devoted your entire high school career to participating in extracurricular activities. On the contrary, most scholarship winners distinguish themselves by the devotion they've demonstrated to a particular activity or activities rather than by how much time they've spent on many activities. In other words, quality is usually more important than quantity.

How to Be a Contender

Scholarship contests demand a modified approach from the college admissions process because contests are characterized by more direct, head-to-head competition. While college admissions officers generally compare students to a predetermined standard, scholarship contests compare students to one another. Because of this heightened competitive environment, students who devise creative techniques to stand out from the crowd have a distinct advantage.

Each scholarship contest has it own biases. This is not to say that scholarship judging is unfair. Rather, it's just that each contest is looking for students with particular qualities. The subjective process of valuing certain qualities over other ones makes the playing field far from level. In this way, the perfect application for one particular scholarship contest may place you out of the running for another. Because of these biases, it's essential to define each contest's ideal applicant and to develop a strategy that emphasizes personal attributes consistent with that ideal. To paraphrase George Orwell, "Everyone is equal, but some are more equal than others."

Third-Party Organizations

Contests administered by third-party organizations often recruit judges from the ranks of current or former teachers, school administrators, and organization staff members. Most third-party organizations have run numerous scholarship contests, and the judging administered by them tends to be highly objective and in compliance with published judging criteria.

High-profile national contests administered by these types of organizations may also employ "blue-ribbon panels" for final judging. The panels generally include celebrities, government officials, and other notable individuals. The Prudential Spirit of Community Awards honor young people in middle level and high school grades for outstanding volunteer service to their communities. Created in 1995 by Prudential Financial in partnership with the National Association of Secondary School Principals (NASSP), the awards constitute the United States' largest youth recognition program based solely on volunteering. Over the past 12 years, the program has honored more than 75,000 young volunteers at the local, state, and national level. You can apply online for their annual Prudential Spirit of Community Awards at their website (www. prudential.com/community/spirit/awards).

Action Plan

Merit is often only in the eyes of the beholder or, in the case of scholarships, in the eyes of the judges. If you understand what the judges are looking for and tailor your approach to each scholarship you apply for, you'll dramatically increase your chances of winning.

On the local level, such blue-ribbon panels typically include television and radio personalities, successful entrepreneurs, and professional athletes.

In contests that employ blue-ribbon panels for judging, a limited number of finalists are usually preselected via more mundane judging channels and then are presented to the blue-ribbon panel for final evaluation.

Corporations

For contests administered by a participating corporation rather than by a third-party organization, public relations personnel may be the ones to select the winners. When judging is conducted by a public relations department, other factors, such as geographical balance, can sneak into (unpublished and unannounced) judging criteria.

Service Organizations

Scholarship programs sponsored by service organizations, fraternal lodges, and veterans' associations are likely to be judged by members of the particular organization. In this way, the key tenets and values of the sponsoring organization frequently play a role in the judging.

Perhaps the most subjective judging occurs when scholarships are sponsored by small family or historic institutions, each of which has a unique set of biases and viewpoints.

How Many Aid Sources Should I Explore?

Explore as many sources of financial aid as you can. Because the amount of aid you receive will be determined partly by the cost of the school you attend, don't rule out any school as being too expensive.

Once the financial aid office has determined your level of need and you've been notified of the amount and type of aid you'll receive (grants, scholarships, or loans), begin negotiating financial aid options with the schools that have accepted your child. Should you need more aid, seek out and apply for loans such as those offered by banks and credit unions. See Chapter 15 for more on loans.

 Warning

Don't think that getting financial aid will be an easy undertaking. Students who understand the details of financial aid and the application process reap the most benefits.

When Should I Submit Applications?

Submit applications for aid well before their deadlines. Paying for education is often a family effort. When students begin working on their applications, parents should organize their income, asset, and tax records. Family need is determined by a federal formula that considers this information as well as tuition and other costs. See Chapter 18 for more on how the formula works.

All applicants for federal aid must complete a need-analysis form, and some colleges also require that students submit some type of financial aid form. These forms can be submitted between January 1 and May 1. It's best to submit them as soon after January 1 as possible.

The sooner you apply, the better chance you have of being considered for aid with early award dates. Always contact the financial aid administrator at each school to verify specific deadline dates.

Where Can I Get More Information and Guidance?

The following individuals and organizations are good sources of information and advice about financial aid:

1. High school counselors can help you research sources of aid, complete college applications, and obtain financial aid forms.

2. College financial aid officers have information on a variety of aid packages you may be eligible for.

3. State financial aid offices can provide you with information about the types of financial aid they offer. These offices are listed in Appendix C.

4. Libraries have guides that list the financial aid available from private, state, and federal sources.

5. Employers may offer employee tuition benefits and assistance for family members.

Warning

Even though grants, scholarships, loans, work-study programs, and financial aid packages may be more plentiful than ever before, the key is to not wait until the last minute—or even the last year, when your child graduates from high school—to become aware of the high costs of sending him or her to college.

Other sources of financial aid include private and public businesses, professional associations, philanthropic organizations, credit unions, labor unions, religious organizations, fraternities and sororities, and civic organizations. As the college years approach, students and parents need to be alert to announcements for financial support offered by these organizations.

You'll find the addresses, phone numbers, and websites of many financial aid sources listed in Appendix B.

When Should I Begin Planning for My Kid's Education?

Do it now! You can never begin to plan too early to meet future college expenses. Most financial analysts recommend that as soon as your child is born, you should initiate some form of college financial program. Early planning can mean more savings and gives families more options that can make a difference in the college selection process.

How Can I Find Out If I Qualify for Assistance?

No one can tell a family with certainty whether it will qualify for federal financial aid. The federal government frequently changes the rules and regulations that determine eligibility. Some schools have a service that provides families with an estimate of what their aid will be if the student is accepted. Ask all the schools you're considering if they have this service. If you know at the time of application what you can realistically expect to receive from all sources, you can determine whether you can afford to send your kid to that particular school and what your financial contribution is expected to be.

Is There an Income Cutoff for Federal Aid?

There is no income cutoff to receive federal financial aid. All families, regardless of income, should file the application for federal aid. Always remember, eligibility for funding from all sources is determined in part by university or college costs. Attending an expensive school may actually mean that a family will qualify for more aid than if the student attended a lower-cost institution. That's why it's so important for students to make college selections based primarily on the academic strengths and other appealing factors of the institutions—not on what they cost.

Another essential reason why all families should file for federal financial aid is that most colleges and universities will not consider a student for institutional aid unless a federal application form is on file.

Do I Need to Reduce My Asset Base to Qualify?

The federal aid formula that is used to determine a family's ability to contribute to a college education expects parents to hand over as much as 47 percent of profits realized from investments, such as stocks and bonds. If you're thinking about unloading stocks or bonds, it's unwise to do so right before your son or daughter begins college. Time your investments so that profits don't show up on your income tax return for the year preceding the one in which you apply for aid.

Isn't the Federal Government Reducing Financial Assistance Programs?

No. The federal government still provides about 75 percent of all aid. Although it's true that aid from the federal government has not kept pace with annual tuition increases, it's incorrect to state that the federal government no longer supports higher education.

Financial assistance is still available; however, funding sources have shifted from grants to loans, and at some schools, student employment allocations have decreased. Although deficit budgets will probably prevent the federal government from substantially increasing financial aid to college students, there are many other sources of funding, including state and institutional programs (see Chapters 10 and 11). It's the responsibility of the family to locate those sources.

What Are the Alternatives to Federal Aid?

Starting a savings plan and an investment program a long way in advance to finance your kid's college education may mean that aid won't be essential. If it is, as is often the case, there are many ways to finance college costs.

Most schools and many states award scholarships based on academic achievement. Many private organizations offer financial assistance to students who meet specific criteria. Banks generally have college financing programs. The PLUS program (see Chapter 15) is awarded on the basis of creditworthiness, not financial need.

What's the Best Savings Plan?

No one single savings or investment program is best for all families. Each family must design a savings plan that will best meet its particular financial needs. The age of the kid and the parents, as well as the financial resources of the family, will help determine the appropriate college savings program. The federal formula currently used to determine a family's ability to pay for college assigns greater weight to current income than to assets, so families are not unjustly penalized for having started to save early for their kid's college education.

Prepayment plans allow families to purchase a fixed, discounted tuition at many colleges. The money is then invested by the institution or the state to cover the future cost of tuition.

Prepayment plans relieve families of the anxiety of escalating tuition bills. However, since these plans are a new type of financing option, don't invest any money in one before you find out whether the plan covers all college costs or just tuition expenses.

Also, determine the maximum amount you can invest and what happens to your investment if your kid decides not to attend that college, or any college, or drops out after the first year.

What Are Tuition Stabilization Plans?

Tuition stabilization plans are similar to prepayment plans, but the amount paid into the plan is generally less than four years of tuition. Most tuition stabilization plans require the family to pay a portion of the educational costs in advance. The advantage of this type of plan is that tuition is capped for all subsequent years that the student is enrolled at the college.

Who Can Help Me Get Through This Process?

The first person to look to for help is you. The process of finding the money for your kid to attend college will seem very complicated unless you take the time to investigate, educate yourself, and explore all of your financial options.

Compare college costs. Seek the advice of your accountant, banker, or investment broker. Get to know a financial aid counselor at the local college or university. The more knowledge you have, the less complicated the process will be.

Find out as much as you can about financing a college education. If you bought this book, you've already learned something about financial aid and where to go to learn more.

The Least You Need to Know

- There are a lot of myths out there about college financial aid. Know how to separate fact from fiction.

- Doing as much research as you can will help you get through the process and reap greater aid benefits.

- Understanding the basic steps you need to take to get started is key. If there's something you don't understand about the system, ask questions until you get the answers you need.

Part 2

Planning Is Everything

Tuition increases over the last several years are enough to scare any parent with kids to put through college. Only a few families can afford to foot the bills by themselves; yet if the kids don't get through college, they'll have a tough time surviving in today's job environment. Before you give up the hope of sending a child of yours off to college, take the first painful step: find out what it's going to cost so you can sit back and determine where you're at financially. How much can you afford to spend, how much do you need in the form of financial aid to make ends meet, and what kind of financial plan will you have? That's what these chapters are all about.

4

So, Kid, You Want to Go to College?

In This Chapter

- ◆ Discovering why it's important to get your kids to start thinking about college at an early age

- ◆ Making sure your kids take the proper level of courses in high school so that they're better prepared to get into college

- ◆ Learning what kids need to do in their freshman year of high school to get ready

- ◆ Finding out how to preplan for important tests like the SAT to improve your kids' results

If you have older kids, you've probably asked them the question, "So, you want to go to college?" Chances are they didn't have the foggiest idea of whether they wanted to go at all, much less what they wanted to do when they got there. And the situation seemed to get worse as they got older. At least when they were little, they would tell you they wanted to be a cowboy or a nurse or a racecar driver. As parents, many of us keep trying to get a feel for our children's potential interest in going on to college. We know that they have a better chance of making it in the real world if they have a college degree.

Even though parents know college is going to be an expensive proposition, many of them encourage their kids to think about the benefits of a college education. If you have a child who's considering college, you should begin to coach him or her on how to prepare for it early on, no later than at the beginning of freshman year in high school.

Minimum Course Work Required

Students and parents often wonder how the level of course work affects college admission. In other words, would colleges rather see a B in an honors course or an A in a regular course? The answer isn't straightforward, but usually colleges prefer a B in an honors course. Students should choose courses based on their abilities. If a student is good in math or science, then he or she should take challenging courses in these areas.

Action Plan

College admissions officers use high school profiles that list the courses offered and other school data to evaluate an applicant's record.

However, the same individual might be better off taking "easier" courses in subjects where he or she isn't as strong. In any case, students should avoid taking unreasonably difficult courses in which they have no chance of getting good grades. A grade of D or F in a challenging course will hurt a student's chance of admission to a college. It could also cause enough frustration to discourage a student from pursuing higher education altogether.

Parents and students often worry about their high school's limited course offerings, but most colleges evaluate each applicant in light of the courses available at the student's school. For example, colleges will take into account that a small rural high school might not be able to offer advanced courses in many subjects. However, students who do have the opportunity to take more advanced courses will have an advantage, and they will be better prepared for college work. The minimum course work required for admission to most colleges is outlined in the following sections.

Language Arts

Colleges require four years of English. Fortunately, at most high schools, this is also a requirement for graduation. If a student can do work at a more challenging level, such as an honors course or one specifically labeled college prep, he or she should be encouraged to do so.

Math

Students are often prevented from pursuing certain options because they didn't take the appropriate math courses. The minimum requirement for most colleges usually includes three years of math, including algebra I and II and geometry. Students who are able should take advanced algebra, trigonometry, precalculus, or calculus.

Science

Most colleges look for at least three years of study in science. Two years of science, usually biology, physics, or chemistry, are typically required. Taking courses that are beyond the minimum requirements, such as physiology, biochemistry, or anatomy, will give a student more options.

Social Sciences

Colleges expect a minimum of two years of study in social sciences or history. As is the case with English, students will satisfy the minimum requirement in this area by meeting high school graduation requirements. However, students with ability and interest should certainly be encouraged to take more courses.

Foreign Languages

Most colleges expect a minimum of two years of study in a single foreign language and prefer more. Students who cannot meet this requirement for reasons such as a serious learning disability may be offered alternative programs and opportunities. Students should concentrate on a single language and not jump from one language to another. As is the case with math, insufficient foreign language preparation can limit a student's choices. Advanced work will enable a student to consider colleges that require more than the two-year minimum in language study. Because the world is constantly changing, so, too, are the particular foreign languages studied that impress college admissions committees. Nowadays, the study of Chinese, Japanese, and Arabic are looked upon with great interest.

Other Courses

Finally, colleges expect students to have some exposure to the fine arts and the performing arts, as well as an introduction to the world of computers. Once again, these courses may also be required for high school graduation.

All students enter high school with the potential to continue their education after graduation. Not everyone will attend college, but all students should be encouraged to keep their postsecondary school options open. They should plan a program of study during high school that preserves choices after graduation. Those students who think ahead will have many opportunities available to them.

Advice for High School Freshmen

Some simple steps taken early in high school can have great value in broadening your kids' college and financial aid prospects.

Make sure they understand the level of courses they'll need to take in high school to qualify for college. Help them select high school courses with advice from their guidance counselor. Encourage them to focus on building strong academic, vocabulary, mathematics, and critical-thinking skills. These skills can have a positive effect on their college entrance exam scores.

Suggest to your kids that they discuss their academic plans with their guidance counselor. Talk to your kids to get their ideas about what they want to do and where they want to go to college. Help them research the types of colleges that might be of interest to them and send for catalogues and brochures.

Constantly encourage your kids to study hard, get excellent grades, and become involved in extracurricular activities that will help them learn skills that they can't learn in classrooms. However, do not forget about the interest factor. If a young person is good at something, it does not automatically mean he or she is interested in studying it. When choosing which classes to take, you should consider both aspects.

> **Getting Started**
>
> The **College Scholarship Services (CSS) PROFILE** is an institutional need-analysis service developed by the College Scholarship Services. It assesses all of your family's assets, including equity in your home. The profile also assesses student income and expected summer earnings contributions.

Some schools require you to fill out their own aid application in addition to a *College Scholarship Services (CSS) PROFILE* and a FAFSA. Be sure to find out whether the school you're interested in requires this. Some do because they figure a family's expected contribution and ultimate need using two different systems; they'll use the Federal Methodology system for the FAFSA and the Institutional Methodology system for the CSS. Some colleges will even request financial data on parents' retirement accounts, cash values of insurance policies, and the like to satisfy their award policies.

The one good thing about the CSS PPROFILE is that there's a relatively short waiting period for finding out how much money you and your family will have to contribute. That's because you send the CSS forms in at the same time you file your application for admission. The quick response time will help if you're shopping for an affordable college.

Advice for High School Sophomores

Okay, you've just started your sophomore year of high school, and you want to go to college. But college is three years off, so you don't need to think about it now. Wrong. *Now* is the time to start practicing for the Scholastic Aptitude Test (SAT) by taking preliminary tests. The score you get on the SAT can literally make or break your chances of getting into the college of your choice. So get with it, kid, and always remember what Yogi Berra said: "Practice makes perfect." You can learn all about the SAT, ACT, and other tests in Chapter 6.

Sophomore Fall Checklist

Sophomores should take the PSAT and PLAN tests. These are preliminary preparation tests for the SAT and the ACT. High scores on these preliminary tests can qualify you for academic recognition and possible scholarships. Both tests are scheduled from October through December. You'll need to register and prepare several weeks in advance, so ask the counseling center at your high school about test dates as soon as you begin your sophomore year.

The PSAT and SAT have similar questions, so consider the PSAT as practice for the SAT. Your PSAT scores from your junior year qualify you for the National Merit Scholarship Competition. Take the test seriously and take it as often as you can so that you become familiar with the format and the questions. Your final test score will benefit from taking these practice tests.

The Scholastic Aptitude Test is used to measure a student's ability in math, verbal comprehension, and problem solving. SATs are administered during the junior and senior years in high school.

The ACT Assessment test is designed to assess high school students' general educational development and their ability to complete college-level work. The tests cover four skill areas: English, mathematics, reading, and science reasoning.

Sophomore Winter Checklist

Meet with your guidance counselor to review the results of the PSAT and PLAN tests. Review the material that's included with your results.

- ◆ Read challenging and interesting books over winter break to strengthen your vocabulary.

- ◆ Visit your college guidance office to research colleges, view literature, read guidebooks, and discover Internet resources.

- ◆ Read good books over spring break to strengthen your vocabulary. Keep a vocabulary journal to help you master the words you've learned.

Sophomore Spring Checklist

Visit your guidance counselor to discuss registering for the June SAT Subject Test. There's some disagreement about whether students should take the test as early as sophomore year, before they've had a chance to learn more about a subject. Taking more tests also means more expense, but we strongly recommend taking the SAT Subject Test in June of your sophomore year. This specialized test evaluates you on academic course work that you've already completed.

> **Action Plan**
>
> Read a variety of fiction, nonfiction, and drama over summer break to strengthen your vocabulary and for pure enjoyment.

Discuss with your guidance counselor options for enrolling in summer school or in a summer course or program at a local college or community college.

Sophomore Summer Checklist

Some colleges require three SAT Subject Tests, which are given in early June. Two of the tests should be in a math and a writing subject. You'll be taking these tests again in your junior year, and you'll have the option of sending your best scores to colleges. PSATS will be taken in October. Consider taking a summer PSAT/SAT prep course.

Advice for High School Juniors

Going to college is almost a requirement for increased earning potential and career satisfaction. The opportunity to study at the college of your choice is both an honor and a privilege. To find the most appropriate schools in which to invest your time and to find the best sources of financial aid to fund your education, follow a few simple steps to make negotiating the course to college more manageable and more promising.

> **Warning**
>
> At many colleges, scholarship and grant applications need to be received early in the student's senior year to be considered for the freshman year of college, so don't delay. Learn everything you can about scholarships by visiting the websites listed under Scholarships in Appendix B and by state in Appendix C. You'll discover a variety of sources for financial aid that you didn't know existed.

Junior Fall Checklist

Complete the necessary requirements to take or retake the SAT or ACT tests. Take practice tests again before going to the exams so you can be familiar with the format of the questions.

- **Start evaluating your college choices.** You're looking for qualities ranging from academics to dorm life, and you'll want to know which schools offer what you want. Be prepared to identify what is important to you, such as a specific degree program, a big-city or small-town campus, a college that's close to home or far away, an atmosphere that's culturally diverse, or a school with special recognition. This search can be free and is always fun.

- **Apply for every scholarship you think you have a chance to win.** College can be very expensive and most likely will require financial assistance from numerous sources. The more informed you are about sources of college funding, the easier it will be to attend the college of your choice. Know where to start so you can find and qualify for grants, loans, and scholarships. But don't let the quantity of forms and applications tempt you to skimp on providing complete and accurate information. Take your time when applying and be sure to set aside time so that each application is filled out properly.

- **Discuss and review your courses for this year and your plans for next year with your guidance counselor.** Make certain you'll be meeting your college requirements with the courses you're taking and have completed.

- **Register for the October PSAT.** This PSAT will qualify you for the National Merit Scholarship Competition. With high PSAT and SAT scores, good grades, and a recommendation from your school, you may become a National Merit Scholarship Finalist. Finalists qualify not only for academic distinction but also for scholarships.

Warning _____

Watch out for the avalanche of "junk" mail that will start appearing in your mailbox during your junior year. Everybody who has anything to do with the financial aid process will contact you for a variety of related reasons, offering consulting services, scholarship search services, and many other "deals." Some of what you receive will probably contain false advertising claims, but there may also be some mail worth following up on, so don't throw it all in the trash.

Junior Winter Checklist

Begin financial aid research by exploring grants, scholarships, and work-study programs with college financial aid offices and with your high school counselor.

- Do research on your own via the Internet.

- Review your PSAT test results with your guidance counselor and consult with him or her about taking the ACT or the SAT. You'll have to determine which tests are required for the colleges you're considering.

- Make sure you have a Social Security number. If necessary, visit the Social Security office in your area to obtain one.

- Prepare a preliminary list of colleges you would like to investigate and possibly attend. Visit with your guidance counselor to discuss your list of colleges.

- Write to the colleges on your list and ask for catalogues, community activity information, and special financial aid options.

- Register for the March SAT.

- Purchase an SAT prep guidebook to read over winter break and consider taking an SAT prep course.

Action Plan _____

Contact each school to explore the financial aid possibilities. Write to the school's financial aid office as soon as you apply for admission. Applying for financial aid should not affect your chances of getting accepted.

Junior Spring Checklist

Make sure your spring checklist includes the following items, and don't let spring fever keep you from getting them done!

- Check the SAT I and ACT test dates.

- Narrow the list of colleges that you're considering down to perhaps a top five.

- Contact the colleges on your short list and request admission literature.

- Consider your summer plans, including summer job options, summer school, and a summer course or program at a local college or community college.

Junior Summer Checklist

Enroll in summer school at a local college, apply for an internship, or work as a volunteer in the field of your career choice.

- Review literature received from the colleges on your short list.

- Pursue other information resources about these colleges. Visit each college's website.

- Consider planning visits to colleges during the summer.

- Inquire about attending an interview session with one of the college admissions counselors. They book up quickly, so set up appointments as early as possible. Include family members on your college tours. Incorporate these visits with your family's summer vacation plans.

- Begin preparing for the application process by assembling your portfolio, collecting writing samples, and drafting application essays.

- If applicable, contact the coaches at the college to inquire about athletic scholarships.

Advice for High School Seniors

Now that you're a high school senior and on the fast track to college, it's time to find out just how fast you really can run. You have to take the SAT and perhaps the ACT before the year is over, so now's the time to fine-tune your testing skills. Go to the library or a local bookstore and get a good book that shows you how to ace these tests. If you like computers, you can also get application software that will show you how to improve your overall score. Practice taking these tests before you take the real thing!

Senior Fall Checklist

Register for the October or November SAT and ACT tests. You can do this through your high school's student guidance office or online. (See the "Scholastic Aptitude Tests" section in Appendix B for website addresses.)

◆ Send for college applications and information from the schools on your short list. Check on application deadlines and any special requirements.

◆ Ask teachers, coaches, and employers to write you letters of recommendation. Give these people at least two weeks to write you the best letters they can and be sure to thank them. Sometimes the person you ask will want you to explain what sorts of things the college will be looking for in a letter. Simply explain as clearly as possible what you think would reflect well and honestly about yourself as a potential college student.

◆ Visit with your guidance counselor to review your list of colleges, making sure your choices are appropriate for your academic and personal record.

◆ Update your personal records.

◆ Visit the scholarship websites listed in Appendix B to discover and research private scholarships. Apply for every scholarship you think you have a chance of winning.

◆ Visit your library, bookstore, and the Internet to research any additional sources of scholarships and financial aid.

◆ Plan visits and set up interviews at those colleges you did not visit during the summer.

◆ Develop a schedule of admissions and financial aid deadlines for yourself.

◆ Update your personal profile to include any changes or last-minute additions.

◆ Visit your guidance counselor to make sure your transcript and test scores have been sent to the colleges you selected.

◆ If you already know which college you want to attend, submit applications for early decision/early action programs.

◆ Prepare applications for your backup college choices.

Warning

Be prepared. Students and parents should file their income tax returns early in the year in which they're applying for financial aid. You'll need information from income tax forms to complete your financial aid applications.

◆ Check with your high school guidance office, bank, or public library to find out about any scheduled financial aid presentations.

Senior Winter Checklist

Discuss and review your final list of colleges with your school counselor.

◆ File all remaining college applications. Have your test scores sent to those colleges.

◆ Obtain all financial aid forms that may be required by the colleges you've applied to.

◆ Update your personal profile to include any changes or last-minute additions.

◆ Complete the FAFSA form, make a copy of it, and submit it as early in January as you can.

Action Plan

Obtain a Free Application for Federal Student Aid (FAFSA) at high schools, colleges, and libraries or by calling 1-800-4-FEDAID (1-800-433-3243). FAFSA is also available online, along with additional college information. Get more information at www.fafsa.ed.gov (also see the "FAFSA" section in Appendix B).

◆ Parents and students should compile income tax information and then complete and file income tax returns early to complete the FAFSA application.

◆ Determine whether any other financial aid forms are required by your state or the colleges you are applying to.

Warning

Monitor your applications to be certain that all materials are sent and received on time and that they are complete. Be aware of all deadlines. Miss a deadline and your application will automatically be rejected. Contact the colleges to which you are applying to see if they have a mechanism in place that acknowledges receipt of your application material. Just be sure you get confirmation that the college did indeed receive all your materials. Another factor to consider—now that so much paperwork is done via the Internet—is whether the school has requested an electronic application. If so, be sure that the institution's virtual application is filled out properly and is electronically conveyed so that it reaches its destination. There have been stories of students who *thought* they had applied to schools, only to find out their electronic application was never received.

Senior Spring Checklist

Review your list to make certain you've submitted all required financial aid forms. Many private scholarships have March 1 application deadlines.

 ◆ Update your personal profile and apply for any new scholarships.

 ◆ If required, send copies of your income tax returns to financial aid offices.

 ◆ Receive your Student Aid Report (SAR). (It should arrive about four weeks after you submit the FAFSA.) Contact your school's financial aid office to ask whether it needs a copy of the SAR.

 ◆ Sign and return financial aid forms.

 ◆ Receive admissions notifications and compare your financial aid packages.

 ◆ Choose a college. Send final transcript and student loan applications to your chosen college.

 ◆ Contact your financial aid office to check status.

 ◆ Contact admissions and financial aid offices of schools whose enrollment offers you've decided to decline, informing them of your final decision. Never burn your bridges with any college you apply to!

Now that you've chosen a specific college, you may discover other sources of aid for that school.

Senior Summer Checklist

Complete any remaining financial aid forms. New awards are added regularly. It's never too early to start looking for next year.

Ten Financial Aid Tips

The financial aid tips that we include in this section are certainly not meant to be all inclusive. They will, however, help you stay on top of the financial aid process so you can get the best possible support out of the program.

1. Prioritize your efforts, beginning with the federal government. Explore the private sector for additional financial assistance programs. Use websites like Scholarship.com to locate the private sector funds to apply for.

2. Contact each school to explore the financial aid possibilities by writing its financial aid office as soon as you apply for admission. Applying for financial aid will not affect your chances of getting accepted.

3. Be prepared. Students and parents should file their income tax returns early. You'll need information from income tax forms to complete your financial aid applications.

4. Try to get to know the financial aid administrators (FAAs) at the various colleges you've applied to. Take notes whenever you talk to them so that you'll remember their names and what you've talked about in the past. The help of the FAAs will be valuable if questions arise later on in the year.

5. Submit a FAFSA even if you don't think you'll qualify for aid. Being rejected for federal aid is sometimes a prerequisite for private awards. Some schools require you to fill out their own aid application as well as a CSS profile. Be sure to find out what each school needs.

6. Apply for aid as early as possible. Deadlines vary, but your application for federal student aid can be sent any time after January 1. An early application will help you get the best financial aid package possible.

7. Take advantage of tuition prepayment discounts. Many colleges offer up to a 10 percent discount for early payment.

8. Money from grandparents could be paid in your name directly to the school. This avoids gift tax liability.

9. Investigate company-sponsored tuition plans. Many employers will invest in the education of their employees or children of employees.

10. Apply for financial aid each and every year you are in school. Even if you receive aid during one year, you must reapply to get it for the next year. Use the renewal FAFSA form to reapply for aid and save time. See your FAA for assistance.

To get the most out of financial aid, parents and students need to have a plan that starts in the student's freshman year. Go to your public library and check out the latest scholarship books. There are lots of them out there, and the research librarian can help you find them. They will give you listings of available scholarships and contact addresses for applying. Check out the Internet for scholarship opportunities. If you don't have access to the Internet at home, use the public library or your high school's computer lab.

The Least You Need to Know

- ◆ Parents and kids should start thinking about college as early as possible.

- ◆ Students should choose courses that match their capabilities and will result in good grades.

- ◆ Important tests, such as the PSAT, PLAN, SAT, and ACT, should be taken several times to improve results.

- ◆ High school students who make plans using the checklists in this chapter will greatly increase their chances of acceptance at colleges of their choice and of obtaining financial aid.

Where Do You Want to Go, Kid?

In This Chapter

- Gathering the information you need for determining which college is right for you

- Finding out how to ask the right questions to be sure you're informed about every aspect of financial aid

- Comparing college alternatives using failsafe selection criteria

This chapter is about ways to get the most out of every dollar you spend on college. Look for colleges that have innovative programs to help you meet their ever-increasing tuition cost. Many even have unique programs that will help you find room and board at very competitive rates. Remember: tuition is just one part of the total cost line.

Choose Wisely, Kid

The process of choosing a college or university can be both exciting and frustrating at the same time. If you're a parent, the last thing you want is to face a confrontation with a son or daughter who wants to attend a college

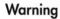

Warning _____

This chapter makes some general assumptions about the subject matter that is discussed. For example, what may be an advantage to one student can be a disadvantage or have no effect on another student.

that you don't think is right for him or her or, worse yet, one that you flat out can't afford.

Although it's not the intention of this book to get into the philosophical reasons for selecting one college over another, it is within its charter to discuss the value issues that parent and student should consider jointly. Then you can select the college options that make sense in terms of meeting both your budgetary and educational objectives. This chapter covers all of those issues.

Start by Gathering Information

Write for school catalogues, financial aid brochures, and any other information they may have such as the placement of their graduates. It may be more appropriate to request information over the phone because you'll have a chance to query the person you're talking to about what information is available. After you've obtained the information, you and your family can compare the various schools and decide which ones deserve further investigation.

Your in-depth investigation might include a visit to the campus and interviews with the admissions officer, the financial aid administrator, and the placement director. Make sure you ask the admissions officer questions regarding the academic quality of the programs that are of most interest, and find out what the student/faculty ratio is. A small student/faculty ratio may mean more personal attention by teachers and staff.

Questions to Ask the Admissions Officer

When you meet with the admissions officer, your objective should be to find out everything you can about what the college requires before it will admit a student into the institution. For example, you might ask the following:

- ♦ How much emphasis is placed on a student's high school GPA or SAT score?
- ♦ Which high school extracurricular activities are more important?

Ask the admissions officer to profile for you his or her "ideal" student applicant so that you can get a good picture of exactly what he or she is looking for.

Questions to Ask the Financial Aid Administrator

Questions posed to the FAA should cover the types of financial assistance programs that are available, application deadlines, and any special aid programs offered. Also ask the following:

- How are awards made, and how does the appeals process work if a student feels he or she deserves a better financial aid package?

- What percentage of students receives financial aid, and what is the average amount of annual assistance per student?

These two critical financial aid numbers, when compared with the annual cost for the college, will give you a good idea of how much financial aid you can expect.

Action Plan

A quick formula for calculating the amount of financial assistance you can expect is to compare the percentage of students on financial aid and the average amount of aid per student with the annual cost of the college. For example, if one of your top colleges is, on average, awarding $4,300 to 57 percent of its students and another of your top choices is awarding less than half that, you can narrow your selection process based on the probability of the award you may receive.

Other questions you may want to ask an FAA are …

- What's the total cost of attending your school for one year?

- What's been the average increase in tuition over the past three years?

- How do you calculate a student's financial need?

- Do you have a "need-blind" admissions policy, meaning that equal opportunity is given to students for admission regardless of their financial needs?

- Do you meet the full need of every admitted student?

- What percentage of the freshman class is paying full tuition?

- What scholarship opportunities are available?

- Is my financial aid package renewable each year?

- What applications are required, and what are the deadlines?

- When will I receive my financial aid award letter?

Questions to Ask the Placement Director

When you meet with the placement director, ask ...

- ◆ What placement services are available?

- ◆ What is the profile of recent graduates? (For example, what percentage had Bachelor's versus Master's degrees?)

- ◆ What percentage was able to find jobs through the placement office?

- ◆ What was the average starting salary in the various career fields? (Consider, however, that salaries may be linked to the geographical location of a school and are not necessarily indicative of an inferior education or poor placement practices.)

If you can't get answers to these basic questions, you're probably dealing with a school that has a mediocre placement office; or worse yet, they may not even have one. If it's not possible to visit all of the schools, get the information over the phone.

Look for Creative Payment Plans

The fact of the matter is that more and more colleges are looking for ways to take the sting out of paying the costs. For many of them, this means offering plans that make it possible to get around paying for college in one formidable annual chunk.

Many colleges now offer a range of innovative payment programs. Some of the programs are as simple as allowing you to pay for tuition and room and board in interest-free, equal installments over 12 months instead of having to fork over whopping payments at the start of every quarter or semester.

Some colleges offer tuition stabilization programs. If you're willing to pay them the full four-year tuition up front, future tuition hikes do not apply to you.

> **Action Plan**
>
> Never forget the fact that your kid is still the customer when he or she starts searching for the right college to attend. The college business is a competitive business, although you'll seldom hear college administrators admit this fine point. All colleges need students in order to survive. Consider yourself a consumer: tell them what you're willing to pay for their service and listen to what they have to say.

Become a Wise Consumer

For both parents and kids, getting a college education is a major investment of time and money, so make sure that the school your student attends is right for him or her. When choosing a school, a student should consider things like these:

- ◆ The quality of instructors and school facilities.

- ◆ Information about students at the school, such as …

  - ◆ The percentage of students who complete the program.

  - ◆ The percentage of students who find jobs within a short time after graduation.

  - ◆ The percentage of students who default on their student loans.

The school is required to inform you of its aid procedures and deadlines, and how and when you'll receive your aid award. Be sure that you read and understand the school's satisfactory-progress policy and keep copies of your enrollment agreement, the school's catalogue, and all loan documents that you've received.

Count Your Credit

If you have an excellent credit history, some colleges offer very-low-interest loans for financing your kid's four-year education over as many as ten years. The point is that there are as many flexible college finance programs out there as there are colleges.

As you and your son or daughter begin your search for viable college alternatives, make sure you ask the question, "Do you offer flexible finance programs?" If they tell you "No" and cannot provide a good rationale, scratch them off your list and proceed to your next college option.

HELP!

The College Opportunities Online Locator (COOL) is brought to you by the National Center for Education Statistics in the U.S. Department of Education. It was authorized by Congress in 1998 to help college students, future students, and their parents understand the differences between colleges and how much it costs to attend college. The site is www.nces.ed.gov/ipeds/cool and is found in the "Career Guidance" section in Appendix B.

It May Be Cheaper at the Top

As a result of doing such extensive research into the financial aid possibilities available for his second child, my friend George was literally stunned to find out how much aid he was eligible for. Even more surprising was that top institutions were among his most viable choices.

George had uncovered a little-known fact: the more expensive the institution, the more likely it is to offer need-based financial aid. He said, "When we looked through the guidebooks, we found colleges that met about 90 percent of our need." George discovered that he had more choices for his children than families whose incomes were $20,000 to $30,000 higher than his.

For example, let's say your expected family contribution (EFC) toward college tuition is $10,000, and you're eligible to receive $1,000 in aid. For a college costing $20,000 in tuition, you could be eligible for $11,000 in aid. The amount you're expected to contribute is the same, regardless of the total cost of the school. What changes is the amount that different colleges will provide you in financial aid.

If you can get your kid into an Ivy League college, and if you have financial need, the college might actually cost you less than a state-supported university. Ivy League institutions don't typically give merit-based aid, so if you can get accepted and have need, they may provide you with enough money to make up the difference. It's all based on your financial resources.

Too many students eliminate colleges from their "preferred list" before determining their financial aid eligibility. Before they address cost issues, students should make choices based on the attributes of the colleges and where those choices fit into their career plans. That's the whole philosophy of financial aid. Thus, highly talented students from low-income families may qualify for significant amounts of aid and have the opportunity to attend institutions they otherwise might not have even considered. If you can be admitted, you can figure out a way to go.

At the other end of the misinformation scale, families often assume there is some income cutoff level that turns off the financial aid tap. That's not true because, even though financial aid is driven by a family's ability to pay, that ability is affected by special circumstances, size, and how many of their children are attending college.

Selection Criteria

Less-selective colleges focus on whether applicants meet minimum requirements and whether there is room for more students. Grades are not overlooked, but acceptable grades might be the only requirement beyond an interest in college study. The SAT I or ACT may be required, but test scores might be used for course placement rather than admissions decisions. Other factors might be considered, but they probably won't play a major part.

At more-selective colleges, course work, grades, test scores, recommendations, and essays will be considered. There may be additional considerations, but the major factor will be whether a student is ready for college-level study. Students could be denied admission because of some weakness in their academic preparation, less-impressive grades or test scores, or a lack of interest in higher education.

At the most-selective colleges, as many as 10 or 15 students might apply for each opening. Nearly every applicant has the necessary academic qualifications, but they can't all be accepted. Therefore, admissions officers at such schools look carefully at every aspect of a student's high school experience. Applicants must have academic strength and impressive SAT or ACT scores. Since so many applicants are strong academically, other factors become quite important in the admissions decision.

Although the most-selective colleges receive a great deal of publicity, there are actually very few of them. Sometimes a college will have a reputation as a select institution that may not be warranted. Try to develop the ability to discern the facts from the hype.

Extracurricular Activities Do Count

The importance of what a student does outside of school has been exaggerated. Selective colleges may look at extracurricular activities, but they're only interested in applicants who've shown long-term commitments to one or two activities. These colleges aren't trying to enroll a class of well-rounded students; they want to admit a well-rounded *group* of students. An applicant with achievements in a specific area may have an advantage, but it's hard to tell which areas might be of interest to a college in any given year.

 Warning

Don't believe what you hear about the importance that colleges place on your extracurricular activities. Less-selective colleges rarely look beyond test scores and grades, and those that are more selective tend to change their interest in specific activities from year to year.

Fill a College's Need

At the most-selective colleges, you must fill a need in the freshman class. Otherwise, you might not be admitted despite outstanding academic records. That need might be something as arbitrary as the student's home state, intended major, desire for housing on campus, or ability to play a specific musical instrument in the college orchestra.

If there's housing for only part of the freshman class, then admissions decisions must reflect this limitation. If there's room for only 25 new engineering majors but 75 new accounting majors can be accommodated, this must also be considered as admissions decisions are made. On the other hand, if a college wants geographic distribution and an ethnic balance of students, admissions decisions will reflect those needs.

Basically, the admission process is unpredictable and holds many potential surprises.

Find the Right Match

Remember that "more selective" does not necessarily mean "better." Our society often associates exclusivity with higher value. However, college is one area where that notion is wrong. If you focus on the most-selective colleges, you risk overlooking your personal needs. Try to find colleges that provide a good match with your interests, objectives, characteristics, and needs. Such colleges may be found anywhere. If you consider only the most competitive college within your area, you may overlook more appropriate possibilities.

The best-prepared student will have the most options. That doesn't necessarily mean attending the most-competitive college. The overriding concern should be finding the right match. If you're well prepared, you will have many options to choose from.

Some Do's and Don'ts

Parents: be candid with your kids about the financial aid process. Many parents are reluctant to discuss finances with their children because they don't want to unduly concern them. The degree to which you involve your children should be based on your assessment of how much they should know. But your children will be better prepared to help make wise family decisions if they have information about the factors you are dealing with. They'll have to become involved sooner or later in their college years as they take over paying back college and graduate school loans.

The Do's

Keep these do's in mind as you and your son or daughter go through the process of choosing a college:

- ◆ **Do make sure the information you're using to apply for aid reflects your parental status.** This tip applies to a divorced as well as either a custodial or a noncustodial parent. Some institutions don't specifically ask about this on their forms. It could make a difference in the financial aid you might receive.

♦ **Do have an organized plan in place to keep track of applications.** Note deadlines and what you have to do to follow up. Some high school counselors can give you forms that will help you compare financial aid packages.

The Don'ts

The list of don'ts is longer:

♦ **Don't wait to apply for financial aid until your child is admitted.** This common misperception among parents sets them to scrambling when an offer of admission is made. At this late date, a lot of the available money has already been allocated. Many families don't realize how time-sensitive admissions are. Your financial package could get cut by as much as 50 percent if you don't meet deadlines.

♦ **Don't assume you have to wait until you get current tax information to begin applying for financial aid.** Estimates of your income that are based on the previous year are acceptable. Many people miss out on the full funding they could have gotten because they were waiting for tax returns.

♦ **Don't assume you'll be penalized because you've saved for college tuition.** Legally, you can be asked to contribute only 5.6 percent of your savings toward tuition. You will get slightly less aid, but you'll also end up borrowing less money and paying less interest.

♦ **Don't start the process of seeking aid when your financial house is a mess.** Clean up your credit history before starting to apply for loans. Have all your financial records handy and in order.

Online Applications

Save time and paper by submitting your school application online. At the Peterson's College and Career Quest (www.petersons.com/schools/ccq-6.html), you can apply to more than 1,200 colleges using a single application. You enter all of your application information once, and then it's available for use on each new application that you open. Once you've completed your applications, you can print and mail them, or you can submit them electronically and securely to colleges that accept electronic applications. Make sure you have a copy of everything you have submitted and proof of when you submitted it. You don't want to be that one individual in a thousand whose records have been misplaced.

HELP!

> CollegeNET was launched in 1995 and lets college applicants complete, file, and pay for their admissions applications entirely through the Internet. Over 350 colleges and universities have contracted with CollegeNET to serve as their official web-based admissions application site. For websites to check out, see the "College Admission Requirements" section in Appendix B or CollegeNET's website at www. collegenet.com.

College Admissions Criteria

For many years, admissions policies were "need-blind," reflecting the belief that students who needed financial aid should be treated the same as those whose families could afford the total cost.

However, much has changed in recent years. A number of colleges still maintain "need-blind" admissions policies, but other colleges include the family's financial situation in the admissions process. This doesn't mean that only students with enough money are admitted, but rather that these colleges know they can't satisfy the financial aid needs of all applicants.

Most colleges accept the strongest applicants without regard to need. Then, as financial aid resources begin to run out, students who don't have as much academic strength are evaluated for their family's ability to pay. This may sound unfair but so is accepting a student who cannot afford the school without financial help.

Other colleges have a policy of meeting a portion of every accepted student's need. A certain amount of need is left unmet for all. Unfortunately, students and parents have no control over the policies or the resources at any college. If a student needs financial aid to attend college, he or she should consider each school's policy when deciding where to apply. Each college has a different approach to admitting qualified applicants and has different factors that it considers.

At most colleges, admissions criteria might include the following:

Courses taken in high school

Counselor or teacher recommendations

Overall grade-point average

Answers to application questions and the quality of submitted essays

Ethnicity

Location of the student's home

Personal interview

Alumni relationship

Rank in class

Activities outside the classroom

Major that the student is applying for

Admissions test results

Special talents and skills

Family's ability to pay for college expenses

These are not arranged to reflect any specific priorities. In fact, there is no general agreement about how criteria should be ranked. Most likely, the chief admissions factor is a student's high school record—both the student's grades and the courses taken.

Colleges evaluate applications in very different ways, depending on how selective, or competitive, the college is. At one extreme are "open admission" colleges. These schools require only a high school diploma and accept students on a first-come, first-served basis. At the other extreme are very selective colleges that consider all of the factors listed. These colleges admit only a small percentage of applicants each year. Most colleges fall somewhere in between.

International Considerations

The idea of an international experience excites many American students until they find out how difficult it is to get any financial aid from foreign institutions. Obtaining aid at a foreign institution is challenging for U.S. citizens because you're obviously competing with students who are citizens of that institution's country. About 100,000 Americans study away from U.S. shores each year, and many have been able to find the financial aid they needed to make it abroad. If you wish to study abroad, be prepared to work hard at locating aid sources.

See Chapter 14 for more on studying abroad and on study for foreign students in the United States. Also check out the websites listed in the "International" section of Appendix B. The best one I've found is www.petersons.com/finaid.

Selecting the Winner

Choosing the right school is difficult; even narrowing your choices down to a few likely candidates can be an exercise in frustration. With thousands of schools in the United States, how will you ever find the right one for you?

Petersons' website at www.petersons.com is an online service that profiles and can help get you through the selection process. This service offers profiles of every undergraduate institution accredited in the United States, along with specially designed tools to help you manage the college admissions process. It also allows you to search for schools by location, major, difficulty level, and other factors, and then compare them side by side and apply online. The website provides informative articles about college selection and admissions.

If you're thinking about graduate or professional school, see Chapter 14 and also look to Peterson's Graduate Planner at www.petersons.com/graduate for detailed information on 35,000 programs, including business, law, medical, and dental school. *Peterson's* is an annual publication that offers a wealth of information about planning for college and about distance learning programs, and it also has a discussion area for graduate students. Check out their site at www.petersons.com. You'll also find more websites in Appendix B in the "College Admission Requirement" section.

> **Action Plan**
>
> Network with your friends. Reach out for information that your friends and their friends have discovered in their respective searches for the perfect college to attend. If you have the opportunity, take a "walkabout" on the campuses of your preferred colleges and survey the current students who are also on "walkabouts." Ask them what they think about the college to get invaluable insight and information.

The Least You Need to Know

♦ To make sure you pick the college that's right for you, look at the full spectrum of offerings for each college that you're considering.

♦ Don't let high tuition at your favorite institutions scare you. Find out what they're willing to offer you in their financial aid package.

♦ Know what your favorite college is looking for in its admissions requirements so that you can customize your application accordingly.

Chapter 6

Take the Tests

In This Chapter

- ◆ Learning what admissions tests are all about and why you must take them
- ◆ Discovering how you can improve your score with a little practice
- ◆ Understanding how test scores are used to get you into college and to win you merit scholarships

There are many thousands of high schools in this country, each with its own grading policy. Years ago, colleges determined that they needed a common measure, such as a standard test, to evaluate applicants. Many college students and parents are confused about the role that college admissions tests play in both the admissions and the merit scholarship awards process. To better understand these tests, students and parents should consider all the factors that influence scores, and that is the topic of this chapter.

By the time many students start to think about college admissions tests, it's too late. These tests measure skills developed over a long period of time—skills that cannot be acquired through short-term preparation. Last-minute intensive courses may help students demonstrate their abilities, but they won't help students develop the skills that the college admissions tests measure.

What can students do early on that may have an impact on test results? Check out the section "Scholastic Aptitude Tests (SAT, PSAT, ACT)" in Appendix B.

The Almighty Scholastic Aptitude Test (SAT)

The *Scholastic Aptitude Test* (*SAT*) is taken by over two million high school students each year. SAT scores, course grades, and other information about your academic background help college admission officers evaluate how well prepared you are to do college-level work. Because course content and difficulty as well as grading standards vary widely from school to school, scores on standardized tests such as the SAT help colleges compare the academic achievements of students from different schools.

The SAT test was revised in 2005, and this more recent version has come to be known as the "new SAT." It differs from the previous SAT test in a number of ways. The next section will explain how the new test differs from the older version.

Colleges often require applicants to take the SAT as a prerequisite for admission. This test is designed to measure critical-reading skills, math reasoning skills, and writing skills that students have developed over time. The new SAT helps predict a student's success in college. Some colleges require students to take the American College Test (ACT), although many will accept either the SAT or the ACT. While these tests are somewhat different, the objectives are similar. Each provides an indication of a student's potential for academic success. The ACT test measures a student's ability in math, critical-reading skills, and problem solving. Usually students take this test during their junior or senior year of high school.

What Exactly Is the New SAT?

The new SAT is a three-hour-and-45-minute multiple-part test used by many colleges as a factor in undergraduate admissions and placement decisions. It has eight sections placed in random order.

The test contains three scored math sections for a total of 60 questions. Two of the math sections are 25 minutes each, and the third section runs 20 minutes.

The math questions appear in two formats:

- Five-choice problem-solving questions
- Grid-in questions

Grid-ins are non-multiple-choice questions; you're asked to find a numerical answer and mark it on a grid.

The new SAT also contains three scored critical-reading sections for a total of 78 questions. Two of the critical-reading sections are 25 minutes each, and the third is 20 minutes.

The two 30-minute sections consist of sentence completions and critical reading; the 20-minute section consists only of critical-reading questions.

The new SAT contains a third section, called the writing section, that is 60 minutes long and contains two parts. There is a 35-minute multiple-choice section; the first group of multiple-choice questions requires that you read 18 sentences, determine if there is an error in any of them, and identify the error if there is one. You will also be asked to read a sentence and try to improve it without changing its meaning. The second group of multiple-choice questions requires that you read 6 paragraphs, determine if they have errors, and if so, improve the paragraphs you've found to have mistakes. Finally, there is a 25-minute essay section in which you must write an essay in response to a writing prompt that demonstrates you can effectively communicate a viewpoint and define and support a position.

The eighth section on the SAT is an experimental section composed of either math or critical-reading questions. It's used to test questions for future tests and is not scored. There is no reliable way of knowing which of the seven sections is experimental since the sections are randomly ordered.

You'll find more about the writing, critical reading, and math sections later in this chapter.

Getting Started

The Scholastic Aptitude Reasoning Test is a three-hour-and-45-minute test, primarily multiple choice with a writing section, a critical-reading section, and a mathematical reasoning abilities section—all of which are skills that develop over time. Colleges often require SAT scores as part of the admissions application. Scholastic Aptitude Subject Tests (SAT II) are one-hour, primarily multiple-choice tests in specific subjects. Unlike the SAT, which measures more general abilities, Subject Tests measure knowledge of particular subjects and the ability to apply that knowledge. Many colleges require or recommend one or more of these tests for admission or placement. SAT scores are one of the main selection criteria used by college admissions officials to assess a student's academic qualifications and abilities.

How Important Is the SAT?

Unfortunately, your SAT score is often one of the most important pieces in your admissions portfolio. If your score falls below a school's acceptable range, the admissions officers may look very critically at the other parts of your application; if your scores exceed the school's acceptable range, you'll have a leg up in the applicant pool for that college.

Larger schools tend to rely heavily, or even base their admissions decisions entirely, on SAT scores and high school grade-point averages. Smaller and more selective schools tend to place more weight on other factors such as your interview (if one is required), your personal essays, and your extracurricular activities. Some schools have begun to de-emphasize the SAT, and a few have even made it optional as an entry requirement.

What Is the PSAT?

The PSAT is a test that's very similar to the SAT. In fact, the PSAT is composed of previously administered SAT questions. It is given to high school students in their sophomore and junior years. The test is used to help select National Merit Scholars, but unless you're one of the very few who are in contention for these scholarships, it's really only a practice test. Colleges will not see your PSAT scores, only your high school will. If you're interested in doing well on the SAT, make sure you practice by taking the PSAT first.

> **HELP!**
> There are many websites that address every aspect of SAT and ACT testing. They are listed in the "Scholastic Aptitude Tests (SAT, PSAT, ACT)" section in Appendix B.

Who Created the SAT?

The SAT and SAT II are written by the Educational Testing Service and administered by the College Entrance Examination Board (better known as the "College Board"). The people who work at the College Board are average folks who just happen to make a living writing and administering tests. But the questions are often confusingly worded, and the Educational Testing Service (ETS) has planted plenty of trick choices to seduce you into picking incorrect answers. You may get the feeling at times that the ETS has rigged the game against you—and you're right.

Preparing for the Test

The best academic predictor for most college admissions offices is the student's high school record. In other words, high school courses and grades are usually the most accurate and comprehensive factors considered in the admissions process. The admissions tests do give the college another valuable piece of evidence about a student: how well the student measures up academically to other students from all the different high schools throughout the United States.

Long-Term Preparation

True success on these tests is based on long-term preparation. Experiences in the classroom will affect how well a student does on admissions tests. But students spend only six hours or so each day in school for 180 days a year, so what they do outside the classroom is important, too.

Students who have good reading habits and strong reading skills do well on the critical-reading part of the SAT. There is no substitute for reading about a variety of subjects on a regular basis. Students who have consistently received A and B+ grades on their English papers should do well on the writing section. Both the SAT and ACT contain questions and reading passages that reflect subjects that students encounter in many areas, including the social sciences, humanities, literature, and physical sciences. Students who read a lot generally do better.

Admissions tests emphasize critical reading skills and vocabulary strength. Students develop most of their vocabulary through reading, but they may also benefit by learning to attack new words. Knowing prefixes, suffixes, and root words will be helpful in some situations. Studying a foreign language can help a student figure out new words as well.

Students who hope to do well on the math portions of these tests should take challenging math and science courses to help them further develop the math reasoning and problem-solving skills that will be measured. This is particularly important with the new SAT since it includes math questions that are based on college preparatory high school math.

Warning

Unfortunately, by the time most students begin to worry about admissions tests, it's too late to do much preparing for them. Preparation should begin well before the required test date, like in the first year of high school.

Short-Term Preparation

During the later high school years, students should begin short-term preparation for taking college entrance tests. They should take practice tests such as the PSAT, which gives students a chance to become familiar with the SAT format and types of questions. After they take the test, students receive a score report that shows how they did on each type of question. They should use the report to pinpoint where they need to do more work. Taking the PSAT will help students feel more relaxed about taking the SAT. There's a similar warm-up for the ACT.

Test Preparation Courses

Students may also consider taking a test preparation course. However, they need to realize that these "coaching" courses aren't meant to help them develop the skills the tests measure; they try to help students demonstrate skills they already have.

Coaching courses usually try to help students keep the test in perspective so they'll be more relaxed. The courses also teach test-taking strategies. Some students need help in these areas, and their scores should improve after taking a coaching course.

Free guides and practice tests are available in most high school guidance offices and online. Also, counselors and teachers are usually happy to help students prepare.

Some students' test scores won't improve when they take a special preparation course simply because they have modest abilities in the areas being tested. Their scores may even go down, adding to their frustration and probably diminishing their self-confidence.

What's Inside the SAT?

As explained earlier, the SAT is a three-hour-and-45-minute test that consists of seven scored sections and one unscored equating section for test research. The majority of the test is multiple choice; however, there is a variety of question types.

Within the two main parts of the exam, the questions are arranged in order of difficulty from least to most difficult. It is to your advantage to answer the easier questions first and then tackle the more difficult ones in your remaining time.

The Critical-Reading Part

The first section of the critical-reading exam is primarily a test of your vocabulary skills. The second part is composed of essays taken from a variety of topics, including social sciences, natural sciences, and the humanities. The passages can be either fiction or nonfiction. It is intended to measure reading comprehension skills. There are three types of questions in the critical-reading section:

1. **Explicit questions.** These ask you to refer to specific facts or words in the passage.

2. **Inferential questions.** These ask you to draw conclusions from the passage.

3. **Line reference questions.** These ask you to refer to a specific line in the passage.

 Action Plan

Check out the sample PSAT questions at www. princetonreview.com/home. asp. Other website addresses are listed in Appendix B under "Scholastic Aptitude Tests (SAT, PSAT, ACT)".

To enhance your reading comprehension skills, you should be reading articles in quality periodicals and newspapers. When you finish an article, always ask yourself, "What was the main point of what I just read?" There will be at least two paired passages in the critical-reading section of the exam. The questions based on the pair of passages will ask you to compare or contrast them.

The sentence completion section of the exam tests your vocabulary skills and your ability to understand sentence structure. Note the use of conjunctions such as *not*, *but*, *though*, and *although*, which change the direction of the sentence. The two parts of the sentence will contrast with each other, and the answer you choose should fit the logic of that contrast. If a sentence has two blanks, make sure both answers fit the logic of the sentence.

Some of the sentence completion questions will have two blanks rather than just one. To solve these questions, do them one blank at a time. Pick one blank or the other, whichever seems easier to you, and figure out which word should go in the blank. Often, but not always, the second blank is easier to figure out. Then cross off all of the choices that don't work for that blank. If more than one choice remains, pick a word for the other blank and see which of the remaining choices works best.

Take a look at this example and select the appropriate words to fill in the two blanks:

The scientific community was _____ when a living specimen of the coelacanth, which they feared had become _____, was discovered by deep-sea fishermen.

A. perplexed   common

B. overjoyed   dangerous

C. unconcerned   exterminated

D. astounded   extinct

E. dismayed   alive

Let's review some of the logical steps you would go through when you search for the correct answer (that is, the two words to insert): Who is the audience that's addressed by the opening words of the sentence? The answer is "the scientific community," which we know intuitively is not perplexed (Answer A), unconcerned (Answer C), or dismayed (Answer E) as a group in general. We have quickly ruled out three of the five choices for the fill-ins.

Wouldn't it be logical to conclude that the scientific community would be overjoyed (Answer B) or astounded (Answer D) at the discovery? That's a tough call until we take the time to look at the second insert word to find the correct answer (Answer D). They feared that the animal was extinct rather than that it was dangerous; to be dangerous it would still have to be running around the earth in great numbers.

The point of this exercise is to show you how to carefully dissect the important segments of a sentence so that you can quickly arrive at the right answer and move on to the next part of the test.

The Math Part

The math part of the exam will test your knowledge of arithmetic, geometry, algebra, and logical reasoning. Most of the questions on the math portion of the exam will be questions you recognize from your school textbooks. However, there may be questions that are unfamiliar to you and that require you to think about a problem in an unfamiliar way. Here are some examples of math questions that might appear on your SAT test:

A. If a student scores 70, 90, 95, and 105 on four tests, what is the average test score?

B. If a student has an average score of 80 on four tests, what is the total of the scores received on those tests?

C. If a student has an average of 60 on tests whose totals add up to 360, how many tests has the student taken?

D. If the average of 4 and x is equal to the average of 2, 8, and x, what is the value of x?

E. The average (arithmetic mean) of four numbers is 80. If two of the numbers are 50 and 60, what is the sum of the other two numbers?

F. What percent of 5 is 6?

G. 60 percent of 90 is the same as 50 percent of what number?

H. A group of 30 adults and 20 children went to the beach. If 50 percent of the adults and 80 percent of the children went swimming, what percentage of the group went swimming? (A) 31% (B) 46% (C) 50% (D) 62% (E) 65%

The answers to the questions are …

A.   90

B.   320

C.   6

D. $x = 8$

E.   210

F.   120%

G.   108

H.   31%

The student-produced response section of the exam (also known as grid-in) is unique. There are no answer choices to select from. The most important thing to understand about this section is how to enter your answers on the answer sheet grid. You use a pencil to shade the area on the grid that you feel is the answer to the question.

The standard multiple-choice section of the exam will cover a variety of mathematical concepts. Read each problem carefully. Translate any word problems into mathematical notation and begin to solve the problem. Review the answer choices and find the solution that fits best. If you're unsure of an answer, use the process of elimination. If you're completely unsure of the correct answer and cannot make an educated guess, skip the question and move on. There is no penalty for omitted questions. However, there is a penalty of one-fourth point for an incorrect answer.

Warning _____

Before you take the SAT, be sure you know what the penalties for incorrect answers are in each section. It will help you decide whether to make a guess or just not answer a difficult question.

How Much Time Should You Spend on Each Question?

It depends. The amount of time needed varies from student to student, from section to section, and even from question to question. As a result, it is very important to monitor the time you spend on each type of SAT question while taking practice exams. This will allow you to make informed decisions about the order in which you should answer questions, and you will be able to determine when you're wasting too much time on a single question.

In the case of the critical-reading portion, most questions increase in difficulty as you progress through each section of the test.

The easier sentence completion questions may require only a few seconds' work, whereas the later (or harder) ones may take a minute or more to answer. The critical-reading questions are not arranged in order of difficulty, but the reading passages often are. In other words, if two reading passages are contained within a single critical-reading section, the latter passage, as well as the questions associated with it, will probably be the more challenging of the two. Also, critical-reading questions generally take more time to answer than other questions on the critical-reading section. An entire passage generally takes 10 to 15 minutes. So what does this all mean for you? Essentially, if you find yourself struggling to finish the critical-reading section within the given time limits, you should probably answer the questions in the following fashion:

1. Answer the easier sentence completions first.

2. Return to the sentence completions that require more effort.

3. Finally, tackle the critical-reading passages.

The math questions are also arranged in order of difficulty. For the most part, however, you will not have subgroupings of question types comparable to those in the critical-reading portion of the SAT.

In two of the sections, you'll be given regular multiple-choice problems; in the third section, you'll need to answer the grid-ins. In both cases, however, the subsections are a mixture of problems designed to test your knowledge of arithmetic, algebra, geometry, and the more difficult college preparatory math such as calculus. So you may want to focus your attention on questions that deal with your areas of strength before working on questions involving mathematical topics that are relatively difficult for you—even if the questions that are easier for you appear later in the exam.

The multiple-choice writing component of the writing section will provide you with brief sentences or paragraphs. You will be asked to select the multiple-choice response that is the best option to make each writing sample grammatically correct or to improve its syntax and structure. However, some of the selections presented in this section may be perfectly fine and will not require any correction on your part. But you must be able to identify them as such.

In the second part of the writing section, you will be provided a prompt. This will be in the form of a sentence or several sentences that make an assertion. For example, "Since the economy of Town XYZ improved during the four years that Mayor Smith has been our mayor, we should re-elect her to a second term." Your task will be to develop an essay identifying why the statement is not necessarily an accurate one and provide your reasons. Your essay will be graded both for the sophistication of your ideas and your mastery of the mechanics of writing, such as punctuation, subject-verb agreement, syntax, and organization.

How Does SAT Scoring Work?

Scoring on the SAT is very different from what you're accustomed to in school. In school, you usually receive a certain number of points when you answer a question correctly, and you lose an equal number of points when you answer a question incorrectly or when you skip it. On the critical-reading part of the SAT, you receive one point for each correct answer, and you lose a quarter point for each incorrect one. Questions that you skip don't count against you, but they won't count for you either.

A scoring sheet for an SAT test will have the following basic formula for each critical-reading section: the scoring system is designed so that one correct answer compensates for four incorrect choices. The reason for this is fairly simple: if you randomly guessed from among five multiple-choice solutions provided for a problem, you would have a one-in-five chance of choosing the correct answer. Given these odds, a student who made random guesses throughout this portion of the exam should end up with a *raw score* of zero on the test. If you can eliminate even one answer, however, you've put yourself in a position that betters those odds.

Theoretically then, you should be able to improve your score through random guessing when you're choosing from among four or fewer answers. (However, our experience shows that students who are able to eliminate only one or two answers don't really have enough information to answer the question; they usually guess wrong and are thus better off skipping to the next question.)

If, however, you can eliminate all but two (or maybe three) answers, take the chance and guess. Think of it this way: if you guess one answer correctly for every two you get wrong, you're still ahead in the game (unlike when you make a random guess without

Getting Started _____

The **raw score**, as the name implies, is the score you get on the SAT after your wrong answers are deducted from your right answers. Fortunately, your right answers receive more points than your wrong answers, as we explained in the introduction to this section.

eliminating, in which case you should simply break even). This is because the one correct answer netted you one point, whereas the two incorrect answers cost you only a half point combined. The resulting half point will round up to a whole point, canceling out your incorrect guesses. In other words, you should consider guessing if you can narrow your choices down to three answers and always guess if you can eliminate all but two answers.

Although the same scoring scale applies to the regular math sections of the SAT, the grid-in portions of the math exam are slightly different.

The grid-in section carries no guessing penalty. Of course, since your answers are self-generated, it's very unlikely that you'll get the correct answer by just taking a shot in the dark. On the other hand, if you've worked on a grid-in problem but feel unsure about your solution, you should still enter it on the answer grid since there is no penalty.

To Guess or Not to Guess

If you're faced with a critical-reading question you cannot answer, you'll have to decide whether to guess or skip the question entirely. All incorrectly answered questions on the critical-reading section of the SAT I result in the deduction of one-quarter point from your final score. There is no deduction for omitted questions.

If you're faced with a math question you can't answer, it's a little more complicated. Deciding whether to answer or skip a question will depend on which type of question you're working on and your sense of what is being asked. For incorrectly answered questions, the point deductions are as follows:

    Student-produced response = no deductions

    Standard multiple choice = one-fourth point deduction

Skipping should always be done in conjunction with elimination. When you cannot eliminate enough choices to comfortably guess, skip that question.

When you skip a question, it's a good idea to circle the question number in the test book so that you can find it later. If you do return to the question during your review and answer it, darken in the circle so that you know it's been taken care of. If you are skipping the question, be especially careful about filling in the next answer on the answer sheet, making sure you've left a blank and haven't messed up the order of answers. This is not an error you'll have time to fix later on!

Many students are unwilling to skip questions for fear of costing themselves points. When you take an English or math test at school, your teacher deducts points for each question you leave blank in addition to deducting for the ones you have wrong. Remember that, on the SAT, you receive one point for each correct answer and lose only a fraction of a point for incorrect answers. There are no penalties for skipping, so it makes sense to skip the questions you're likely to get wrong.

Action Plan

Because of the SAT's scoring system, if you have no idea what the answer to a question is, you're better off skipping it.

The questions you'll be most likely to skip are the sentence completions. These questions require more proficient vocabulary and math skills, take the most time to answer, and thus give you the least chance of success.

It's true that if you don't answer enough questions, you can't expect a high score; on the other hand, answering too many questions incorrectly will also adversely affect your score. If you wisely choose the questions to skip, you can skip over half of the 78 critical-reading questions and still score in the low 500s. If you had answered all those questions and gotten them wrong, your score would have dropped into the 400s. You can even skip 20 of the 78 critical-reading questions and still score in the low 600s. Again, if you had attempted all those questions and gotten them all wrong, your score would have dropped into the 500s.

HELP!

The College Board (www. collegeboard.com) offers a SAT Preparation Center on their website. Sample SAT tests should also be available in your high school guidance office.

Practice Tests

Taking practice exams prior to the actual SAT I is an important part of your exam preparation. An essential aspect of preparing for the SAT I is knowing how to pace yourself. Taking the practice tests should give you a good sense of whether you're answering questions within the allotted time.

Another important aspect of taking practice tests is understanding how to mark your answer sheet correctly.

After you've finished the tests, scoring them using the SAT scoring system will allow you to measure how guessing or skipping a question affects your overall score.

We strongly recommend that you use actual SAT examinations when you practice for the test. Even with the changes to the exam, you should use compilations of old-format tests produced by the College Board rather than the mock exams produced by other organizations. Why? The mock examinations are not similar enough to actual SATs.

Fine-tuning your critical-reading and math skills is a good way to prepare for the SAT, not to mention your college career! However, when it comes to your SAT score, some skills will do you more good than others. There are concepts you can learn, techniques you can follow, and tricks you can use that will help you get the best score possible. Here are 10 tips to help you out:

1. **Make a study plan and follow it.** The right SAT study plan will help you get the most out of this book in whatever time you have.

2. **Learn the directions in advance.** If you already know what to do for each question type, you won't have to waste precious test time. You'll be able to jump right in and start answering questions as soon as the proctor says "Go!"

3. **Make educated guesses.** If you can eliminate one or more answer choices, you have everything to gain by guessing.

4. **Know what to expect.** Learn the SAT question types in advance. They won't change, and you won't have any surprises on test day.

5. **In sentence completions, look for clue words.** These words will reveal the meaning of the sentence and point you in the right direction.

Action Plan

To register for the PSAT or SAT I, ask the college admissions counselor at your high school for an SAT I registration form. The test is offered nationally seven times each year. You can also call the College Board at 609-771-7600, or if you're ready to take the test, you can register online at www.collegeboard.com.

6. **Save critical reading questions for last.** These reading questions take more time than others, but you don't get any more credit for them. So tackle the rest of the section first.

7. **If a multiple-choice math question stumps you, work backward from the answers.** The right answer has to be one of the five choices, and since the choices are arranged in size order, start with (C). That way you'll have to do the fewest calculations.

8. **In grid-ins, blacken the bubbles.** If you don't, the computer won't give you any points.

How Test Scores Are Used

Myths and misconceptions abound about the college admissions process:

What are colleges really looking for?

How do they make admissions decisions?

How much control do students have in this process?

Are there steps students can take that might affect their chances of being admitted?

Check out the "College Admissions Requirements" section of Appendix B for the answers to these and other pertinent questions about what colleges look for and how they make admissions decisions.

Students who have poor grades often have fewer choices. With this in mind, some students do not enroll in challenging classes. On the other hand, these students may not meet minimum course requirements for many colleges. With better planning, all students can have access to the appropriate courses. Also see Chapter 5 for more on required course work.

The Least You Need to Know

◆ Students should start preparing to take college aptitude tests in their freshman year of high school.

◆ There are numerous practice tests and preparation courses kids can take to build their skills for taking the real tests.

◆ Know how test scores are used by colleges for admission purposes, and impress upon your kids how important these tests are to their future.

College Costs and Financial Planning

In This Chapter

- ◆ Getting a college to help you determine what it will cost
- ◆ Discovering the hidden cost of going to college
- ◆ Determining the best college value for your kid
- ◆ Considering ways that kids can help finance their college education

By the time your kids are seniors in high school, they should have completed a school search and conducted comparative analyses of colleges they want to attend. The next step is to apply to the schools that meet their academic needs and your financial abilities. A careful analysis of school costs at this time is essential. You should know what it will cost for your kid to attend each of the schools he or she is considering and what resources will be needed to meet those costs. This chapter covers the steps for arriving at an accurate estimate of what it costs to go to college.

Get All of the Facts

Once your kids decide on a career path, the next step is to locate appropriate colleges that offer the specific programs they're seeking. Take the following factors into consideration. Establish the importance of each one, to you and to your college-bound kid. Then use your own ranking system to determine which school is right for both you and your son or daughter.

Gather Information

Make comparisons of what the different colleges and universities cost and have to offer by writing for their catalogues, financial aid brochures, and information on the placement of their graduates.

HELP!

If it's not possible for you to visit all the colleges on your kid's preferred list, obtain answers to your questions about admission, financial aid, and placement over the telephone.

After obtaining this information, you and your family can compare the various schools and decide which ones you wish to investigate further. This investigation can include a visit to their campuses and interviews with their admissions officers, financial aid counselors, and placement directors. The interview at the admissions office can include questions regarding the academic quality of the programs offered and the student-to-faculty ratio. See Chapter 5 for more on this subject.

Ask Questions

The questions you ask the financial aid administrator (FAA) should be about the type of financial assistance programs available, application deadlines, the awarding process, the financial aid appeals process, special aid programs, and the average indebtedness of recent graduates. This last statistic is critical because it can reveal several things such as how wealthy the average student's family is, how expensive the college is, how generous its scholarship programs are, and how closely the financial aid office monitors its students' debt burden. If this information is not available at the time of your meeting, ask when it will be made available. If the FAA can't tell you, scratch that college off your list.

What's the Best College for Your Kid?

Meet with the college placement director and ask what placement services are available. Questions to ask the placement director are covered in Chapter 5.

Here are some suggestions for subjects to discuss with an FAA or admissions officer:

Cost competitiveness with other comparable schools

Academic programs offered

Faculty-per-student ratio

Number of faculty with Ph.D. degrees

Special programs offered

Library facilities

Research opportunities

Financial aid policies

Work-study opportunities

Student body profile

Athletic opportunities

Extracurricular activities

Housing options

Crime rate in the area

Graduation rate

Average student indebtedness

College placement rate for graduates

Action Plan

The more you know about the financial aid system, the better prepared you will be to pay for college. Start with Financial Aid Facts (www.ais.fsu.edu) and Twenty Things You Need to Know About Financing College (www.collegeboard.com/prof/counselors/pay/16.html).

Get Colleges to Tell You What the Cost Is

Before you can think about how you're going to pay for your kid's college education, you need to know what it will cost. This section discusses the different types of expenses you should expect and how to get colleges to disclose their costs.

The cost of attendance is the total amount it will cost your son or daughter to go to school, which is usually expressed as a yearly figure. Each college is responsible for determining the annual average cost of attendance for its students by using a standard definition established by the U.S. Congress.

Call every college that's on your child's "preferred" list and ask for an estimate of what it costs to attend the institution annually. This figure is used to calculate your financial aid eligibility. Remember, once your kid is in school, the actual expenses will vary based on his or her lifestyle.

> **Action Plan**
>
> Some expenses will depend on the choices you make, such as whether it's a public or private college, its location, and your kid's decision to live on or off campus or at home. Other expenses, such as the total cost of books, stay relatively constant from college to college.

Direct Cost

The direct cost typically includes tuition, fees, and room and board. You pay the money directly to the college. Tuition and fees vary by college, and if you've selected a state college or university, your tuition will depend on your residency status. The difference between in-state and out-of-state tuition can amount to thousands of dollars per year.

Tuition

Some colleges base their tuition, which is the cost of the student's classes, on the number of credit hours taken during an academic period. Others rely on enrollment status (full time versus half time). These details are easy to find out from the financial aid or admissions officer or from school brochures.

Fees

Colleges often charge additional fees for other services, activities, or facilities. For example, they may charge for health insurance, class labs, or the use of a gymnasium or recreational center. Usually, these fees appear on your tuition bill and are not charged on a per-use basis.

Room and Board

Students may choose to live on campus and eat in campus dining facilities. A variety of meal plans may be offered, and costs may vary significantly based on the particular plan selected. Housing may be in a dorm or in an off-campus rental, which may or may not be associated with the college. In either case, off-campus housing usually involves utilities charges for electricity, gas, water, phone, and possibly Internet access. In a dorm, all of these expenses are typically included.

Action Plan _____

Look into the total cost of each college your kid is applying to. Once you know how much it will cost for tuition, housing, food, books and supplies, travel, and personal expenses, you'll have a better idea of the financial aid you'll need.

Variable Costs

Variable costs are costs that students have some control over since they tend to vary based on what they buy and how much they use it. For example, do they really *need* a laptop as opposed to a less expensive desktop PC? Is it necessary for them to have a car on campus, or would a bike do instead? In short, you have more control over variable costs than you do over direct costs.

Books and Supplies

Individual book costs vary greatly, depending on the courses you're taking. You may be able to purchase used books to lower these costs, but for planning purposes, it's best to assume that you will be paying full cost. Some classes also require more supplies than others, such as course materials or equipment, printing, copying, and computer costs. As mentioned earlier, the rising cost of textbooks has become a controversial issue in the past several years, and a number of states have taken and are taking legal action to help students reduce the cost of their yearly textbook outlays. Remember that any laws or statutes enacted by a state to provide students with ways of saving on textbooks apply to the state in which your college is located, not to the state you legally reside in unless each happens to be the same. For the latest on textbook reform, visit www.inthetext.com.

Computers

Many colleges require each student to have a PC. Check the school's admissions requirements to determine whether you need a basic PC or a more expensive laptop model. And don't forget additional expenses such as software and a printer. If you live off campus, you may have fees for hookup to the school network.

Transportation

Transportation costs cover gas, parking, public transportation, auto insurance, and maintenance. These costs depend on your school's location. If you commute, be sure to factor in the cost of public transportation or gas, car insurance, and parking fees. Some schools provide free parking, while others may require you to pay for a permit. Don't forget the cost of breaks and holiday travel! For example, think about how many times you'll want to go home. You can lower these costs by carpooling or shopping around for student rates on airfare.

Personal Expenses

Lifestyle can have a big impact on the personal expenses category. Consider such living expenses as clothing, laundry, haircuts, phone bills, recreation, and entertainment. When kids live at home, their allowance can, for the most part, be spent on fun stuff. When they get to college, that same allowance may have to fund more essentials than fun. Parents should work with their kids to reevaluate their priorities so their expenses stay within your budget. Maybe that long-distance call that they want to make to their girl- or boyfriend for a half-hour a day can be replaced with an e-mail message.

Action Plan

Going to school is a big investment, so creating a reasonable budget is important. With College Answer (www.collegeanswer.com) budgeting tool, you can easily plan expenses, establish priorities, and make financing your education a less-stressful experience. If you're ready to plug in numbers, go to the Budget Calculator at www.finaid.com. More site addresses are listed in the "Budgeting" section of Appendix B.

Other Costs

Other costs may be unexpected, such as drop-and-add fees to change a course schedule. And don't forget athletic, sorority, fraternity, or other organizational expenses! Always try to keep a little extra money in your budget to cover emergencies. Other costs that your kid may want to include on his or her checklist are …

◆ Clothing, laundry, and cleaning.

◆ Food costs covering meal plans, groceries, and eating out.

◆ Loan payments for education loans, credit cards, and banking fees.

- ◆ Personal expenses such as toiletries, haircuts, and so on.

- ◆ Medical, dental, and vision care expenses and insurance.

- ◆ Entertainment such as movies, cable television, music CDs, and cultural and sporting events.

- ◆ Miscellaneous gifts and cleaning supplies.

Warning _____

Prospective students and parents sometimes mistakenly assume that payment in full is due upon registration. Don't make that assumption: it may cause you to eliminate a preferred school because it seems too expensive, or you may make a hasty borrowing decision without exploring other college-financing options.

Breaking Down the Expenses

Breaking down college expenses can show you where you can economize, such as by buying secondhand books or living at home and commuting to classes.

You can break down costs into the following categories: (1) tuition; (2) books, fees, and miscellaneous expenses; (3) living expenses. Assuming that financial assistance will not meet all of these expenses, let's further assume that some combination of student, family, and school resources will meet the educational costs of attendance.

Students and their families have the primary responsibility to finance their education. Schools have a responsibility to assist families in this process. Careful planning, resourcefulness, and hard work are the key ingredients, but one other factor is essential: determination. It's important that families and students approach student financial planning with a positive attitude. The earlier you plan, the more information and options you will have.

Action Plan _____

High school kids can work during the summer months to save money to pay a portion of the cost of books, fees, and other expenses. These costs can be estimated. A resourceful student can plan ahead and find employment that will fulfill the objectives of achieving financial survival.

Create an Effective Action Plan

Prior to admission, you should know the institution's financial aid policies and understand its financial aid application and awarding process.

In addition to federal and state programs administered through the school's financial aid office, private or corporate programs can be investigated. Local unions, churches, civic organizations, and charitable institutions often will sponsor needy students. The objective in exploring the various avenues of financial assistance is to attempt to meet tuition costs through a combination of federal, state, and private sources.

No source should be eliminated from consideration. Scholarship assistance should have priority over loan sources, but you should be prepared to borrow a portion of tuition expenses if necessary. This early process of financial planning to meet tuition expenses allows you and your family to organize your finances. The search for financial aid funds can follow immediately after the career analysis and school search have been completed (see Chapter 5) and before you enroll in any postsecondary institution.

Dividing Up the Money

One suggested method of meeting living expenses during the academic year is for parents to apportion the monthly living costs of the family members. By figuring out the average amount of money spent on your kid's food and miscellaneous expenses, you can calculate the amount of money you could contribute to meet these expenses. The money can be set aside and added to the student's monthly income while at college.

Let's say you determine that it costs an average of $250 a month to support your kid when he or she is living at home, and this includes housing, food, clothing, and miscellaneous items. If the kid's monthly living budget is $500 at college, and he or she is contributing $250 per month from summer job earnings, you could provide the rest and break even.

If you can't afford to contribute anything to living expenses, investigate housing alternatives. Many housing offices list low-cost or no-cost housing. Check with the housing officer at the college your son or daughter has chosen to attend.

If low-cost housing is not an option at the school, maybe a high-paying job is possible. The average student can work approximately 10 hours per week without jeopardizing academic studies. A resourceful student can expect to earn about $200 or more a month. Over the course of an academic year, this represents approximately $2,000 that can be used to meet expenses.

Students can seek help in locating employment from the financial aid administrator's office. Most students participate either in the Federal Work-Study Program (FWS) or in the school's employment program. Both programs can assist in employment placement. While some work-study jobs may not be the most exciting in the world, some students have gotten jobs such as cameraperson or carpenter. Check with the work-study office or individual academic departments to see what is available.

Parents can and should help their kids find jobs that pay more than minimum wage. You can encourage them to capitalize on any particular job skills they may possess. Can they tutor, paint, or offer specific computer skills that are in demand? Meeting some expenses through employment is useful in keeping debt levels manageable.

Action Plan

If you're a student, not long after you were born, your parents may have started putting money away for your education. And if you've been working or saving money on your own, you have something to contribute as well. Maybe those savings won't completely cover all costs, but chances are they're going to be a big help. Stay in your savings plan, but don't stop there. Keep searching for other investment options.

If you know beforehand that your son or daughter working part-time is an essential part of your financial plan, you'll be better prepared to incorporate employment into your kid's academic schedule. Over the course of four years, the money your student earns can go a long way toward reducing the amount of money you as parents need to borrow to meet college costs.

What about the student who, for academic reasons, cannot work while attending classes? Your financial plan must consider academic success as the first priority. Special arrangements can be made for students who cannot maintain an acceptable academic grade point average while they're working. Consult with your school's financial aid counselor and academic dean to find a solution to the problem. Some schools have scholarship funds set aside for these situations.

Financial Planning

Reputable financial planners can provide advice for families exploring the various savings and investment programs currently available. However, be aware of others who are not as helpful. In recent years, some people engaged in what might more accurately be described as financial *aid* planning have typically been claiming that they can help a family increase its eligibility for financial assistance. Many of these planners seem to suggest methods that keep a family's assets hidden. This undermines a system designed to help families who most need financial aid. It can also freeze assets that you had counted on to pay college costs, putting your child's education in jeopardy.

Good financial aid consultants can help families develop sound financial-planning strategies, assist in filling out forms, negotiate better offers, and so on. If you want to engage a financial aid consultant and avoid problems down the line, just be sure the "expert" you hire is reputable. See Chapter 17 for information on how to choose a consultant who can greatly increase your chances of receiving the most financial aid possible.

Setting Priorities

If your family is like most families, you'll often spend money on things that you really don't need, or somehow the money you make always seems to be just enough to cover expenses. Your first short-term plan should be to get control over your family's spending habits. Budgeting is an excellent way to get started. You may be amazed at how a budget can help you save on little things that can add up to big dollars.

Let's take a simple example. Suppose you, your spouse, and your two children attend a baseball game once a week. If it costs $35 for the four of you to eat at the game, you're spending about $400 on food during the season. Suppose you instead make sandwiches and carry them to the game, along with your own soft drinks. If you invest this $400 savings at 10 percent over a 10-year period, you'll find that your $400 has grown to $6,500 by the time your kids are ready to go to college (assuming their average age is eight years old today). And you have not deprived yourself or your family of anything. Okay, we didn't take into consideration that it still cost you something to make your own sandwiches. That's because we wanted to keep the math simple and focus on the concept!

Action Plan

We often make purchases on the basis of impulses and wants rather than reality. If you want to get serious about planning for your kids' education, you must be prepared to postpone some of your desires. The trade-off is that you're doing without something now so that you can afford to send your kids to college.

By making one minor adjustment to your family's priorities, you can have instant money available to invest in long-term planning for your kids' future. If you're serious about controlling your money, you've got to set priorities and recognize that you can't have everything right now. If you want to have money set aside for their education, you must be prepared to make sacrifices over a period of time.

Part of the budget-prioritizing process is distinguishing between what you need and what you want. For example, you might need a car, but you want a Mercedes. Or you may have to cut your vacation plans back, and that's tough. But in many cases, it simply has to be done.

Emergency Funds

Many families start a program to save money for college and then withdraw the money when emergencies arise. They lose not only their initial savings, but also a part of their investment program because they were forced to terminate their plan prematurely. An emergency fund should be considered a critical part of your overall financial plan. As a rule, your emergency fund should be equivalent to at least three times the size of your family's monthly income, enough to cover job losses, medical problems, or unexpected major repairs.

Money market funds are an excellent place to invest emergency dollars. Your money is readily accessible when it's needed, and it's earning interest at rates considerably higher than traditional savings accounts. Money market funds have become extremely popular in recent years as a way to gain ground in inflationary periods. They are widely advertised and available through savings and loan associations, banks, and brokerage firms.

Use Time Wisely

It's a common misconception that to save a lot of money you have to make a lot of money. In reality, acquiring a substantial sum of money requires only time and discipline. The importance of long-term planning cannot be underestimated. It's a major factor in your overall planning for college expenses. Most families fail to use time to their advantage because they allow procrastination to delay the start of their financial plan. Don't make that mistake: start early and make long-term plans.

Suppose you and your spouse are 25 years old, and you've set a goal to accumulate $50,000 for your kid's college education in 10 years. You could accomplish it by saving only $10 per month at 12 percent! However, if you are 35 and have the same goal, you would have to save $445 a month, or 44 times as much as you needed to amass the same sum at age 25.

In addition to time, the only other factor you need to make money is discipline. Suppose you want to start saving $100 per month over a long period of time, and you are able to earn a 12 percent return on it. The following table dramatically illustrates how much you can earn with enough time and discipline.

 Action Plan

Think of your money as your workforce and put it to work now!

The Rewards of Discipline (Investing $100 a Month at 12 Percent)

5 Years	10 Years	15 Years	20 Years	30 Years
$14,015	$32,940	$58,455	$92,870	$201,910

The Magic of Compound Interest

One of the most exciting facets of financial management—and one of the simplest to understand—is what successful investors call "the magic of compound interest." You've just seen how even a small amount of money ($100 a month), saved systematically over a period of time, multiplies dramatically through the compound interest formula.

No amount of money is too small or insignificant to save for your kids' college education. The important thing is to take advantage of the time portion of the formula and start to invest now. Look at yourselves as employers of your income. The dollars you earn are your "employees." If the two of you own a business, you can't afford to let your employees sit around doing nothing. In today's economy, you can't let that happen to your money either. Your money is your workforce. Get it working now for your kids' future.

Making a long-term investment with a fair rate of return, you can take advantage of compound interest. The previous table shows what happens when you invest $100 each month at 5, 10, and 12 percent, respectively. Again, the difference in the total amount of money you accumulate at the different rates illustrates just how important a few percentage points can be.

Another important concept to understand about compound interest is what is known as the "Rule of 72." If you divide 72 by the rate of interest you're receiving, you can determine when your money will double. For example, if you're lucky enough to find an investment that's earning 18 percent a year, you'll double your money over four years (72 divided by 18 percent is 4).

Putting It All Together

Understanding your benefits and knowing how to use them will help you lay out the foundation of your financial plan. You can see how that's done in this simple example. Let's assume that you and your spouse are both 30 years old and earn a combined yearly income of $75,000. Both of your incomes are covered by pension plans. Your intent is to save enough money over the next 10 years to put your kid through college. What do you need to do to get there? For starters, review the following checklist:

♦ Estimate the annual rate of inflation over the next 10 years.

♦ Determine as best you can whether your kid will go to a state college or a private college. Find out what the tuition rates are today and, using your projected inflation rate, determine what the tuition rates will be 10 years from now.

♦ Contact one of the colleges of your choice and find out what it costs to attend the institution for everything except tuition (room, board, books, etc.).

♦ Estimate how much financial aid you believe your family will be able to qualify for.

♦ Project the rate of return you expect from your investment program.

This example assumes an average inflation rate of 3 percent and a 5 percent average annual increase in college tuition per year over the next 10 years. The return on investment is projected at 10 percent. Here is how the plan comes together in three simple steps:

Step 1: You believe your kid will want to attend a state college as a state resident. Current tuition rates are $2,500, and the college estimates that the average student spends an additional $6,500 for other expenses. The total cost in today's dollars is $9,000. Ten years from now, based on a 5 percent annual increase, you can expect tuition to be $4,070. Other expenses will be $8,735 if the average inflation rate holds at 3 percent. Therefore, you can expect to pay $12,805 ($4,070 + $8,735) for the first year your kid is in college.

Step 2: You've had a conversation with a financial aid person who, based on the information you provided, believes you would be responsible for about 20 percent of your kid's total annual college expenses, or about $2,560 ($12,805 × .20).

Step 3: Your expected cost for your kid's first year of college 10 years from now is $10,245 ($12,805 – $2,560). How much would you have to start saving now to cover that first year of college? The answer is about $50 a month if you assume a 10 percent return on your money.

Don't concern yourself now with whether or not these numbers and assumptions are realistic. You can establish your own assumptions based on your personal requirements and earnings. For the time being, follow the progress of this couple of 30-year-olds who are doing some long-term financial planning.

To support their retirement program and their kids' college education, they need to initiate a $6,000-per-year savings and investment program. Up to this point, all that the family in our example has done is determine where they are today and where they want to be in 10 years when their oldest kid will reach college age. The next step is to map out a way to get there.

Choosing an Investment Program

Before you start to plan your kid's college savings program, you'll need to become familiar with the various aspects of investment vehicles that are available to you. You can reach your savings goal, one payday at a time, by developing a savings habit.

As explained earlier, you need to do short-term budgeting in order to have the funds to invest in long-term financial planning. Budget for savings each month, just as you budget for food or loan payments. Once you've decided to save a percentage of your income, stick to your decision. If your employers offer payroll deduction plans, you can arrange to have money deducted from your paycheck and automatically deposited into a savings account every payday. You could also make regular contributions to an education IRA (tax-deferred earnings) or, better yet, a 529 plan, which is a state college plan with tax-deferred growth and estate tax advantages. (See Chapter 16 for more on this subject.)

Here are several investment points to consider:

- ◆ **Return.** The amount your money can earn in interest.
- ◆ **Security.** The more secure your account is, the less risk you face of losing your investment.
- ◆ **Liquidity.** The speed with which you can obtain your money.
- ◆ **Convenience.** The ease with which you can manage your investment plan. Take into account the location of the financial institution where you save, web access to your account, and the quality of service that you receive.

In choosing investments that are right for you, you'll need to think realistically about your financial situation, your educational goals for your kids, and the period of time in which you want to reach them. Since no single investment is likely to satisfy all of your financial requirements, you might want to consider using a combination of investment vehicles to achieve your goals. You could invest a portion of your money in a passbook savings account and the rest in mutual funds.

Investment Options

In planning for college, it may be a good idea to sit down with your accountant, financial advisor, banker, investment broker, or insurance agent to assess your child's pending long-term educational needs. Even though many financial plans specifically designed to pay for future college costs are of value, in some cases parents may be better off dealing with traditional financial investments earmarked for future college plans. For example, if your kids are young (under 10 years old), you may want to invest in the stock market, which has traditionally earned higher returns than conventional savings programs over the long term.

> **Action Plan**
>
> No matter how young your kids are, it's better to learn what options you have now and begin figuring college expenses into your long-term financial plan.

Investing for Your Preteen

Some financial analysts recommend investing in higher-risk, higher-income-producing vehicles during a kid's preteen years, then moving into more secure and conservative investments as the kid approaches college age.

When you're looking into taxable or nontaxable investments, consider your kids' ages. If they're under 14, consider investing in more aggressive nontaxable investments such as stocks or mutual funds. When they turn 14, you may want to switch over to a more conservative investment, such as municipal bonds, to protect your principal as each kid begins to approach college age.

College Savings Plans

A growing number of colleges and universities offer savings plans in which parents or guardians can invest a certain amount of money that is placed in a certificate of deposit. The interest earned on the investment is based on the anticipated level of that college's inflation rate. The amount to be invested is determined by the age of your child, the type of school (public or private) he or she will be entering, and its cost.

Action Plan _____

Take advantage of tuition prepayment discounts. Many colleges offer up to a 10 percent discount for early payment.

Theoretically, the investment will grow at a rate that will cover all education-related costs when your child is ready to enter college. The downside is that many of these investments may not produce as high a rate of return as your money might have earned on the open market. Additionally, in some cases, if the child for one reason or another does not attend college, the parent may recoup only the initial investment with less than the full amount of interest earned.

Prepaid Tuition Plans

Similarly, some state governments offer prepaid college tuition plans. Some states allow parents or guardians to invest a lump sum for tuition, room, board, and other academic fees, thereby ensuring that the student will be entitled to a prepaid education (provided the youth qualifies for admission). Consult your state department of education (see Appendix C) or the financial aid offices at your state colleges and/or universities for information about any prepaid college tuition programs.

Where to Invest

A wide range of investment programs are available through financial institutions and commercial banks. Programs include savings and time deposit accounts, brokerage accounts, and money market deposit accounts. Credit unions also offer various programs of their own.

Deposits in federal and state chartered credit unions are insured for up to $100,000 through the National Credit Union Administration. Brokerage houses and mutual fund companies offer a wide variety of financial services, including time deposit and money market accounts. The terms and security of these accounts can vary substantially from those of more traditional savings institutions.

Money Market Accounts

If you can meet the minimum deposit requirement, you may want to consider investing in a money market account that combines high yields and liquidity with the safety of federal insurance. They're like regular savings accounts in that you can withdraw your money at any time without paying a penalty. They differ in that they offer a variable rate of interest comparable to money market rates. However, if your balance drops below a specified minimum (usually $2,500), interest rates are reduced accordingly.

Savings Bonds

U.S. savings bonds are among the most convenient bonds to purchase and redeem. They're extremely safe, and the interest isn't subject to state or local taxes. The government offers three types of bonds: Series EE, Series HH, and Series I. They are all easy to purchase. For example, Series EE bonds are available in denominations from $50 to $10,000 and are sold at less than their face value (discounted). They are purchased at 50 percent of the face value printed on the bond and are redeemed for their full value at maturity. The maturity period is determined by how long it takes enough interest to accumulate to double the issue value of the bond. Series EE and Series I bonds can be purchased through most financial institutions.

Bonds that you purchase now earn interest at a fixed rate that increases on a graduated scale for the first five years to a maximum of $7\frac{1}{2}$ percent interest compounded annually.

Bonds held for a minimum of five years earn interest at a rate tied to the money market rates. When you redeem a bond, the interest rate you'll receive will be based on the average rate earned for the term. You are guaranteed a minimum of $7\frac{1}{2}$ percent interest compounded annually. Series EE bonds can be purchased through most financial institutions.

Series HH bonds are no longer available for direct purchase. The only way to get an HH bond is in exchange for an EE bond. They are obtained at face value. Every six months, the U.S. Treasury sends you a check for your interest earnings. Although the maturity period for HH bonds is 10 years, they may be redeemed six months after their issue date.

Mutual Funds and Stocks

The decade of the 1990s was one of the best ever for both stock market and mutual fund investors. Parents continue to draw on mutual funds as a viable investment vehicle to finance their kids' education, and they do so for several good reasons. Mutual funds are still a good investment option in the new millennium, but past performance does not necessarily indicate future returns (as any mutual fund brochure will tell you). So shop around carefully.

Mutual funds are professionally managed by experienced investment managers who provide instant diversification by investing in a broad range of stocks if you invest in the right fund. The AAA funds have provided stellar performance over the last 15 years. Available investment funds range from the super conservative to the extremely aggressive. Almost all of them will outperform the rates of return in savings accounts, bonds, or Treasury bills.

This chapter began with a discussion about the magic of compound interest. A relatively small amount of money, if properly invested, will accumulate into substantial dollars over a period of time. An example illustrated how to determine the amount of savings needed to meet your financial goals. The importance of budget planning was also emphasized.

As your financial situation and goals change, you'll need to make adjustments to your savings and investment programs. When you're just starting out, you may need the liquidity and relatively high yield of a money market account to help provide for a growing family. When your kid approaches college age, you may choose to shift to short-term secured investments to make sure the money is there when you start paying your share of college expenses.

Whichever savings strategy you adopt, you'll see the rewards of your effort as you reach each of your savings goals.

Homework for Your Kid

College is an investment in your kid's future, but it doesn't come cheap. Whether your son or daughter chooses a low-cost community college or a high-priced private institution, his or her education will cost you money. As high as the prices may seem, your family can finance the education that your child deserves. Creating a plan to pay for college takes effort, so you'll need some help and guidance. Financial aid is limited. It's important to start early and investigate all your options. Make sure you have an in-depth discussion with your college-bound kid and other family members about how to go about financing his or her education.

The Least You Need to Know

- Know how much college is going to cost before you start putting together a financial plan.

- Understand all of the hidden costs it takes to go to college so that you are financially well prepared.

- Know what the difference is between fixed versus variable costs so you can accurately project what the total cost of going to college will be.

- Involve your college-bound kids as well as other family members in plans for financing college expenses.

Develop a College Savings Plan

In This Chapter

◆ Learning how to select a tax-deferred college savings plan that's right for you

◆ Knowing how to manage your plan and how to change it

◆ Pulling it all together into a consolidated savings program

The cost of going to college continues to soar with no end in sight. Everybody knows this, so you have no excuse for not planning well in advance to pay for your child's college education. Before you consider opening a savings plan for your kid's college education, you'll need to become familiar with the various educational savings programs available to you.

There are several investment features to consider when you review the savings programs presented in this chapter. What is the return on investment that you can expect from the different savings programs? How secure is your investment in any one plan? The ease with which you can access and manage your savings plan (for example, web access to your account) should also be considered.

When you choose a savings plan that's right for you, think realistically about your financial situation, your educational goals for your kids, and the period of time you have to reach your savings goal. Since no single savings program is likely to satisfy all of your college funding needs, you might want to consider using a combination of savings programs to get to where you want to go. For example, you could invest a portion of your money in savings bonds and the rest in a self-directed savings plan that allows you to invest in mutual funds and stocks.

Introduction to College Savings Plans

What exactly is an education savings plan? It's a savings plan that is operated by a state or educational institution that is designed to help families set aside funds for future college costs. As long as the plan satisfies a few basic requirements, the state and federal tax laws provide special tax benefits to the plan's participants. Most banks and brokerage firms offer college savings plans that include the following standard components:

- There is a plan owner, the person who sets up and manages the plan.

- There is a beneficiary, the potential student for whom the plan is meant to fund his or her postsecondary education.

- There is an institution, the state or educational institute under whose authority the plan exists.

- There is a financial administrator, a commercial entity that is responsible for accepting contributions, investing the plan's money, and distributing the plan's funds per the owner's direction.

The following is a summary of the college savings plans covered in this chapter. We will also tell you how to contact your state to find out more specifics about each plan.

Savings Plan	Plan Description	Advantages	Disadvantages
529 plan	State-run or sanctioned savings plans that have significant tax benefits at both the federal and state levels.	You can open an account for as little as $250. Monthly deposits can be made for as low as $50.	Some plans are open only to parents or custodial guardians.

Savings Plan	Plan Description	Advantages	Disadvantages
Coverdell plan	A custodial account created solely for the purpose of paying qualified educational expenses for the designated beneficiary of the account.	These are very versatile. Not only can the money be used to pay for college expenses, it can also be used for elementary and secondary school expenses.	The total dollar amount of contribution for a designated beneficiary cannot exceed $2,000 per year.
Savings bonds	U.S. Series EE and Series I savings bonds are issued by the U.S. government.	The interest earned by bonds is not subject to federal income tax, and the bonds are guaranteed by the U.S. government.	The proceeds from bonds can only be used to pay for tuition and authorized education fees.

529 Plans

One of the more popular savings plans, 529 plans are covered under IRS's section 529 tax code. They allow you to save money for college expenses in a tax-deferred status for qualified beneficiaries (for example, your children). The plans are administered by the states. Some states allow residents of other states to participate in their plans.

Recent state and federal policies have made these plans easier to understand and more stable for the would-be investor. One change occurred in 2005 when the financial sponsors of the various plans agreed to create a set of "disclosure principles" so that potential investors could see just how each plan operates, the various options available under each plan, and the total costs of a plan for the investor. In addition, the Pension Protection Act that was signed into law in 2006 has broadened the definition of "family members" who could be listed as beneficiaries in the plan so that now first cousins are eligible members for the purposes of rollovers and change in beneficiaries. In addition, the temporary federal income tax exclusion that was to end in 2009 has now been made permanent for qualified withdrawals. State income tax exclusion is now permanent as well, so long as the particular state that administers its 529 follows the 529 federal tax recommendations.

Getting Started

You can access every state's 529 plan website at www.savingforcollege.com to find out what savings plans are available in your state. If you enter your state's name followed by the number 529 in your Internet browser's search screen (for example, Arizona 529), the "find" screen will display the websites that cover your state's 529 plans. You can also utilize this website to inquire about specific 529 plans by name of plan, type of plan, or the name of the program manager or investment manager.

There's a misconception that state-sponsored 529 plans are only geared toward families that send their children to a state school, and this is not true. There are two general types of 529 plans: prepaid programs and savings programs. The states offering prepaid tuition contracts covering in-state tuition will allow you to transfer the funds in your account to private and out-of-state schools. If you decide to use a 529 savings program, the full value of your account can be used at any accredited college or university in the country along with some foreign institutions.

Recent tax law changes now permit higher education institutions to offer their own 529 prepaid programs. These will allow you to target your tuition prepayment to the sponsoring institution or group of institutions. The Independent 529 Plan is the only such program currently in operation. All of the 529 plans offer different features. For example, there are prepaid tuition plans that allow you to save to purchase the tuition to a particular school or group of schools in a specific state ahead of when your student will attend. Some states offer guaranteed savings rate plans for those who are looking for low-risk plans.

When you open a 529 plan and begin making contributions to it, you are not allowed to direct how the money is invested in your plan. That function is performed by the plan's administrator on your behalf. You are allowed to change to a different plan once a year. You're required to maintain separate accounting for each beneficiary that shows contributions (dates and amounts) and how the money was used (date, amount, and what was purchased). Contributions to the plan are not deductible from your federal income tax, but they are deductible from some state income taxes.

Coverdell Savings Plans

Coverdell Education Savings Accounts (ESAs) are another tax-deferred college savings plan that's available to you. ESAs are sometimes referred to as 530 plans, and like their 529 plan counterpart, you can invest money in an ESA in a variety of ways (for example, equities, mutual funds, bonds, and so on). Unlike 529 plans, you have the option to make all of the investment decisions on the funds held in the account. If you are an astute investor, over the years your self-directed investments will hopefully earn a greater rate of return than what you would have earned in a traditional savings plan.

There are strict limits on the annual amount any contributor can make. Contributions cannot be made to a beneficiary after he or she reaches age 18 and currently cannot exceed $2,000 per year per contributor. In addition, any funds you may have in such a plan will incur penalties and taxes if they are not withdrawn by the time the beneficiary turns 30. There are no age restrictions or contribution limits on disabled and special-needs students. ESA assets are considered to be owned by the beneficiary and are therefore counted as the student's assets when financial aid calculations are made. You are allowed to pay for a wide variety of elementary and secondary educational expenses with ESA funds.

U.S. Savings Bonds

U.S. savings bonds are among the most convenient bonds to purchase and redeem. They're extremely safe, and the interest they earn isn't subject to state or federal taxes. The federal government offers two types of bonds: Series EE and Series I, which can be purchased through most financial institutions.

Series EE savings bonds are related to original Series DD savings bonds that were created during World War II to help finance the war. They have come a long way since then, and you can now use them to pay for some college expenses without paying any federal income tax on the interest that they earn. They're issued at 50 percent of their face value at maturity, which means that a $100 bond costs you $50. When it matures at a specified future date, it will be worth $100. They're offered in a variety of amounts ranging from $50 to $10,000 and are guaranteed to reach their face value in 20 years. You can cash in the bond at any time six months after its issue date. If you have owned the bond for less than five years, you will forfeit three months' worth of interest. For example, if you cash in a bond that you have owned for 12 months, you will only be entitled to 9 months of interest.

Series I savings bonds are relatively new and represent a major departure from the U.S. Treasury bonds of the past in that they offer a fixed interest rate and some inflation protection. They're offered in a variety of amounts ranging from $50 to $10,000, but you have to purchase them for their full face value. When you redeem a Series I bond, you will receive the original face value of the bond plus compound interest along with any inflationary adjustments that have been made over the years. If you cash in a Series I bond before it matures, you will forfeit three months' worth of interest.

Finding the college savings plan that's right for you and your student depends on a number of important factors like your tolerance for risk, the age of your beneficiary, and the amount of time you're willing to spend managing the plan you select. Generally speaking, the closer your beneficiary is to attending college, the more conservative you may want to be about how the funds in your plan are invested. The last thing you want to happen is to see the funds in your plan begin to disappear because of a downturn in the stock market where the plan's funds are invested just before your beneficiary is about to attend his or her freshman year in college. Perhaps you would have been better off investing in a guaranteed savings account.

> **Warning**
>
> Mutual funds offer a wide range of risks to consider. A fund that invests in high-quality corporate bonds is considered "low risk" as compared to a fund that invests in aggressive-growth, "high-risk" stocks.

On the other hand, if your beneficiary is several years away from reaching college age, you may decide that it's worth taking the risk of the ups and downs of the stock market to realize a higher rate of return. Perhaps mutual funds are the way to go? They're made up of either equities (stocks) or debt instruments (bonds) or a combination of both. The following table compares the primary features of the education savings plans presented in this chapter:

Education Savings Plan Comparison Chart

Feature	529 Plan	ESA Plan	Series EE Bonds	Series I Bonds
Self-directed investments	No	Yes	No	No
Investments in mutual funds, equities, and bonds offered	Yes	Yes	No	No

Feature	529 Plan	ESA Plan	Series EE Bonds	Series I Bonds
Risk	Medium	High	Low	Low
Contribution limits	No	Yes	No	No
Beneficiary age limits	No	Yes 30 Years	No	No

Savings Strategies

How do you develop a savings strategy that meets both your short-term and long-term savings goals? Let's assume that you intend to save $5,000 a year for your son's college education. Your son is 8 and will enter college at age 18. You have evaluated the various plans available to you and know that you can invest your money in a 5 percent fixed-interest savings account that is virtually risk-free. However, you believe that you can double your rate of return (10 percent) if you invest your contributions in a savings account that allows you to invest in mutual funds. Your savings strategy is as follows:

1. You decide to invest 100 percent of your contributions in mutual funds that have had an average rate of return greater than 10 percent over the past five years, based on your research.

2. As your son gets closer to his first year of college (10 years from now at age 18), you plan to reduce your 100 percent mutual fund contribution by 10 percent per year and invest the difference in a fixed-interest investment.

3. When your son reaches age 9, your savings plan investment formula changes from 100 percent invested in mutual funds to 90 percent invested in mutual funds and 10 percent invested in fixed-income investments. At age 10, your investment formula would be 80/20, and so on as your investments become more conservative with less risk as your son approaches college age.

You need to decide whether to invest in a self-directed savings plan. You can choose one in which you decide how and where you want

Action Plan

If you are interested in learning more about higher-rate-of-return mutual funds, check out Morningstar's excellent websites at www.Morningstar.com to get comprehensive, up-to-date information about mutual funds and stocks.

your money invested, or you can choose a plan in which the plan's institution makes investment decisions on your behalf or a plan that simply guarantees you a certain interest rate of return. In a self-directed account in which you make all of the investment decisions, you are at greater risk. If this is your first venture into the investment world, you may feel more comfortable leaving the investment decisions to a third party. As you gain confidence in your investment abilities, you can always switch your savings plan over to a self-directed plan.

Opening and Managing Your Account

Most major banks, savings and loan companies, and mutual fund and brokerage companies offer educational savings plans. Once you've selected a savings plan and an administrator that you are comfortable with, you need to complete an account setup form, which is similar to an IRA form. You're required to provide the Social Security numbers of the account owner and beneficiary plus the usual contact information. You will be asked if you will remain the account owner after the beneficiary reaches college age or if it will revert to the beneficiary. Make sure you know about any fees you'll be required to pay for account maintenance by the financial institution you select.

Contributions

You contribute money into an educational savings plan simply by writing a check made out to your plan's administrator (Fidelity Investments, Bank America, etc.), and those funds get deposited into your beneficiary's account. Although the federal government doesn't impose any specific dollar limitations on the maximum annual contribution you can make, the states do. State-imposed contribution limits may influence which state program you choose to participate in (high-limit versus low-limit state). So check the laws in the state that oversees your account. You can also deposit money into a savings plan through a payroll deduction program at work.

Placing Orders in Self-Directed Plans

If you select a self-directed savings plan (such as a Coverdell/ESA plan), there are several ways you can place buy or sell orders for stocks and mutual funds. The easiest way is to contact your account administrator and tell him or her what stock or mutual fund you want to buy or sell. For example, your instructions may simply be, "Buy me 50 shares of IBM stock today." You could also have said, "Buy me 50 shares of IBM stock today at a price that is equal to or less than $$." The same basic words are used to sell a stock: "Sell 50 shares of IBM stock today," or "Sell 50 shares of IBM stock today at a price that is equal to or greater than $$."

Qualifying a Beneficiary

There are three primary caveats you need to know about to determine whether your student is qualified to participate in a tax-sheltered savings plan. The first is the age limitation. You have 18 years from the birth date of a beneficiary to set up and contribute into an ESA plan and 30 years from the birth date for a 529 plan. There are no age limits for federal savings bonds.

> **HELP!**
>
> If you are interested in trading stock and mutual funds direct online, visit Fidelity Investment's website at www. fidelity.com. The site offers tutorials on how to trade online and how to use Fidelity's trading tools, even if you don't have an account with Fidelity.

Second, all assets in ESA plans must be totally liquidated once the beneficiary reaches age 30. If you transfer the account to another beneficiary before the original beneficiary turns 30, the age of the new beneficiary cuts in until he or she reaches 30. Obviously, you are not allowed to transfer an ESA plan to a beneficiary who is over 30. There are no age limitations in 529 or educational savings bond plans. Therefore, you could transfer funds from a beneficiary's ESA plan when he or she reaches age 30 into a 529 plan to avoid the age penalty.

Third, you are also allowed to transfer an account from one beneficiary to another beneficiary as long as he or she is a member of the same family as the original beneficiary. The new beneficiary must be related to the previous beneficiary in one of the following ways: brother, sister, grandchild, first cousin, or stepchild.

Withdrawing Funds

The funds you've accumulated in your savings plan can only be spent on what the IRS refers to as "qualified educational expenses" if you want to avoid paying income tax. You also need to know what schools are eligible to receive money for qualified expenses such as tuition. As a general rule, most accredited colleges, universities, and even trade schools qualify to receive funds from educational savings plans. Qualified expenses depend on whether the beneficiary is a part-time or full-time student, as summarized in the following table:

Qualified Expenses for Savings Plans

Expense Category	Full-Time Student	Part-Time Student
Tuition	Yes	Yes
Room and board	Yes	If half time or more, yes; otherwise, no
Institutional fees	Yes	Yes
Books, computers, and supplies	Yes	Yes

Whenever your student takes a distribution from your savings account and uses the funds for qualified educational expenses, you will receive an IRS Form 1099-Q from the administrator of the account at the end of the year showing the total amount of the distribution. As long as you used the distribution to pay for qualified educational expenses, you will not be taxed.

Changing Plans

Let's assume for a moment that you have a 529 or ESA plan that you've set up for your daughter, and it is not performing as well as you expected. You want to switch over to another 529 or ESA plan. What are your options? Tax-free transfers can be made from any plan to any other type of tax-sheltered college savings plan and between states as long as you are covered by their residency and nonresidency requirements. You must complete the account transfer within 60 days from the date the money actually leaves the first account. If you fail to meet the 60-day limit, you will be subject to a 10 percent penalty fee.

You can transfer funds from a 529 or ESA account into a U.S. savings bond without triggering taxes, but be careful about ownership issues. For instance, an ESA is effectively owned by the beneficiary, so it may not be proper to transfer the funds into a 529 account that is owned by you. Also note that the tax-free transfer of U.S. savings bond redemption proceeds into a 529 plan requires that you meet all the qualification requirements for the education exclusion, including the income limits in the year of the redemption.

Closing a Plan

What happens if you close a savings plan before the funds are all used to cover qualified educational expenses? It might happen because your beneficiary doesn't need all the money for his or her education or the person decides not to go to college. The beneficiary or account owner will owe income tax on any accumulated income (such as interest income, asset appreciation, etc.) and a 10 percent penalty for receiving a nonqualified distribution.

One way to avoid the nonqualified distribution tax problem and penalty is to transfer the account to a new beneficiary. Or you may decide to spread out nonqualified distributions over a number of years to minimize a "one-time" hit on your tax bill if you close out 100 percent of a plan in one year. Just keep in mind that ESA accounts must be completely closed out when the beneficiary reaches age 30.

> **Warning**
>
> Check the rules of your plan very carefully before you close it. Every state has its own set of rules, so check out the ones that are specific to your plan. A few prepaid tuition plans don't allow you to receive the money back when you close a plan. Most will allow you to transfer the funds to a new beneficiary.

Financial Aid Implications

One of the major disadvantages of owning an educational savings plan is the effect it can have on your application for financial aid. If you are unable to save the entire amount your student needs to attend college and cannot afford to pay the difference, you may have to submit a Free Application for Federal Aid (FAFSA) form. The completed form is submitted to the U.S. Department of Education to determine a student's eligibility for federal financial aid. (See Chapter 19 on FAFSA.)

The information you provide on the FAFSA is used by the Department of Education to determine if a student is eligible for aid and how much his or her family can afford to pay. If the student qualifies for federal aid, he or she may be eligible for low-interest loans, need-based grants, and scholarships. Unfortunately, if you are the owner of an educational savings plan and the student (in this case, your child) is the beneficiary, your application for financial aid will be affected.

Several factors could affect you. The prepaid tuition plan is counted far more heavily in the financial aid formula than other educational savings plans. The dollar value of the plan must be included as part of your net worth on the FAFSA form, which in effect reduces the amount of aid your student may be eligible to receive.

A new law enacted in early 2006 (Deficit Reduction Act of 2005) made substantial changes to the treatment of 529 plans in the federal student aid eligibility formula. The changes were first effective for the 2006-2007 school year. The law now prevents a 529 account from being treated as a student asset on a FAFSA filed by a dependent student. This means a custodial 529 will no longer be subject to the 20 percent assessment rate. In fact, it shouldn't be included on the FAFSA at all. Along with favorable asset treatment, a 529 account also garners favorable treatment in the income portion of the financial aid eligibility formula. A tax-free distribution from a 529 plan to pay this year's college expenses will not be part of the "base-year income" that reduces next year's financial aid eligibility.

Here is a simplified example of how this all works: You file the FAFSA aid application when your child is a senior in high school. Let's say you have a 529 savings account with $20,000 in it, of which $10,000 represents your original contribution and $10,000 is earnings. Your eligibility for federal financial aid this year will decrease by no more than 5.64 percent of the account value, or $1,128.

Assume there is no further appreciation in the account, and you withdraw $5,000 in the fall to pay for the first semester college bills. If you have $15,000 left in the account when you apply for aid in your child's sophomore year, you will again be assessed up to 5.64 percent, or $846, of the account value. The $5,000 withdrawal brought $2,500 of excluded earnings with it, but as indicated here, none of the withdrawal is counted as financial aid income. The federal aid formula is even more complicated than what is described here.

Another major change in the 2006 law is the way a 529 prepaid tuition plan is treated. Under the old law, your investment would not show up at all on the FAFSA. However, the benefits paid out would be considered by the institution as a resource that reduced your child's overall financial "need." The bottom line effect for most families was a dollar-for-dollar offset in eligibility.

Going forward, a 529 prepaid tuition plan will be treated the same as a 529 savings plan. It will no longer cause a dollar-for-dollar reduction in financial aid. Instead, the reduction will be no more than 5.64 percent of the refund value of the prepayment account.

If this sounds complicated, it is—and we are only talking about the federal financial aid rules here! Each school can (and most will) set its own rules when handing out its own need-based scholarships, and many schools are starting to adjust awards when they discover 529 accounts in the family. Also consider that the federal financial aid rules are subject to frequent change. Finally, remember that most financial aid comes in the form of loans, not grants, so you end up paying it back anyway.

The Least You Need to Know

- Tax-sheltered educational savings programs are everywhere if you know where to look for them.

- The rate of return on the money you invest in a savings account can vary significantly, so make sure you consider all savings plan options.

- The federal and state tax rules that regulate educational savings programs are basically straightforward. Follow them and you will avoid future tax problems.

Part 3

Seek and You Shall Find—Money

Remember when you were a kid, or an adult for that matter, and you went to a treasure hunt party? You and your team were given a list of seemingly impossible items to find, and you eagerly struck out to knock on your neighbors' doors to see if they had anything on your list. You didn't know where to look, which was part of the fun of the game. Whoever returned to party headquarters with all the items on the list won at least a sack of candy.

Finding financial aid isn't that much different from a treasure hunt. There's money to be had out there if you know where to look for it. Fortunately, you have this book: think of it as a financial aid treasure map. Whatever is on your list of needs, these chapters can point you in the right direction to meet them.

Grant Me a Grant

In This Chapter

◆ Distinguishing between merit-based and need-based grants

◆ Searching for grant money

◆ Writing a winning grant proposal

◆ Learning the guidelines for submitting grants

Grants are a type of need-based aid awarded to students who demonstrate the most financial need. Both federal and state governments provide grant programs.

Pell Grants are the largest source of need-based gift aid and are available to undergraduate students who demonstrate financial need. If you apply by the deadline and meet the eligibility criteria, you receive Pell Grant funds. The amount you receive is partly determined by the total funding approved by the U.S. Congress.

The Federal Supplemental Educational Opportunity Grant (FSEOG) program is administered by the financial aid office at your college and is available to Pell Grant recipients. Each school has a limited amount of funding for this program, so it's important to file early for financial aid. You could receive up to $4,000 a year in FSEOG grants. You'll find out more about Pell Grants and the FSEOG program in this chapter.

The Various Types of Grants

According to a survey conducted by Gallup and Robinson, most parents of college-bound students have saved no more than 25 percent of college costs. Before we begin our discussion about how grants can help ease the burden of meeting college expenses, it's important to distinguish between the various types of financial aid for college.

Almost all aid comes in one of two varieties: grants or loans. Both grants and loans can be paid directly to the student, to the student's school, or to the student's parents. The key distinction is that loans have to be paid back, whereas grants do not.

There are several problems, however, for a student who relies solely on receiving need-based aid to finance an education. The major ones are as follows:

♦ There just aren't enough need-based funds to go around. Most colleges have strict financial aid budgets, restricting the amount of need-based grants they can award. The majority of families soon discover that a financial aid office's estimate of need is very different (usually lower) from the realities of a family's cash flow and bank accounts.

Getting Started

A grant is a type of financial aid that does not have to be repaid. Grants are usually awarded on the basis of need, but they can also be awarded for a student's special skills.

♦ Even though a college may claim that a significant percentage of its student body receives financial aid, such statements can be misleading. When loans carry an interest rate below the current market level and don't have to be paid back until after graduation, they're classified as "financial aid." What college students and their families soon discover is that these types of low-interest loans make up the bulk of most financial aid packages. Although such loans are helpful in that they delay repayment, they still have one overwhelmingly undesirable feature: they eventually have to be repaid.

♦ Students from middle-income families often find themselves "caught between a rock and a hard place." Such families aren't wealthy enough to cover all of the costs on their own, but they don't have low enough incomes to qualify for substantial levels of need-based aid. Having to send more than one child to college further aggravates the situation.

Winning grants can help students and their families substantially lower their debt burden or even avoid borrowing money altogether. This is especially important in a debt-ridden era in which increasing numbers of parents resist taking out new loans for college expenses, opting instead for less expensive schools. Grants allow students to take control of their educational destinies by empowering them to choose the right college for them, regardless of the financial situation of their families.

Grants generally come in two flavors: merit-based and need-based:

- **Merit-based grants** are awarded on the basis of student achievement. The judging criteria used to evaluate achievement vary substantially among grant programs, which frequently take into account a wide range of student talents and interests.

- **Need-based grants** are awarded solely on the basis of financial need, as determined by formulas that weigh financial resources against living expenses, parental assets, income, and expenses (if the student is a dependent).

Merit-Based Grants

A merit-based grant is what most people generally mean when they use the word "scholarship." Grants, or scholarships, are awarded by corporations, nonprofit groups, foundations, service clubs, state and federal governments, and other organizations. Some colleges also offer merit-based grants to students who enroll at their institutions, although this is rare at the more competitive schools, which don't have to offer this type of financial incentive to attract students.

An example of a merit-based grant, or scholarship, is the Tylenol scholarship program. It requires that students submit 100- to 200-word essays describing their goals and aspirations, including two or three sentences about their experiences or about people who have contributed to their achievements. Basically, the program's creators expect the student to summarize his or her entire future in less than 200 words. The 2007 Tylenol program (for students planning to begin college in 2008) will award a total of $270,000 in grants ranging from $1,000 to $5,000 to 170 individuals planning to enter the field of health science.

The program's creators are looking for how precise someone can be while writing his or her essay. For example, is the theme of your essay clearly identified in the opening paragraph?

Many merit-based grants are reserved for individuals planning to enter a particular field of study or are intended for students with certain affiliations such as geographic location and family heritage.

Applying for Merit-Based Grants

If you apply for a merit-based grant (scholarship) and the sponsors ask you for information about your extracurricular activities, they basically want a summary of everything you do outside of class time. This includes school clubs, sports, jobs, independent projects, volunteer activities, and everything in between. Sometimes scholarship applications will distinguish between different types of extracurricular activities. In the Tylenol scholarship example, the application requests information about two separate categories of extracurricular activities: (1) school-related activities and (2) community and volunteer service activities.

Action Plan

Make sure you can validate all of your extracurricular activities. For example, if you participated as a volunteer in a United Way program, make sure you keep all of the documentation that confirms your part in the program.

Most applications request information about extracurricular activities in some type of list format. Some contests will limit you to the space provided on the physical application, while others will let you attach additional sheets. In addition to requesting a brief description of the activity itself, contest applications may also ask for information about the time commitment devoted to the activity, any leadership positions or offices held, and any awards or honors received from the endeavor.

Although not all scholarships request information about a student's academic record, a substantial number do make it part of the judging criteria. The way in which this is taken into account can vary tremendously. For scholarships such as the All-USA Academic Team sponsored by *USA Today*, grades are an important part of the judging criteria. On the other hand, many scholarship contests use only activity accomplishments.

Need-Based Grants

The largest need-based grant program is the Pell Grant, which is sponsored by the federal government. The program awards money to students from lower-income families. A relatively small number of grant programs use both merit-based and need-based criteria in making awards.

Institutional aid is also awarded by colleges and universities from their own coffers. The majority of this aid comes in the form of discounts on published sticker prices of, for example, tuition, and it's distributed according to financial need.

Need-based grants are sometimes offered by foundations and other organizations, but such programs are less common.

Federal Grant Programs

The rising costs of higher education, combined with only minimal relief from college financial aid offices, has made federal need- and merit-based grants an even more critical source of funding in recent years.

Quite simply, merit-based grants are monetary prizes awarded on the basis of some measure of achievement. What constitutes achievement depends on who is awarding the money, but you'll soon discover that merit-based grants are targeted at virtually every type of student. An enterprising student can exert tremendous influence over the amount of merit-based grants he or she receives; this is not the case with need-based grants.

Pell Grants

Last year, the *Federal Pell Grant Program* awarded gift money to nearly 4 million students in amounts ranging from $400 to $3,000 yearly. Unfortunately, the grants are off limits to graduate students and to students who have already received a Bachelor's degree but are returning to school for additional higher-education studies.

Getting Started

The **Federal Pell Grant Program** is for undergraduate students who have not completed a first baccalaureate degree. It is designed to financially assist students who are the least able to contribute toward their basic education expenses.

The amount you get depends on your demonstrated need, the costs of education at the particular college you want to attend, the length of the program in which you are enrolled, whether your enrollment is full- or part-time, and the amount of money Congress approves divided by the number of qualifying students. You apply for a Pell Grant by filling out and submitting the FAFSA form.

Supplemental Education Grants

Do you have exceptional demonstrated need? If your answer is "yes," then the Federal Supplemental Educational Opportunity Grant Program, fondly known as SEOG, is for you. To qualify, you must be enrolled at least half-time in an undergraduate program at an accredited institution. Grants in the neighborhood of $4,000 are possible on the basis of pure, unadulterated need. However, most colleges don't receive enough FSEOG funds to pay out maximum eligibility, and $1,000 to $1,500 is considered a good award. Roughly a million students are awarded this crucial funding, which is designed to equalize college opportunity.

The FSEOG program is campus-based, which means that although the money comes from the federal government, the colleges hand it out to students who show exceptional need. Typically, students eligible for Pell Grant awards are also eligible for FSEOG funds.

If you're turned down for a FSEOG grant, you're allowed to borrow an additional unsubsidized Federal Stafford or Direct loan, as long as you submit your parents' rejection letter with your application. Through this process, you can borrow $4,000 for each of the first two years and $5,000 for each of the last two years. Although your parents' interest rate for the new loan can increase, your repayment of the principal begins after graduation or when you're no longer attending college at least half-time. By contrast, your parents' repayment of the principal begins 60 days after they receive their final installment. In short, this type of borrowing is great for your cash flow.

Work-Study Programs

Work-study programs are campus-based programs in which federal dollars are distributed by colleges. To qualify for these jobs, you must have demonstrated need and be enrolled for at least half-time study at either the undergraduate or graduate level. Employment is almost always on campus, although jobs are also arranged off campus in community service programs.

The pay is at least the current federal minimum wage and usually is higher. Compensation for off-campus jobs is left to the discretion of the employer and may be greater than for campus jobs. The military offers a cornucopia of financial aid opportunities, described in Chapter 12.

The federal government tries hard to help your education money numbers add up to an affordable year of college.

Five Ways to Begin Your Grant Search

The grants game is an ever-changing field that requires hard work, persistence, and a little luck. Finding an appropriate grant source takes a lot of work; writing the proposal is actually easier than finding the right grant source.

Unfortunately, there is no master list or 800 number to call for the information you need. Nevertheless, let's get started with some basic resources to find out what's available.

Community Services

Check with your high school, local school district, and county or state agency to see if they have a grants listing service or a grants assistance office. (See Appendix C for resources listed alphabetically by state.) Since these lists are not all-inclusive, you'll still have to monitor grant awards and announcements in other print or online media. Find out if your school district or county office has a reference center where you can go to use reference materials.

The key to finding a grant locally is that you have to take the initiative! Corporations and privately endowed organizations frequently are open to grant proposals from students in their community.

Library Resources and School Districts

Check with your local, regional, and university libraries to see what grant research resources are available to you. Some of the reference materials are very expensive, but they are usually available in a collection that you can use rather than buy. Some school districts have their own professional development libraries, which contain grant research resources. Some of this information is also available on the Internet.

HELP! Check out Grants.gov at www.grants.gov to learn more about grant subscription services. This website and others are listed under "Scholarships, Grants, and Fellowships" in Appendix B.

Subscription Services

Consider subscribing to one of the national services that sends subscribers timely grant information. These services can cost anywhere from $80 to $300 a year. The people who write grant newsletters read through the federal register and check with other sources to provide you with leads to grants and the federal agencies that are offering them.

Subscription services are expensive, and you can often find the materials they provide on your own with a little digging. However, if you're busy, the time saved could be worth the money. Ask your local public librarian about these services. He or she may be able to recommend such services or may even subscribe to these services through the library. If your local library does subscribe to services that you find helpful, chances are the library provides remote access to library card holders, so you can conduct your own research from home via your Internet connection free of charge.

The News Media

Several newspapers and magazines contain grant proposal notices. Some publications print short articles about who was funded for which grant. These are fascinating to read. For example, check out a copy of *Education Week* or the *Chronicle of Philanthropy* for grant information. You'll also find many leads in such magazines as *Electronic Learning* and *Technology and Learning* and in vendor advertisements, mailings, and your local newspaper.

Online Services

The major online services have grant areas that are worth a look. On America Online you'll find useful information in the National Education Association's (NEA) files, the Association for Supervision and Curriculum Development (ASCD) area, and the Reference Service Press (RSP) Funding Focus section.

HELP!

There are many ERIC websites, all linked by a system-wide site run by ACCESS ERIC. Internet users visit ERIC sites at www.eric.ed.gov more than 500,000 times each week.

For background research, use the Educational Resources Information Center (ERIC) on the Internet. ERIC is a federally funded national information system that provides access to an extensive body of education-related resources. These resources will help you find current information about educational issues. Write your projects based on the latest research in the field. Make sure you learn how to navigate ERIC because its database of articles, reports, research studies, and reviews is vast.

Federal Grants

Just a few years ago, grant seekers had two options: live in a big city with a great library system or go to a university library to manually research grant leads. Today, with telecommunications common in schools, many of the traditional library resources for finding grant opportunities are available online. Finding them does, however, take some persistence.

These resources are the cornerstones of any funding program. When searching for federal or national corporate funds, books such as *Barron's Complete College Financial Guide* and websites like www.finaid.com will help you identify which programs are available. In some resources, you simply read all programs available nationwide. In others, the resources are listed alphabetically by state. Federal programs are targeted nationwide.

Corporate and foundation programs often provide funds for areas of the country where their businesses are physically located. Private foundations and nonprofits often fund specific kinds of programs such as technology or professional development.

Resources such as John Schwartz's book *College Scholarships and Financial Aid* include a CD that will give you the details you need for just about every scholarship available. For practical, up-to-date information on federal, state, and individual college financial aid programs, get a copy of *Barron's Complete College Financing Guide* at your local bookstore.

Federal Register

The *Federal Register* is the official publication in which all regulations must be published in order to notify the public of federal agency actions. The U.S. government has committed itself to maintaining a full-text digital database of the *Federal Register* and the *Code of Federal Regulations.* You can find out more about the different ways of accessing the *Federal Register* if you visit the U.S. Government Printing Office site at www.access.gpo.gov.

Action Plan

To see what's available from the federal government for the current fiscal year, check out the Department of Education's site at www.ed.gov. This site and others are listed under "Scholarships, Grants, and Fellowships" in Appendix B. They have links to the latest funding programs and information about future programs.

Catalog of Federal Domestic Assistance

The *Catalog of Federal Domestic Assistance (CFDA)* is the federal government's guide to all funding programs. The catalog is a good place to start a grants search for federal funding.

The CFDA number consists of two digits that identify the agency. For example, the Educational Department is 84.345, and the Health and Human Services Department is 93. A decimal point followed by three digits identifies the specific program. Some CFDA numbers, such as those in the Education Department section, end in letters to indicate multiple grant competitions under a single program.

Programs with numbers ending in 999 have not yet been assigned permanent CFDA numbers.

You can order a free copy of the *CFDA* from the Superintendent of Documents, U.S. Government Printing Office, Washington, D.C. 20402 or through its website at www. access.gpo.gov.

Making the Grant Process Work for You

The Office of Management and Budget (OMB) provides grant management guidelines to help grantees follow the rules and limitations for how the money may be spent and how it must be accounted for.

The OMB, the main overseer of federal grant administration, has set standards and processes for managing federal funds, covering such issues as dealing with audits, cost principles, and indirect cost rates.

The agency publishes a book titled *OMB Grant Programs and Guidelines*, which includes the text of OMB's circulars as well as other circulars, texts, and points of contact. This book is available at federal bookstores or by writing to the Superintendent of Documents, U.S. Government Printing Office, Washington, D.C. 20402. Write for current pricing or check its website at www.access.gpo.gov.

Education Department General Administration Regulations

In their entirety, Education Department General Administrative Regulations (EDGAR) apply only to programs of the U.S. Department of Education. Other federal programs described in the *Guide to Federal Assistance* may be affected by some of the regulations included in EDGAR regarding intergovernmental review, lobbying activities, and the provision of a drug-free workplace.

The *United States Government Manual* describes every agency, commission, and federal department. It lists addresses, telephone numbers, and key personnel. Revised annually, the manual is useful in identifying names and addresses for programs described in the *Catalog of Federal Domestic Assistance*. Order from the Superintendent of Documents, U.S. Government Printing Office, Washington, D.C. 20402 or through its website at www.access.gpo.gov.

Private Funding Sources

The *Foundation Directory* is an annual reference source for information about private and community grant-making foundations in the United States. It provides basic descriptions and current fiscal data for the nation's largest foundations. Check the

Foundation Center's website at foundationcenter.org for a catalogue of products or call 1-800-478-4661 for a free catalogue.

The Foundation Center is a national nonprofit organization established in 1956. Its mission is to collect, organize, and disseminate factual data on foundation and corporate philanthropy.

The center offers free public access to this information by means of four center-operated libraries and a nationwide network of more than 180 cooperating collections. In addition, the center's publications program features over 50 titles on philanthropic giving and other nonprofit sector concerns. The latest edition is in two volumes and can be found at many cooperating collections around the United States. For more information, check out the center's website.

 Warning

Proofread! Spelling and grammar errors do not convey a positive image. Great grant ideas, when they're submitted laced with spelling and grammar errors, are automatically rejected.

The *Foundation Grants Index* is an annual source for determining the current funding priorities of the nation's largest foundations. It is useful to develop an initial list of potential funding sources based on a foundation's giving program and its application procedures before submitting grant requests. However, you should know that most foundations fund organizations, not private citizens, so make sure you focus on funding earmarked for individuals.

The *National Guide to Funding for Elementary & Secondary Education* is a starting point for grant seekers looking for foundation and corporate support for organizations serving elementary and secondary education. This resource is also available from the Foundation Center. This guide is aimed at grant-seekers looking for foundation and corporate support for libraries and information services.

Grant-Writing Tips

The most important thing for grant writers to remember is that they might submit a perfect application and still receive a rejection. Most foundations have limited resources with which to fund projects. Do not get discouraged if you get a rejection from a possible funding source.

Understand the Guidelines

Read the grantor's guidelines and instructions carefully. Do not try to make the grantor's program fit what you want to do; your program must be in line with the funding agency's priorities. Follow the grantor's instructions to the letter. Applications are turned away when they do not exactly meet the funding agency's requirements.

Be Innovative

Grant ideas should be innovative, creative, and educational. Grantors will rarely fund operating expenses. They usually invest in supplemental programs. Private foundations often seek creative solutions to problems or needs in the community, but they usually do not wish to fund risky projects. Try proposing a project that puts a fresh spin on a controversial but popular topic, such as controlling wildfires through increased logging activities.

Action Plan

Clarity in communicating the ideas in your grant request is very important. Have someone who is not involved in the project read and critique your draft application.

Don't assume that you can't qualify for a grant if you're a freshman. Many corporations are eager to offer grants to freshmen on subjects that address issues that are unique to freshmen students. For example, I was awarded a grant from Computech Corporation to write an essay titled "What Every Freshman Must Learn in the First 30 Days at College." Computech wanted to offer this advice to their employees who had kids who were about to enter college.

Back Up Your Goals with a Budget

Keep your goals realistic! It's important to have an evaluation plan. Grantors want to know if the projects they fund are viable. They also want to know if your project is meeting its goals.

Have a reasonable and detailed budget. Do your homework on costs prior to submitting your application, and be sure to explain your budget even if there are no requirements to do so.

If your project is rejected, ask the grantor for reviewer comments. The comments can offer invaluable tips for improving your future grant applications. Never forget to write thank-you notes, even if your project is not funded.

The Least You Need to Know

- Be prepared to work hard to find grants made to students for specific projects.

- The most common federal government grants are the Pell and FSEOG grants.

- There are numerous private funding sources for grants if you know where to find them.

Chapter 10

State Aid Programs

In This Chapter

◆ Taking advantage of your state's aid programs if you can't get federal aid

◆ Learning about types of state aid and how they differ from federal aid programs

◆ Finding out about special programs available in your state

States are usually more generous than the federal government in determining whether you qualify for financial aid. Federal awards are based on your adjusted gross income and your asset base at the time of your application for aid. In contrast, most states consider only your adjusted gross income. This means that if you have a relatively low gross income but live in a posh home and own expensive assets, you may still be able to qualify for state aid if your income falls within your state's guidelines.

Last year, total state aid was more than $50 billion. Savvy students who took the initiative to obtain as much information as early as possible about state financial aid programs were the ones who benefited the most from state-directed financial aid programs.

This chapter gives you an overview and a sampling of the types of programs available in individual states. It covers the basics and points you to Appendix C, where you can get information about specific programs in all states. Programs are constantly changing, so be sure to ask your state aid office for its most recent information on financial aid opportunities.

Overview of State Aid Programs

All state educational agencies provide need-based financial assistance, and all states award merit-based scholarship assistance. Most states have created a guaranteed tuition plan or educational savings program for their residents. About a quarter of the states have adopted the Taylor Plan, which guarantees that the state will pay the tuition costs of eligible moderate- and low-income students who meet the state's minimum academic qualifications to attend college. Also, check to see if you can take a state grant with you if you enroll in an out-of-state college or university. Many states have reciprocal agreements with other states.

Action Plan

Tuition and fees are still a bargain at most state colleges. About 16 percent of the actual cost of a public college education comes from tuition. The state and federal governments make up the rest.

Unfortunately, only about 30 percent of the states are currently offering work-study programs, though the number of states endorsing the programs increases every year. Many states offer loan-forgiveness programs for specific professions such as education- or health-related careers. Under this program, the state will pay off your loan if you graduate in a certain profession and reside in the state for a specified period of time after you graduate.

A Sampling of State Aid Programs

Several federally funded aid programs are administered by individual states. This gives a little more consistency to the crazy quilt of state aid programs and gives you some program names to look out for when going over state aid information.

Student Incentive Grants

Although the states administer the program and decide individually whether the grants apply to full- or part-time students, the Student Incentive Grant program is partially funded by the federal government. It awards an annual maximum amount of $2,500.

Robert C. Byrd Honors Scholarships

The Robert C. Byrd Honors Scholarship program recognizes 10 students from each congressional district for outstanding academic
achievement and provides $1,500 for their
first year of higher education.

The addresses and tele-
phone numbers of all the
state aid offices can be found
listed by state in Appendix C.

Paul Douglas Teacher Scholarship Program

The Paul Douglas Teacher Scholarships are a merit-based, state-administered program. This program is intended to encourage students who graduate in the top 10
percent of their class to enter the field of teaching. States may give each student up to
$5,000 a year for up to four years. Participating students are then obligated to teach
for two years.

Getting Started

According to the National Association of State Student Grant and Aid Programs,
the top 10 spenders of need-based grant aid per full-time undergraduate student in
1999 were as follows:

New York $850	Vermont $570
Illinois $815	Indiana $410
New Jersey $790	Washington $380
Pennsylvania $710	Iowa $370
Minnesota $685	Virginia $355

State Aid Offices

State aid offices are the central clearinghouses for the aid programs provided within
the state. Since even programs that sound similar can vary in their particulars from
state to state, these offices can help you sort out the differences. You can get current
information from counselors at your high school or at the college financial aid office.
However, if the world isn't working as well as you would like and local sources aren't
helpful, the state financial aid agencies have the most up-to-date and comprehensive
information.

How Much Aid Comes from the States?

States vary widely in the amount of aid that each gives to education, according to the authoritative New York State Higher Education Services Corporation, which keeps track of state financial aid expenditures on students.

Last year, states awarded over $3 billion in aid to more than 2 million students. About 85 percent of that amount went to need-based aid. The New York State Higher Education group predicts that the numbers will continue to rise.

Some states spend more than others on their students. Last year, five states (California, Illinois, New Jersey, New York, and Pennsylvania) dispersed a total of $1.5 billion in need-based awards to undergraduates—a whopping 50 percent of the total for that category.

The less populous states will argue that citing the raw dollar amounts spent overall is misleading because they end up spending more per capita on their smaller numbers of students. They'll also tell you that the full extent of their aid doesn't show up in the standard measures used by the federal government. Here's their argument: if their schools are relatively inexpensive, then students don't need as much financial aid as they do in the more expensive schools in other, larger states. Thus, they say, the less populated states are to some degree penalized in the rankings for helping students out with lower tuitions.

Types of Programs Administered by the States

The range of state aid is broad and shows the political process at work. Along with the standard varieties of need-based aid, states are now moving heavily into non-need-based aid programs that reward students for outstanding academic achievement, regardless of their need for funds.

State legislatures also try to influence future careers by offering money to students who pursue certain areas of study or professions that are in demand within a respective state, just as the federal government rewards students entering certain professions. Many states push math and science studies for students who intend to go into teaching, whereas others boost a wide array of professions ranging from physical therapy to teaching.

Other state programs try to reward people less for what they do than for who they are. Minority group programs and programs to aid the dependents of prisoners of war or children of police officers killed in active duty all fall under this broad heading.

Many states also offer low-interest loan programs, which are similar to federal loan aid.
To make their private colleges more attractive, several states now offer "equalization"
money to help the tuition grants of private
colleges match those of the state's public institutions.

The best benefit a state offers is the protection it gives its own citizens in the form of in-
state tuition at its public institutions. Resident
status also provides eligibility for certain aid
programs.

Action Plan

Most state financial aid programs apply only to state
residents. Check the residency
and transfer requirements of each
program, and find out if your
state has any reciprocal financial
aid agreements with other states.

If you plan to attend an out-of-state public college, it may be worth your while to take
the time to establish residency in that state first. Before you take this action, make sure
you understand the particular state's residency requirements. In some states, it takes
two years to establish residency. If you're attracted to an academic program offered in
another state, but you don't want to give up possible aid from your own state, check
Appendix C to see if your state has an established agreement with the other state to
allow you to take advantage of your home state's aid while studying elsewhere.

The Non-Need Aid Trend

There's a growing trend toward non-need-based aid. In 2001, 37 states had such programs, and they paid out over $425 million. Those programs have been growing,
though over 90 percent of the grant dollars awarded to undergraduates by states is need-
based, according to the National Association of State Scholarship and Grant Programs.

Of the non-need pool, the biggest chunk of cash went into academic scholarships, so
maintaining good grades still pays big dividends. Non-need-based aid is broken down
into three categories:

- **Tuition equalization programs.** These programs help reduce the difference in
  tuition costs between public and private schools.

- **Scholarship programs or merit awards.** This category rewards academic
  achievement and is largely aimed at charming academic talent into staying in
  state.

◆ **Categorical aid programs.** This type of aid encourages students to go into particular fields of study such as math and science. It also helps special constituencies like veterans and police officers.

Action Plan

According to the National Association of State Scholarship and Grant Programs, adding new non-need programs has contributed little to the growth of state financial aid. Of course, a million dollars here and there is not pocket change, and any student would be very happy with just a fraction of that money.

As with all state programs, some states award a lot more in non-need aid than others. Last year, for example, most of the growth in non–need-based programs was attributed to Florida and Georgia, which increased their spending by more than $26 million. The spurt in non-need monies is still minor compared with the massive $2 billion in need-based funds that goes to undergraduates annually, but non-need aid is out there if you're willing to go after it.

Starting new non-need programs makes good political sense. Giving non-need programs enough money to make a difference makes state legislators look decidedly good to their affluent constituents. As a result, if you deduct the expenditures for such behemoth programs as New York's Part-Time Tuition Assistance Program (Part-Time TAP) and Ohio's Student Choice Grant Program, the remaining allotment for less visible non-need programs drops off dramatically.

State Guaranty Agencies

A state guaranty agency is a nonprofit organization that administers the Federal Family Education Loan (FFEL) and Stafford Parent Loans for Undergraduate Students (Stafford PLUS) loans that are covered in detail in Chapter 15.

HELP!

The address and phone number of each state's guaranty office is listed in Appendix C.

The federal government sets the loan limits and interest rates for these programs, but the states set their own limitations and conditions. You'll want to contact your state guaranty agency for the latest information on loan availability and repayment and deferment conditions; the agency can also put you in touch with willing lenders.

Special State Programs to Consider

All state educational agencies provide need-based financial assistance, and many state agencies award merit-based scholarship assistance. Over 60 percent of all states have created some kind of guaranteed tuition plan or educational savings program for their state residents.

Prepaid Tuition Plans

Prepaid tuition plans allow parents to pay a certain sum of money, years in advance, for their children's education; tuition savings plans are usually in the form of tax-exempt bonds or zero-coupon bonds. The following states offer prepaid tuition plans or tuition savings plans:

> Alabama, Arkansas, Colorado, Connecticut, Delaware, Georgia, Hawaii, Illinois, Indiana, Iowa, Kentucky, Louisiana, Maine, Maryland, Massachusetts, Michigan, Minnesota, Missouri, New Hampshire, New Jersey, New York, North Carolina, North Dakota, Ohio, Oklahoma, Oregon, Pennsylvania, Rhode Island, Tennessee, Texas, Virginia, Washington, West Virginia, Wisconsin, and Wyoming

Guaranteed Tuition Plans

The Taylor Plan, which guarantees that the state will pay the tuition costs of eligible moderate- and low-income students who meet the academic qualifications to attend college, has been adopted by these states:

> Louisiana, Florida, Texas, and Ohio

Action Plan

The amount of state aid for academically talented students is growing faster than aid for financially needy students. However, the competition for academic scholarships is tough.

Work-Study Programs

The following states offer work-study programs:

> California, Colorado, Connecticut, Florida, Iowa, Indiana, Kansas, Louisiana, Massachusetts, Michigan, Minnesota, Nevada, New Mexico, North Carolina, Pennsylvania, Rhode Island, South Carolina, Texas, Vermont, and Washington

Loan Forgiveness Programs

The following states offer loan forgiveness programs for specific professions such as education or health-related careers. The particular professions that fall under this category vary from state to state, so be sure to learn which professions are included based on the location of the institution to which you are applying:

Alabama, Arkansas, California, Connecticut, Delaware, Florida, Georgia, Hawaii, Illinois, Indiana, Iowa, Kentucky, Louisiana, Maryland, Massachusetts, Mississippi, Missouri, New Jersey, New Mexico, New York, North Carolina, Ohio, Oklahoma, Oregon, Pennsylvania, South Carolina, Tennessee, Texas, Utah, Vermont, Virginia, Washington, West Virginia, and Wisconsin

Western Student Exchange Program

Fourteen states participate in the Western Undergraduate Exchange (WUE) program administered by the Western Interstate Commission for Higher Education (WICHE). This program allows students to participate in tuition reciprocity agreements. The following states participate in the WICHE program:

Alaska, Arizona, Colorado, Hawaii, Idaho, Montana, Nevada, New Mexico, North Dakota, Oregon, South Dakota, Utah, Washington, and Wyoming

Highlights of State Financial Aid Programs

Each state offers a wide variety of scholarship, grant, work-study, and loan programs. Appendix C describes selected programs in each state to give you a better idea of the different types of state aid that might be available to you.

Keep in mind that states are constantly adding and deleting programs. Contact your state's financial aid office to get the latest list of state aid programs.

The Least You Need to Know

- ◆ State agencies may be able to offer you financial aid even if you don't qualify for federal aid.

- ◆ Because state aid programs are dynamic and change rapidly, check with your state's financial aid office for the latest information on what is available.

- ◆ Contact your state's financial aid office to apply for a grant or scholarship. See your state's guaranty office to apply for a student loan. In some states, the two offices are combined.

Playing the Scholarship Game

In This Chapter

◆ Learning what scholarships are all about and how to get one

◆ Finding out how to increase your odds of getting a scholarship

◆ Knowing how to spot and avoid scholarship scams

A scholarship is a form of financial assistance that doesn't require repayment. This type of award is usually given to students who demonstrate potential for distinction in academic performance or who show special talents in other areas.

Scholarship dollars can come from many sources: federal and state governments, the school you'll attend, or private sources such as corporations, fraternal organizations, local professional associations, unions, and high school or college alumni associations, to name a few. They can also come from your parents' employers or, if you're working, your own employer.

Scholarship awards are either need-based or merit-based and do not have to be repaid. Many scholarships are initially awarded for one academic year but are renewable if you continue to meet certain requirements.

Need-based scholarships are awarded to those who need more help paying for school. Merit-based scholarships typically are awarded to students who excel in academics, the arts, or sports, so don't give up on those violin lessons! Merit scholarships typically have qualifiers attached to them, such as religious affiliation, intended field of study, ethnic background, or leadership skills. To renew these scholarships annually, you may be expected to maintain a specific grade-point average or pursue a specific major.

Surfing the Web for Scholarships

The best way to search for a scholarship is to use personalized search tools on the web that will compare your background with a database of available scholarships. Only scholarships that fit your profile are identified in the matches.

With more than $1 billion in scholarships available annually, FastWeb (www.fastweb.com) is the largest, most accurate, and most frequently updated scholarship database. If you supply an e-mail address, FastWeb will notify you when new awards that match your profile are added to its database. You can even submit an electronic application to some of the scholarships listed on FastWeb, saving you time and money. The site also includes college websites and numerous other student resources that are available on the web.

Getting Started

FastWeb is able to offer its services for free, in part because of the willingness of its users to be reached by FastWeb's marketing partners. The information you supply to FastWeb may be made available to leading companies, so you'll receive free information on college financing and admissions, as well as offers and promotions designed just for students, including coupons from campus bookstores, retail store freebies, and more. It doesn't take much time to search, and again, it's free.

To find small local awards that aren't listed in any book or database, look for notices posted on bulletin boards at your school's guidance office, the public library, and outside the financial aid offices at nearby colleges and universities.

Don't waste your money on scholarship matching services that charge you a fee. You won't get any better information than you can get from the free services available on the web.

Scholarships that sound too good to be true usually are. Learn how to recognize and protect yourself from the most common scholarship scams. The number-one tip is that if you have to pay to get scholarship money, it's probably a scam.

Scholarship Databases

In addition to searching FastWeb, you should also search at least one of the other large scholarship databases such as www.scholarships.com or www.college-scholarships.com. Search each database to make certain that you've found all the awards for which you qualify.

You'll notice a significant amount of overlap among the databases in that they all use similar methods to compile their listings. Each database usually includes a few awards not listed in others. If the type and number of databases seems a bit overwhelming, consult your local library or school counseling office. They can often save you time in finding the best databases for you. In addition, some high schools and public libraries subscribe to fee-based services so you can avoid paying a personal fee.

HELP! Students who are awarded scholarships often need additional financial assistance. See the "Lenders of College Loans" section of Appendix B for websites and information on student and parent loans.

Peterson's Scholarship Search

Peterson's Award Search (www.Petersons.com) makes it quick and easy to find the right scholarships for you. The database covers over 2,000 scholarship sources in 70 academic subject areas.

Peterson's is one of the most trusted names in education and careers publishing. Its dedication to providing the best possible information guided the design of its scholarship database.

SmartStudent Guide to Financial Aid

The SmartStudent Guide to Financial Aid's website at www.Finaid.com includes a scholarship database that lists scholarships and other types of financial aid programs from over 3,000 national, state, public, and private sources. The database is updated annually. You'll find its website at www.collegeboard.org/fundfinder/html/ssrchtop.html. Also check the other scholarship chapters in Part 3.

SRN Express

SRN Express at www.srnexpress.com is a free web version of the Scholarship Resource Network (SRN) database. The SRN database focuses on private sector, non–need-based aid and includes information about awards from more than 1,500 organizations. The database is updated annually.

CollegeNET MACH25

CollegeNET MACH25 at www.collegenet.com/mach25 is a free web version of the Wintergreen Orchard House Scholarship Finder database. The database lists awards from over 1,500 sponsors and is updated annually.

In addition to the scholarship databases listed in this section, several other free scholarship databases are listed in Appendix B. These databases are smaller but more tightly focused, providing information for specific majors or career interests such as art, computer science, journalism, or nursing. You'll also find the website addresses for all of the scholarships covered in this section under "Scholarships, Grants, and Fellowships" in Appendix B.

Searching for scholarships does take time, but this book makes it easy. Spend about 30 minutes on the web completing a profile, and let computer technology begin working for you. You can also use the web to quickly send away for scholarship applications that you're interested in. Soon your mailbox will be filled with scholarship applications, and you'll be well on your way to applying for a scholarship. Here's a sampling of some of the great scholarships out there:

♦ **American Chemical Society (ACS).** Better education through chemistry is the motto of the ACS. It offers science scholarships to minorities. Its website at www.acs.org also lists many other sources of academic scholarships.

♦ **American Indian College Fund.** The American Indian College Fund supports over 30 tribal colleges and helps thousands of Native Americans get scholarships.

♦ **America's Junior Miss Scholarship Program.** The country's largest and oldest scholarship program for high school girls offers academic scholarships to young women.

♦ **AmeriCorp Scholarships.** Do some good for others, like build homes or clear hiking trails, and qualify for a college scholarship or loans through AmeriCorp.

- **Army ROTC.** Learn all that you can learn and let the Army help pay for it through their generous ROTC scholarship program, which is covered in detail in Chapter 12.

- **Coca-Cola Scholars Foundation.** Coca-Cola awards thousands of dollars in college scholarships each year to over 250 high school seniors.

- **Discover Card Tribute Awards.** The Discover Card folks have teamed with the American Association of School Administrators for a scholarship program. Apply when you're a high school junior.

- **Easley National Scholarship Program.** The Easley Foundation offers academic scholarships. It also publishes a newsletter about the other forms of financial aid it offers.

- **Elks National Foundation.** The Elks give away over $3 million a year in college scholarships to top high school seniors.

- **Fulbright Scholarship Program.** Teachers, students, and scholars in a wide array of fields can apply for these academic grants to study overseas.

- **Harry Truman Scholarship Foundation.** The bucks start here for college students looking to enter public service. The Truman scholarship program will help you get there.

- **Hispanic College Fund.** This minority scholarship program is looking for Hispanic business leaders of the future, and it's willing to offer you a scholarship to help you get there.

> **Action Plan**
>
> Scholarships are a great way to finance your education. Because they are gifts, these funds do not have to be repaid.

- **Hispanic Scholarship Fund.** Hispanic students in high school, community college, or four-year colleges can apply to the Hispanic Scholarship Fund program for awards.

- **Imagine America Scholarships.** The Career Training Foundation's program for technical schools offers numerous scholarships.

- **Intel Foundation.** Each year, the Intel Foundation provides undergraduate scholarships and graduate fellowships to outstanding engineering and computer science students at colleges and universities around the world.

- **Jackie Robinson Foundation.** The Robinson Foundation offers college scholarships for talented minority youths.

◆ **National Action Council for Minorities in Engineering.** The council offers scholarships for African Americans, Latinos, and Native Americans majoring in engineering.

◆ **National Collegiate Athletic Association (NCAA) Scholarships.** Student athletes in college can continue their education with the support of athletic scholarships that are sponsored by the NCAA.

◆ **Rhodes Scholarships.** The best and brightest college students apply to spend a couple of years at the University of Oxford in England. The Rhodes scholarship is one of the premier scholarships to get you there.

◆ **Rotary Foundation Ambassadorial Scholarship.** The Rotary Foundation gives out more than a thousand academic scholarships a year worldwide. It's the biggest program of its kind.

◆ **United Negro College Fund.** A mind is a terrible thing to waste and so is an opportunity like this for African American students who can qualify for United Negro College scholarships.

Scholarship Programs for Minorities and Special-Interest Students

In addition to the preceding scholarships focusing on minority students, literally thousands of additional opportunities are out there for both minorities and special-interest students. This section covers just a few of them to give you an idea of what's available.

Children's Scholarship Fund

The Children's Scholarship Fund helps provide educational opportunities for low-income children. Siebel Systems, which is a California-based software company, has donated over $3 million toward the mission of providing more students with access to colleges. Its Children's Scholarship Fund has awarded over $160 million in scholarships to about 40,000 such children around the country since 1998. The scholarships pay up to 75 percent of their tuition.

Educational Opportunity Programs (EOPs)

EOPs are administered through California State University (CSU), the University of California (UC), and California's community colleges. They provide grants, counseling, and tutorial services to low-income, disadvantaged students. At UC and some CSU campuses, counseling and tutorial services are provided through the campus Equal Opportunity Programs (EOPs), but grants come from the financial aid office.

To be eligible for the EOPs, a student must be disadvantaged according to criteria established by California regulations and be enrolled full-time at a community college or at a CSU or UC campus.

William Simon Foundation

The William Simon Foundation provides support for scholarships and fellowships for academically qualified students in need of financial assistance. These awards, which support a portion of the expenses of tuition and room and board, are made through grants.

 Warning

Follow the instructions for application forms to the letter. Use a word processor to write the applications or, if you still have a typewriter, type them out. Handwritten applications don't cut it!

How to Win a Scholarship

When requesting information on a particular scholarship, send a personalized letter to the scholarship provider with a self-addressed, stamped envelope. When you get the application, make sure you follow the instructions—to the letter—for completing the form. The biggest mistake you can make when applying for scholarships is to overlook the fine print. If the provider requests your high school transcripts, send them. If the application says to include an essay on how to live "La Vida Loca," do it. And, most important, don't miss the deadline. Deadlines are deadlines, and organizations that provide scholarships have an obligation to run in a timely manner.

If you are asked to send a letter of recommendation, ask the person writing it to take the time to focus on your personal assets, and to print it on his or her personal or organizational letterhead since presentation is very important. Scholarship providers do not like to see generic recommendation letters. If at all possible, submit only word-processed applications. Make copies of everything you submit to scholarship providers. That way, in the rare instance an original is misplaced, you will be able to provide a copy in a timely manner.

If you're a school leader, such as president of your class, there are many additional scholarship opportunities for you to explore. The William Randolph Hearst Foundation has a scholarship program that acknowledges students who have been

HELP!
Send your completed scholarship application packet via certified mail to ensure that the scholarship provider receives it.

elected to leadership offices in their high school's student government. The program distributes $2,000 each to over 100 students a year. The makers of Tylenol (the headache medicine) offer a similar program to high school leaders. The awards are based on leadership credentials, academic records, and extracurricular activities. Each year, 500 students receive $1,000 awards and 10 individuals get whopping ones of $10,000 each.

Can Students with Average Grades and Credentials Get Scholarships?

Of course average students can get scholarships. Not all scholarships are based on grades or test scores. For example, you can get a scholarship because you were born in New York or just because your dad works at US Airways. You'd be surprised to know just how many awards exist for all types of students.

Scholarship searching is an ongoing process, not a one-time project. Just as your academic status, qualifications, and interests change, so will the scholarships in the databases. In any scholarship database you use, be sure to update your profile and search for new awards frequently to increase your chances of obtaining one.

Scholarship Scams

Every year, several hundred thousand students and parents are defrauded by scholarship scams. The victims of these scams lose more than $100 million annually. Be wary of direct mail offers or Internet sites that seem suspect.

Scam operations often imitate legitimate government agencies, grant-giving foundations, education lenders, and scholarship matching services, using official-sounding names containing words like "National," "Federal," "Foundation," or "Administration." If you have to pay money to get a scholarship, it's probably a scam.

Fellowships

Fellowships are like scholarships in that they require no repayment or service in return for the reward. Fellowships provide money to cover the cost of tuition, books, fees, and even nondiscretionary expenses. They can be awarded based on a student's demonstrated need, academic merit, or any combination of variables that meet the objectives of specific fellows. Fellowships are primarily for graduate and postdoctoral students. To learn more about them, see Chapter 14.

Private School Scholarships

Parents seeking assistance with private school tuition for their children might get help from the school the child would like to attend. It may have scholarships available or be able to direct you to local sources of assistance. Also, many corporations offer extensive scholarship programs that are worth checking into.

The Least You Need to Know

- ◆ Scholarships are everywhere if you know where to look.

- ◆ Routinely search the scholarship databases listed in Appendix B to find new and exciting scholarship and grant opportunities.

- ◆ You will win a scholarship only if you follow the application instructions to the letter.

12

Military and Veteran Scholarship Programs

In This Chapter

◆ Learning about the many financial aid opportunities available through ROTC and other military programs

◆ Finding out how you can qualify for a military scholarship

◆ Discovering the educational options that are available to you as a veteran

The GI Bill, which was passed after World War II, has helped to finance the education of millions of military personnel and veterans. If you qualify, financial assistance programs offered by the military services are a way to reduce your college costs. This chapter examines the numerous scholarship and tuition programs offered by the military financial assistance programs for their personnel and their dependents.

Reserve Officers' Training Corps (ROTC) Scholarships

The ROTC scholarships are offered to qualified men and women who are enrolled in either two-, three- or four-year college programs (based on the length of time remaining for students to complete their degrees). Candidates must be U.S. citizens between the ages of 17 and 21 when they apply for a scholarship. There are physical requirements for acceptance into the program, and applicants must take either the ACT or SAT test. A personal interview is required.

ROTC scholarships pay for tuition, fees, and expenses up to $20,000 per year. Tuition and fees are paid directly to the school and are considered financial aid. The monthly stipend paid to the student is considered income, and it's taxable.

Recipients are required to study military science while in college, participate in summer training sessions, and maintain satisfactory academic progress as determined by their schools. Upon successful completion of the program and graduation, a recipient is awarded a military commission. Scholarship recipients must enlist in the Army, Navy, Air Force, or Marines and must agree to serve for four years on active duty and two years on reserve status after graduation.

Over 600 colleges and universities participate in this program. Speak with the school's ROTC representative to obtain specific information, program obligations, and application materials. Contact the following for additional information:

Air Force
Air Force ROTC Scholarship Program, JQ Recruiting Division
Maxwell Air Force Base
Maxwell, AL 36112-6106
205-953-2091

Army
Army ROTC Scholarship Program
Gold QUEST Center Box 3279
Warminster, PA 18794-0128
1-800-USA-ROTC (872-7682)

Marine Corps
Command General
Marine Corps Recruiting Consul Code MRON, 2 Navy Annex
Washington, D.C. 20380-1775
703-614-8541

Navy
Navy Opportunity Information Center
P.O. Box 9406
Gaithersburg, MD 20898-9979
1-800-327-NAVY (327-6289)

Military Academy Scholarships

Military academy scholarships are awarded each year to qualified students for attendance at the Air Force Academy, the Army Academy, the Naval Academy, the Merchant Marine Academy, and the Coast Guard Academy. Nominations are usually made by the applicant's U.S. senator or congressional representative. The scholarships are competitive and are based on a number of factors, including high school grades, SAT or ACT test scores, leadership qualities, and athletic ability.

Action Plan

All of the U.S. military academies offer Ivy League–quality educational programs that will serve you well throughout your career. The trick is figuring out a way to get into an academy. It starts with your congressman or congresswoman, who must first nominate you for entrance. Get to know these people well and be prepared to network your way through the political system. If you can find out from those in the know exactly how the entrance system works and what you need to do to crack it, you'll be miles ahead of your competition.

Applicants must apply separately for each academy. Students enrolled in this program receive their undergraduate education at the respective academies. Begin the process very early, especially the securing of a nomination from a senator or congressperson. Contact the following military offices for further information:

Air Force
Director of Admissions HQ USAFNRRS
U.S. Air Force Academy
2304 Cadet Dr., Suite 200
Colorado Springs, CO 80840-5025
719-472-2520

Army
Director of Admissions West Point
600 Thayer Rd.
West Point, NY 10996-1797
914-938-4041

Coast Guard
Director of Admissions
U.S. Coast Guard Academy
15 Mohegan Ave.
New London, CT 06320-4195
203-444-8501
1-800-883-8724

Merchant Marine
Director of Admissions
U.S. Merchant Marine Academy
300 Steamboat Rd.
Kings Point, NY 11024
516-773-5391
1-800-732-6267

Navy
Candidate Guidance Office, U.S. Naval Academy
117 Decatur Rd.
Annapolis, MD 21402-5018
410-293-4361
1-800-638-9156

Military Financial Assistance Programs

Each branch of the armed services offers numerous programs for both enlisted and officer personnel interested in continuing their educations. Most military bases have education officers who can provide information on specific programs offered during your period of service and after active duty is completed.

Service programs pay a portion of the cost of college attendance, which usually ranges from 75 to 90 percent of undergraduate or graduate school expenses. At the graduate level, commissioned officers are selected to attend a graduate school, where all of the educational expenses are paid.

As an incentive for enlistment, certain branches of the armed forces will repay a borrower's student loan. Under the Veterans' Educational Assistance Program, the government will double the monthly education contribution of the serviceperson. The military services offer excellent opportunities to learn new skills and save for higher education at the same time. Follow these procedures if you're interested in learning more about the educational benefits offered by the armed services:

1. Speak to a local recruiting officer. He or she can provide specific information on the educational benefits offered by each branch of the armed services.

2. If possible, contact the local military base education officer to obtain more information on specific programs.

3. Determine whether the education benefits offered by the military match your long-term career plans and objectives.

There are so many military college financial aid programs to consider that this chapter can't possibly cover all of them. Check out the "Military and Veteran Programs" section in Appendix B for additional programs and options. Military aid programs are constantly changing, so you may discover options that were not available at the time this book went to press.

Here are some examples of what you'll find when you visit the websites listed in Appendix B in the "Military and Veteran Programs" section.

Air Force Aid Society

The Air Force Aid Society provides educational loan assistance to the children of qualified Air Force personnel. Candidates for the program must be enrolled or accepted for enrollment as full-time students in an approved college. Contact the National Headquarters, Air Force Aid Society, 1745 Jefferson Davis Highway, Arlington, VA 22202 or call 703-607-3072 for further information.

> **HELP!**
> If you contact the Air Force Sergeants Association, make sure you ask about special scholarship programs that are available to dependents of Air Force personnel.

Air Force Sergeants Association/Airmen Memorial Foundation

The Air Force Sergeants Association/Airmen Memorial program offers approximately 40 academic and technical grants ranging from $1,000 to $3,000. Applicants must have a cumulative GPA of 3.5 to qualify and are accepted between November and March. To apply, send a self-addressed, stamped, 9-by-12-inch envelope to AFSAIAMF Scholarship Program, P.O. Box 50, Temple Hills, MD 20757-0050.

Army College Fund

The Army College Fund provides a way for Army personnel to finance their college educations while still on active duty. Under the plan, army personnel on active duty contribute $100 per month for the first 12 months to their education fund. The Army also contributes to the fund based on the length of enlistment. If you serve for four years, the Army will give you its maximum benefit of $18,000. Contact your local Army recruiter for further details.

Army Continuing Education System

The Army Continuing Education System provides numerous educational programs for Army personnel. A variety of academic and nonacademic educational opportunities are available. The following programs are offered: Basic Skills Education Program, High School Completion Program, English as a Second Language Program, Advanced Skills Education Program, Army Apprenticeship Program, and Defense Activity for Nontraditional Education Support. Contact your local Army recruiter for further information.

Army ROTC

The Army ROTC four-year program provides college-trained officers for the Army, Army Reserve, and Army National Guard. The Army ROTC program is offered at more than 600 colleges and universities throughout the nation. As the largest single source of Army officers, the ROTC program fulfills a vital role in providing mature young men and women for leadership and management positions in an increasingly technical Army. Even though the Army is getting smaller, it still needs thousands of new officers each year.

Scholarships pay up to $20,000 a year for college tuition and education fees, *or* room and board, whichever is chosen by the student. An additional scholarship benefit is a designated book allowance. Army scholarship winners also receive a tax-free subsistence allowance that increases as they progress through military science, for up to 10 months for each year the scholarship is in effect. You can find all the information you need about the army ROTC scholarship program, and even apply online, by going to www.goarmy.com/rotc/index.jsp.

Army Nurse Corps

The Army Nurse Corps program enables nursing students interested in careers as Army nurses to participate in Army ROTC while in college. Nursing cadets who meet all of the professional requirements and successfully complete the program are commissioned as second lieutenants upon graduation from college. Contact your local Army recruiter for further information.

Army Loan Repayment Program

The Army Loan Repayment Program offers special financial incentives to regular and reserve Army enlisted persons. Under the program, the Army will repay the Stafford Federal Loans and Federal Perkins Loans (see Chapter 15) of persons who enlist in areas specified as critical by the Army. Contact your local Army recruiter or military base education officer for further details.

Servicemembers Opportunity Colleges (SOC)

Colleges that are members of the Servicemembers Opportunity Colleges allow service people to transfer credits and pursue programs of study, regardless of location, in a coordinated network of junior colleges, community colleges, and four-year colleges. Flexible course hours and entrance requirements make it possible for military personnel to continue their educations and obtain college degrees wherever they may be stationed. Contact your local recruiter for further details.

Broadened Opportunity for Officer Selection and Training (BOOST) Program

The BOOST program is designed for high school seniors who have good academic grades but not the required College Board test scores for the four-year Navy ROTC scholarship program. Students selected for the BOOST program attend a training school. After graduation, a student either is granted a four-year Navy ROTC scholarship or receives an appointment to the Naval Academy. Contact your local Navy recruiting office for further information.

Navy's Dependents Scholarship Program

The Navy's Dependents Scholarship Program offers scholarship assistance to the dependent children of Navy, Marine, and Coast Guard personnel. Recipients must be enrolled as full-time students in accredited programs. Write to the Naval Military

Personnel Command, Department of the Navy, Washington, D.C. 20370-5121 for additional information.

Navy Student Loans

The Navy Federal Credit Union Student Loans program offers federal Stafford Loans and federal Parent Loans for Undergraduate Students (PLUS) to qualified Navy personnel. For information and application forms, contact Navy Federal Credit Union facilities or write to the Navy Federal Credit Union, Security Place, P.O. Box 3350, Merrifield, VA 22119-3350.

The Marine Corps Scholarship Foundation

The Marine Corps Scholarship Foundation provides scholarship assistance to the dependent children of active service Marines, as well as to the children of discharged and reserve status Marines. The awards are based on financial need, and the amounts of the scholarships vary. Contact the Marine Corps Scholarship Foundation, P.O. Box 3008, Princeton, NJ 08543 for further information on this program. The application deadline is February 1.

Montgomery GI Bill

The Montgomery GI Bill is a federal program that provides financial assistance to all military personnel who joined one of the armed services after June 30, 1985. Under the terms of the program, the government contributes to the serviceperson's education fund in the amount of $275 a month after two years of service and $350 a month after three years of service. The college fund for some military persons can exceed $10,000. For further information, contact your local recruiter, base education officer, or local Veterans Administration Office. The following opportunities are available under the Montgomery GI Bill:

> **Action Plan**
>
> The Montgomery GI Bill applies to those who entered active duty after June 30, 1985. To receive the maximum benefits the program offers, you must serve on active duty for three years.

- Courses at colleges and universities leading to associate, bachelor, or graduate degrees, and independent study or cooperative training programs.

- Courses leading to a certificate or diploma from a business, technical, or vocational school, or an apprenticeship or on-the-job training program.

♦ Flight training programs for qualified veterans. Before beginning training, a veteran must have a private pilot's license and meet the physical requirements for a commercial license.

Veterans Programs

The Office of Student Financial Assistance (OSFA) provides information and special services specific to the needs of veterans, servicepersons, and eligible dependents in the community. The OSFA office will help you apply for educational assistance benefits under the provisions of the GI Bill and other programs of the Veterans Administration, as well as state veterans programs. Contact the OSFA office for further information and assistance.

Veterans Education Assistance Program (VEAP)

The Veterans Education Assistance Program (VEAP) allows enlisted men and women as well as officers to contribute from $25 to $100 per month to an educational fund. When the person enrolls in a postsecondary program, the federal government matches the contribution with $2 for every $1 contributed by the military person. The tuition assistance program pays the serviceperson up to 75 percent for undergraduate courses and 90 percent for job-related courses. For those who have been out of school for a while, remedial, deficiency, and refresher courses may be approved under certain circumstances. Contact your local recruiter or military base education officer for further details.

Disabled American Veterans Auxiliary National Education Loan Fund

The Disabled American Veterans Auxiliary education fund provides interest-free loans to undergraduate students. Academic achievement and financial need are considered when making the awards. Children of fully paid life members of the Disabled American Veterans Auxiliary are eligible to apply. Loans of up to $12,000 can be awarded to students during each year of college. Repayment begins 90 days after graduation or immediately upon withdrawal from school. The application deadline is March 1. Write to the National Education Loan Fund Director, National Headquarters, Disabled American Veterans Auxiliary, 3725 Alexandria Pike, Cold Spring, KY 41076.

Veterans Administration Dependents Education Assistance Act

Through the Veterans Administration Dependents Education Assistance Act, the federal government provides financial assistance to the dependent children and spouses of veterans who have died or who are totally disabled as a result of service-related injuries, as well as to the spouses and children of living veterans. Survivors of deceased veterans, spouses of living veterans, and their children between the ages of 18 and 26 are also eligible for benefits. For application forms, contact any Veterans Administration Center (see Appendix C). For further information, write to the Division of Student Services and Veterans Programs, 400 Maryland Avenue, SW, Room 4010, Washington, D.C. 20202.

Knights of Columbus Educational Fund

The Knights of Columbus Supreme Council offers financial assistance to the children of veterans who were members of the Knights of Columbus and who were either killed in action or permanently disabled as a result of military service. For further information, write to the Director of Scholarship Aid, Knights of Columbus, P.O. Box 1670, New Haven, CT 06507.

Noncommissioned Officers Association Scholarship Foundation

The Noncommissioned Officers Association Scholarship Foundation awards renewable scholarships to the children and spouses of noncommissioned officers who are members of the association. For further information, write to the NCOA Scholarship Foundation, P.O. Box 33610, San Antonio, TX 78265 or phone 512-653-6161. The application deadline is March 31.

Retired Officers Association Scholarship Loan Program

Children of active-duty or retired members of the military can receive financial assistance from the Retired Officers Association Scholarship Loan Program. Loans are made for up to five years of full-time undergraduate study at accredited colleges or technical schools. For applications, write to the Administrator, Scholarship Loan Program, 201 N. Washington Street, Alexandria, VA 22314. The application deadline is March 1.

Warning _____

If you contact one of the Veterans Administration Centers, don't limit your questions to just a few specific subjects. There's a wealth of VA programs out there that you may not be aware of, so ask general questions like, "I want to go to college. Can you provide me with information that shows me all of the financial aid that might be available to me through the VA?"

Veterans Administration Centers

For a complete list of state addresses for Veterans Administration Centers that can provide information on all programs for veterans and their dependents, look up your state in Appendix C.

HELP! _____

The military offers a series of examinations that can help service personnel receive credit for life experiences. Ask for information on Defense Activity for Nontraditional Educational Support (DANTES) from your local recruiter. DANTES also offers correspondence courses and certificate programs that range from high school level through postgraduate study.

Publications

Many excellent publications provide information on programs offered by the armed services and Veterans Administration. Best of all, most of them are free. The following publications can be used to obtain further information:

Army ROTC Scholarship Program (Free)
Army ROTC Department of Military Science
73 Harmon Gym
University of California at Berkeley
Berkeley, CA 94720

Federal Benefits for Veterans and Dependents
Veterans Administration
Government Printing Office
Washington, D.C. 20402

Financial Aid for Veterans, Military Personnel, and Their Dependents
Reference Service Press
1100 Industrial Rd., Suite 9
San Carlos, CA 94070

How the Military Will Help You Pay for College
Don M. Betterton
P.O. Box 2123
Princeton, NJ 08543-2123

Need a Lift?
The American Legion
P.O. Box 1055
Indianapolis, Indiana 46206

Scholarship Pamphlet for USN-USM-USCG Dependent Children (Free)
Naval Military Personnel Command, NMPC-121D
Navy Department
Washington, D.C. 20370-5121

Some of the best education in the nation is available to those who qualify for admission to a military academy. However, enrollment is limited, and full-time military careers are not necessarily for everyone. Nonetheless, if you are willing to devote a part of your life to military service, there are many ways in which the federal government can help pay your way through college. The four branches of military service—the Army, Navy, Air Force, and Marines—provide in-service educational assistance. Ask your local military recruiter about these and other programs. Your high school's guidance counselor should have information on these programs as well.

The Least You Need to Know

- Each branch of the military offers its own unique financial aid program.
- ROTC programs offer you a way to go to college and get paid at the same time.
- Dependents of military personnel are eligible for many types of assistance.
- The Office of Veterans Affairs offers numerous educational assistance programs.

Minority and Other Special Programs

In This Chapter

- ◆ Discovering some of the excellent financial aid programs available to minorities

- ◆ Finding out about special aid programs for women, adult students, and handicapped students

- ◆ Learning where to look for the kinds of scholarship programs you could qualify for

- ◆ Finding out how to tap into private sources to get the funds you need

Over the past several years, it has become apparent that the "traditional" college student—defined as white, 18 years old, and middle class—has changed. Minority students, women, adult students, and part-time students who were previously classified as "nontraditional" are fast becoming the majority on many college campuses. Federal legislation now includes these students as eligible to receive financial aid. This chapter looks at programs targeted for nontraditional and handicapped students.

Financial Aid for Minority Students

Unfortunately, minority students looking for financial aid will not find much support at the federal level. Federal monies are concentrated in counseling for minority students or are transferred to the states for administration. All of the states therefore have minority financial aid programs and can direct you to funds available at the schools you're most interested in attending. State financial aid offices are listed in Appendix C. For a list of reference guides to the more prominent scholarships for minority students, look under "Minority Programs" in Appendix B.

To enhance opportunities for minority students, states have funded various programs ranging from the California Grant B program to the Florida Seminole-Miccosukee Indian Scholarship Program. Contact your state's Department of Education for more information. (The offices are listed by state in Appendix C.) Colleges are trying to fulfill their federal commitment to affirmative action programs by working harder to recruit and retain qualified minority students.

There's a category of minority student aid you should know about that often doesn't get publicized as much as it should. Broad areas of minority financial aid contributions are kicked in from many financial aid sources, including the federal and state governments, the schools themselves, and private groups.

Another area of minority aid involves programs that are attempting to correct a different type of imbalance: the lack of minority students entering certain professions such as teaching and health care. To get more minority students into these areas, government and private organizations are offering lucrative scholarships. Minority students with the right qualifications should not pass up the opportunities these programs offer.

Action Plan

For a list of schools that offer scholarships to minority students interested in pursuing degrees in engineering, write to the National Action Council for Minorities in Engineering, 440 Hamilton Ave., Suite 302, White Plains, NY 10601, call 914-539-4010, or visit the council's website at nacme.org.

We obviously can't list every minority program offered in the nation; otherwise, the list of programs would fill the entire book. Instead, we will concentrate on the state level where much of the money is. We will also cover scholarships offered by religious organizations, civic groups, and professional associations, which provide many of these awards. The best-known program sponsored by a professional association, the National Action Council for Minorities in Engineering, aids minority students interested in engineering careers. Most nongovernmental programs are funded through the schools.

For more programs, review the minority scholarship programs covered in Appendix B and in Chapter 11. Also check with your high school counselor or college financial aid office for more information.

Nontraditional Students

Colleges and universities are required to allocate a minimum of 5 percent of their campus-based aid to their nontraditional student population. Institutions are also required to use a reasonable amount of their administrative funds to provide financial aid services to part-time and adult learners. These services are to be provided at times and in places that are convenient to this type of student.

Federal Pell Grant eligibility is extended to students who are enrolled in less-than-half-time programs. An allowance for child care or for disability-related expenses might be added to the cost of school attendance.

Financial Aid Programs for Women

There are many financial aid programs for qualifying women. Note that the qualifications are often circumscribed. That's one reason you need to research funding possibilities carefully. They might be located right in your hometown, but since they are not heavily advertised, you may not be aware that they exist. Here is just a small sampling:

♦ **The Verda White Barnes Memorial Scholarship Fund.** This program provides scholarships to qualified junior and senior students at Idaho State University. Applicants must be Idaho residents and must be full-time students. Preference will be given to students majoring in political science. Awards are based on academic merit, financial need, and feminist views. For further information, write to the Scholarship Office, Idaho State University, P.O. Box 8391, Pocatello, ID 83209.

♦ **The Business and Professional Women's Foundation (BPWF).** Various scholarship and loan programs focus on women enrolled in health professions, engineering, and graduate business schools. Applicants must be at least

HELP! In addition to the regular federal, state, and institutional financial assistance programs that are available to students, regardless of gender, many financial aid programs are funded specifically for women. Women needing financial assistance should seek the advice of their school's financial aid director.

25 years old, U.S. citizens, and enrolled at least half-time at an approved school. The amounts of the awards vary and are based on financial need.

The BPWF sponsors several financial aid programs, including the following:

- New York Life Foundation Scholarship for Women in Health Careers
- Loan Fund for Women in Engineering Studies
- Sally Butler Memorial Fund for Latina Research
- Lena Lake Forrest Fellowship Program
- Clairol Loving Care Scholarship Program
- The Avon Foundation Scholarship Program for Women in Business Studies

For further information, write to the Business and Professional Women's Foundation, Attn: Scholarships and Loans, 1900 M St. NW, Suite 310, Washington, D.C. 20036, call 202-293-1100, or visit their website at www.bpwusa.org.

- **Ada Comstock Scholars Program.** Affiliated with Smith College, this program provides need-based financial assistance to students of nontraditional age admitted to Smith. Applicants should have completed at least one year of liberal arts work before applying. An interview is required, and the application deadline is February 10. For more information, write to the Ada Comstock Scholars Program, Smith College, Northampton, Massachusetts 01063. Fax: 413-585-2123. E-mail: comstock@smith.edu.

Action Plan

The money for women in higher education comes almost exclusively from colleges and private sources. College money most often takes the form of athletic scholarships; for an up-to-date listing of such awards, write for general information to the Women's Sports Foundation, Eisenhower Park, East Meadow, NY 11554 or call 1-800-227-3988.

- **Daughters of the American Revolution (DAR).** The DAR sponsors financial assistance programs for qualified women students. Most of the scholarships are administered by individual state societies, which have their own requirements, deadlines, and application procedures. There are several scholarships offered to graduating high school seniors as well as to students already enrolled in college or university degree programs. Scholarships are offered for certain subjects, and eligibility will depend on the student's declared major.

♦ **The Society of Women Engineers.** This professional organization offers
scholarships and loans to women students. It can also provide you with a list of
scholarships for women that are not widely publicized. For more information,
write to The Society of Women Engineers, 230 E. Ohio St., Suite 400, Chicago,
IL 60611 or call 312-596-5223.

If you're a female student with small children, you should find out whether your college offers day care for free or at low cost. Regardless of whether it does or not, the
expenses associated with raising kids should be reflected in your financial need, which
could get you more aid.

Handicapped Students

Handicapped students will find financial assistance programs offered by both the federal government and individual states.

Federal legislation forbids discrimination on the basis of handicap and encourages
handicapped persons to enroll in postsecondary institutions. Colleges and universities
must meet the needs of their handicapped students or risk losing their federal financial
aid funds.

The U.S. Department of Education Rehabilitation Services Administration administers the Rehabilitation Act, which determines financial eligibility for handicapped
persons. However, each state has its own programs for the handicapped. Addresses for
state rehabilitation services are listed in Appendix C.

Handicapped students have expenses not usually incurred by other students, and these
should be considered when calculating financial need. These costs include special
equipment needs, transportation, interpret-
ers, note takers, and personal attendants.
The student's financial aid director should
be informed of any additional expenses, and
information should be coordinated with the
institution's director for handicapped or disabled persons. Here are three programs that
offer financial assistance to handicapped students:

> **(HELP!)** The U.S. Department of
> Education is ultimately
> responsible for the overall admin-
> istration and disbursement of
> financial aid funds to the states.
> Its website is www.ed.gov.

♦ **AMBUCS Resource Center (AMBUCS).** This organization offers scholarships
to U.S. citizens in their junior or senior year of college. Applicants must
be accepted into an accredited program by the appropriate health/therapy

profession authority in physical therapy, occupational therapy, music therapy, speech language pathology, hearing audiology, or recreational therapy. Awards are based on financial need and a GPA of 3.0 or above. The deadline for applications is April 15. Awards are announced in June. For further information, contact AMBUCS Scholarship Committee, P.O. Box 5121, High Point, NC 27262 or call 800-838-1845.

- **American Foundation for the Blind.** Scholarship assistance for blind women is the focus. Awards range from $1,000 to $3,000 per academic year. Contact the American Foundation for the Blind, 15 W. 16th St., New York, NY 10011 for additional information and application forms.

- **Alexander Graham Bell Association for the Deaf.** This association funds scholarships for deaf students who use speech and speech reading to communicate and who are attending or planning to attend a regular university or college for students with normal hearing. Applicants must use speech and residual hearing and/or speech reading as their primary form of communication. Applications are mailed in November, and the deadline is April 1. For further information, write to the Alexander Graham Bell Association for the Deaf, 3417 Volta Place NW, Washington, D.C. 20007-2778, call 202-337-5220, or visit its website at www.agbell.org.

A Sampling of Minority Aid Programs

Many organizations provide financial assistance to minority students. Seek advice from high school counselors and college financial aid officers in locating sources of funds. There are many church-sponsored minority programs. Ask church officials to help you locate these funding sources.

American Institute of Certified Public Accountants

The American Institute of Certified Public Accountants provides scholarships to undergraduate minority accounting majors. To be eligible for the scholarships, minority students must be citizens of the United States and must be enrolled in an undergraduate accounting program. For further information, write to the Manager of Minority Recruitment, American Institute of Certified Public Accountants, 1211 Avenue of the Americas, New York, NY 10036-3775 or visit its website at aicpa.org.

Association of University Programs in Health Administration

Qualified African American, Native American, Asian American, Mexican American, and Puerto Rican students can participate in internship programs offered by the Association of University Programs in Health Administration. Recipients must be either second- or third-year undergraduate students. Academic ability is considered in awarding the internship. For further information, write to the Association of University Programs in Health Administration, 2000 14th St. North, Suite 780, Arlington, VA 22201.

Action Plan

If you're a minority student and you file for financial aid correctly and on time, you'll receive some kind of financial aid. It's almost guaranteed!

Bureau of Indian Affairs Higher Education Grant Program

Grants from the Bureau of Indian Affairs Higher Education program provide financial aid to eligible Native American students. The awards are based on financial need. For further information, write to the Bureau of Indian Affairs Higher Education Grant Program, Bureau of Indian Affairs, 18th and C Street NW, Washington, D.C. 20245.

Congressional Hispanic Caucus

The Congressional Hispanic Caucus provides qualified Hispanic students with fellowships to work with members of Congress. The fellowships are for one academic term. For further information on this program, write to the Congressional Hispanic Caucus, 911 2nd St. NE, Washington, D.C. 20002, call 202-543-1771, or visit its website at www.chci.org.

General Motors Scholarship Program

The GM Corporation provides scholarship assistance to qualified minority undergraduate students through several U.S. colleges and universities. For more information, write to the General Motors Scholarship Program, General Motors Corporation, 700 W. 5th Ave., Naperville, IL 60563 or call 1-888-377-5233.

Action Plan

Most of the Fortune 100 companies offer scholarship programs for minorities. Contact their public relations department to find out how to apply. The research librarian at any public library can provide you with a directory of Fortune 100 companies, giving addresses and telephone numbers.

Indian Education and Psychology Fellowship Program

The Indian Education and Psychology Fellowship Program, which is supported by the U.S. Department of Education, provides scholarship assistance to Native American or Alaskan Native students who are enrolled in accredited undergraduate or graduate school programs in education, psychology, or related fields. Contact the U.S. Department of Education, Indian Education and Psychology Fellowship Program, 400 Maryland Ave. SW, Washington, D.C. 20202 for additional information.

Indian Fellowship Program

The Indian Fellowship Program awards fellowships to Native American students enrolled in undergraduate and graduate degree programs in business administration, engineering, education, law, medicine, and related fields. The awards are based on financial need. For further information, write to the Indian Fellowship Program, Office of Indian Education Programs, 1849 C Street NW, MS-Room 3525, Washington, D.C. 20242.

National Achievement Scholarship Program

Outstanding African American high school students can receive assistance from the National Achievement Scholarship Program. Over 800 scholarships are awarded each year. For further information, write to the National Achievement Scholarship Program, One Rotary Center, 1560 Sherman Ave., Suite 200, Evanston, IL 60201-4897.

National Action Council for Minorities in Engineering (NACME)

The NACME organization provides financial assistance to qualified undergraduate minority students pursuing degrees in engineering. The major funding is directed through corporate scholarships administered by NACME. For more information, write to the National Action Council for Minorities in Engineering, 440 Hamilton Ave., Suite 302, White Plains, NY 10601, call 914-539-4010, or visit its website at nacme.org.

National Merit Scholarship Program

The National Merit Scholarship Program is the largest academically competitive scholarship program in the United States. Each year, more than 3,000 scholarships are awarded among 5,000 finalists, and an additional 650 scholarships go to African American students. Fifteen hundred of these awards are one-timers of $1,000, and another 1,500 are four-year awards for the same amount per year.

Competition for the four-year award is strong, but if you win, your harvest is more abundant than the $1,000 award. Schools that value lustrous reputations lure National Merit winners with additional financial aid awards.

To qualify, take the Preliminary Scholastic Aptitude Test (PSAT) or the National Merit Scholarship Qualifying Test (NMSQT), usually given in your junior year of high school. Ask your high school guidance counselor for details. Finalists are chosen based on scores. Write to the National Merit Scholarship Corporation, One Rotary Center, 1560 Sherman Ave., Evanston, IL 60201-4897 for additional information and application forms.

Action Plan

If you want to win merit or sports scholarships, keep your nose in the books. The people handing out these awards love to give them to athletes who have great GPAs and SAT and ACT tests. You have to be able to leap over a high bar if you want to win a sports scholarship. Both talent and academic achievement must be stellar to win one.

United Methodist Church

The Board of Higher Education and Ministry of the United Methodist Church awards scholarships to qualified undergraduate and graduate minority students. Applicants must be U.S. citizens or permanent residents; must be Hispanic, Asian, or Native American; and must be active members of the Methodist Church. The United Methodist Church also sponsors several scholarship and loan programs for graduate students. Church-sponsored loan programs are available to undergraduate and graduate students. For additional information, write to the United Methodist Church, Board of Higher Education and Ministry, Box 871, Nashville, TN 37203.

United Negro College Fund Schools

Over a thousand scholarships a year are given to students attending United Negro College Fund schools. The awards are based on financial need and academic merit. For more information, write to the United Negro College Fund, 8260 Willow Oaks Corporate Dr., Fairfax, VA 22031. If you're interested in a specific school, contact the school for more information. Here's a listing of United Negro College Fund schools:

Paine College
Augusta, Georgia 30901

Paul Quinn College
Dallas, Texas 75241

Philander Smith College
Little Rock, Arkansas 72202

Rust College
Holly Springs, Mississippi 38635

Saint Augustine's College
Raleigh, North Carolina 27610

Saint Paul's College
Lawrenceville, Virginia 23805

Shaw University
Raleigh, North Carolina 27601

Spelman College
Atlanta, Georgia 30314

Stillman College
Tuscaloosa, Alabama 35403

Talladega College
Talladega, Alabama 35160

Texas College
Tyler, Texas 75702

Tougaloo College
Tougaloo, Mississippi 39174

Tuskegee University
Tuskegee, Alabama 36088

Virginia Union University
Richmond, Virginia 23220

Voorhees College
Denmark, South Carolina 29042

Wilberforce University
Wilberforce, Ohio 45384

Wiley College
Marshall, Texas 75670

Xavier University of Louisiana
New Orleans, Louisiana 70125

Financial Aid Publications for Minority Students

A number of excellent publications are available to minority students who are interested in applying for financial aid. This section introduces you to what we believe are some of the better publications that you may want to seek out at your local library, local bookstore, or purchase outright through www.amazon.com.

Directory of Financial Aid for Minorities
Reference Service Press
1100 Industrial Rd.
San Carlos, CA 94070

Garrett Park Press Publications
Garrett Park Press
P.O. Box 190
Garrett Park, MD 20896

Hispanic Financial Resource Handbook
The Ohio State University
Hispanic Student Programs
347 Ohio Union
1739 N. High St.
Columbus, OH 43210

Minority Student Opportunities in U.S. Medical Schools
Association of American Medical Colleges
Office of Minority Affairs
Division of Student Programs
1 Dupont Circle
Washington, D.C. 20036

The following titles are available from the Superintendent of Documents, U.S. Government Printing Office, Washington, D.C. 20402:

Financial Aid for Minority Students in Allied Health

Financial Aid for Minority Students in Business

Financial Aid for Minority Students in Education

Financial Aid for Minority Students in Engineering

Financial Aid for Minority Students in Law

Financial Aid for Minority Students in Mass Communications and Journalism

Financial Aid for Minority Students in Medicine

Financial Aid for Minority Students in Science

Minority Organizations: A National Directory

The Big Book of Minority Opportunities

Higher Education Opportunities for Minorities and Women

To be honest, if you're a minority student with outstanding qualifications, you have a good chance of getting an excellent scholarship. That's because most scholarship programs favor awarding minorities money for college. Although this chapter discusses specific programs directed at minorities, don't ignore all of the other "non-minority" scholarship programs, such as those in Chapter 11. Our advice to you is to apply for every scholarship that you have a chance of getting.

The Least You Need to Know

◆ Know where to apply for specially targeted scholarships for which you are qualified.

◆ Many professional organizations offer financial aid for minorities and women studying in specific professional fields.

◆ Federal aid programs grant special allowances for such expenses as child care for children of adult students and special equipment for handicapped students.

◆ Don't overlook church-sponsored minority programs. Seek the advice of church officials to help you locate these opportunities.

◆ In general, scholarship programs favor minorities, so go after every one with a vengeance.

Chapter **14**

Adult, Graduate, and International Programs

In This Chapter

◆ Finding the few adult financial aid sources and options

◆ Learning how to dig for hidden aid opportunities for graduate students

◆ Discovering unique financial aid opportunities to study abroad

◆ Getting the details on employee tuition assistance and learning how to get some from your employer

◆ Understanding why you must have a plan to spend less and save more for college

The nontraditional student, as described in the preceding chapter, is one or more of the following: an adult student, a graduate student, and/or a student who wants to study abroad. If you fall into any of these categories and are seeking financial aid to help you get the education you want, you have one thing in common with your peers. It's going to be tough to get aid.

Why is it so hard? Because, unfortunately, most financial aid programs have been designed to help the under-24-year-old demographic. They also cater to students trying to earn baccalaureate degrees rather than Master's degrees. In the case of foreign study, the various agencies that administer funds are very selfish about using taxpayer dollars to fund educational institutions that are located outside the United States.

We don't want to discourage you from pursuing a degree as an adult or a graduate student, whether you study stateside or in another country. We just want you to be aware of the facts before you start your search for financial aid.

Adult Student Programs

Let's take a step backward and review what the Federal Government's original intentions were when, in all its wisdom, it created financial aid programs for colleges. Quite simply, the program was constructed to help parents pay for their kids' education if they could show that they truly needed supplemental funds.

With rare exceptions, you won't find the words "adult aid" listed anywhere in program brochures. Why is that? Well, for one thing, the feds have another program for adults that they call "welfare."

> **Action Plan**
>
> If you think the task of getting financial aid for a foreign university is overwhelming, remember the words of the poet Henry Wadsworth Longfellow: "Perseverance is a great element of success. If you only knock long enough and loud enough at the gate, you are sure to wake up somebody."

Federal welfare programs cost the government substantially more than the college aid program, and the welfare programs' funds are awarded primarily to adults. Welfare grants are made to adults who qualify for welfare and want to attend college or technical, vocational, or trade schools. The clear intent of the program is to help people find viable employment that will take them off the welfare rolls.

If you're on welfare or can qualify for being on welfare, contact your state's welfare office to discover the educational opportunities it may be able to offer you.

Graduate Student Programs

Graduate study means study that follows a Bachelor's degree in a given academic field such as chemistry or business. The Doctor of Philosophy (Ph.D.) is a graduate degree, as is the Master of Business Administration (MBA). On average, only about 20 percent of the graduate students in the United States are receiving any kind of financial aid. And most of the aid that is available is flowing into the scientific and engineering disciplines.

The admissions requirements for most graduate programs include at least one exam. See the "Graduate Tests (GMAT, GRE, LSAT, MCAT)" in Appendix B.

Graduate Student Loans

Unfortunately, loans are the chief source of funding for most students who pursue graduate and professional studies. Graduate student loans are acquired from the same places that are open to undergraduate students (see Chapter 15). Some colleges will award money for fellowships and teaching assistantships, which carry teaching and research responsibilities (see Chapter 9).

HELP!
Several institutions offer special loan programs for graduate students. You'll find them listed under "Graduate and Professional Student Loans" in Appendix B.

Fellowships

Fortunately, if you're a graduate or postdoctoral student, you have a chance at getting a *fellowship*. Most fellowships are issued by universities and private foundations and are typically based on merit. The reason is clear: the school or foundation wants the student to accomplish something that contributes to the prestige of the sponsoring institution. If you have a sterling academic record and are pursuing research projects that are attractive to a particular school or foundation, you have a good shot at a fellowship.

Getting Started

Fellowships are grants of money to a student from private and public organizations that generally require something in return, such as conducting research or teaching. Fellowships are usually awarded to postgraduate students, but there are an increasing number of them that are being awarded to undergraduates.

The National Service Fellows Scholarship Program was announced in 1997, and 12 fellowships were awarded that year after a competitive selection process. The fellows who have been selected annually since then contract with the Corporation for National and Community Service to produce a product or outcome of value to the corporation or, broadly, to the field of service.

Although fellows are not employees, they are attached to an office of the corporation or an affiliated state organization. In addition to producing the outcomes specified in their proposals, the fellows comprise a self-managed team that assesses progress, considers synergies among projects, and promotes further individual development.

The mission of the Corporation for National Service is to improve the quality of service through the talents of a diverse, self-managed team that will learn with the corporation and will contribute to the future of national service. The National Service Fellows Program has become a high-quality program that has strengthened national service through continuous learning, new models, stronger networks, and professional growth. You can contact the organization at its website (www.cns.gov) to learn more about the program.

International Student Programs

As mentioned at the beginning of this chapter, finding financial aid to supplement your education abroad will be difficult. Most of the financial aid funds have been allocated to stateside programs, and there are a disproportionate number of students trying to get at the crumbs left over for international study, so competition is stiff. However, don't allow yourself to get discouraged: you'll find some suggestions in the following sections.

International Co-Op Programs

If you want to study abroad and you're looking for some financial support to get there, the deepest pockets can often be found in the college or university you're already attending. Many institutions across the country have established student co-op programs with international schools that allow their students to attend foreign colleges at substantially discounted rates.

HELP!

Check out the "International Financial Aid Directory" section in Appendix B for key agencies that may be able to help you get financial aid to study abroad. For a comprehensive list of federal financial programs for study abroad, check out www.iefa.org.

Unfortunately, these programs are generally not available to you until you've completed your sophomore year of college. The exchange periods are typically limited to one or two semesters, when you'll be required to return to your home-base college. If you take courses that have been preapproved by your sponsoring college while you are on your international tour, you'll receive full credit. Here's a partial list of colleges that award significant aid to international students:

Harvard University

Radcliffe University

University of Miami

Massachusetts Institute of Technology

University of Pennsylvania

Princeton University

Brown University

Stanford University

Arizona State University

U.S. students who attend accredited U.S. institutions overseas that are an extension of their stateside institution are eligible for the full range of federal financial aid programs.

How International Co-Op Programs Are Administered

Colleges set their own policies for institutional aid abroad.

U.S. students who attend an international institution overseas are eligible for federal and private loan programs only, not for any gift aid.

Students from other countries can find out about U.S.-sponsored aid that may be available to them by contacting the U.S. embassy or consulate in their home country.

NAFSA, previously called the National Association of Foreign Student Affairs, has a membership of international educators who promote international educational exchange between the United States and the rest of the world. However, the organization offers virtually no direct grants to international students. It does provide links to international financial aid through its website (www.nafsa.org), along with online searches you can do to find other sources of potential aid. Also see the "International Financial Aid Directory" section in Appendix B for relevant addresses and websites.

Support from Abroad Does Happen

Eleven American college students recently were awarded scholarships by the Winston Churchill Foundation for graduate study in mathematics, engineering, and the sciences. The students were drawn from the 50 accredited institutions participating in the program. They will study for one year at Churchill College, Cambridge University, in Great Britain, receiving $23,000 toward tuition, travel, and living expenses there. The Churchill awards come from the Winston Churchill Foundation of the United States, which is located in New York City.

> **Warning** _____
>
> Don't expect the governments or private funding sources of other nations to be too generous with study money for noncitizens (with a few exceptions, such as Japan, Germany, and Canada). Get your cash at home before you take off to schools abroad.

International Student Loans

Loans are difficult to come by for students who want to study in other countries. That's probably because lenders are afraid the students won't come back to pay off their debts. But if you have an excellent credit history, you have a fair chance of getting a loan. The International Finance Corporation is a unique private firm that specializes in global student loans. If you want more information, contact the group at International Finance Corporation, 2121 Pennsylvania Ave., Washington, D.C. 20433, 202-473-3800, or www.ifc.org.

They May Want *You*

Believe it or not, there are a lot of colleges out there that want adult students in the same classroom with the younger students. It adds a level of maturity to classes because adults tend to ask tougher questions, a fact that was so elegantly demonstrated by Rodney Dangerfield in the movie classic *Back to School*. If you're an older student, the experience you can offer gives you a potential negotiating edge that you may not have known you had.

> **Action Plan** _____
>
> You never know what the answer will be until you ask the question! If you never ask the question, you are wrongfully assuming that the answer would have been "no."

Walk into the admissions office of the college of your choice, and ask to speak to the director of admissions or whatever title the college uses for the person who manages admissions. Better yet, make an appointment with this person. When you meet with him or her, briefly explain why you want to go to that college, why you need financial support, and what you can contribute on your own in return for the favor.

For example, suppose you have some expertise in counseling young people on how to find jobs, on how to do difficult searches on the web, or whatever. Bring up these offerings when you talk to the admissions officer, and you could solicit a very favorable response. The officer may ask you to chair a discussion group with students in one or more fields of your expertise in return for a substantial reduction in tuition and fees.

Employee Educational Assistance Packages (EAPs)

Can you get your boss to pay the bills while you attend college part-time? That's an easy question if you're working for a company that offers its employees an educational assistance package (EAP), which comes complete with reimbursement of tuition, books, and fees. You simply sign up for the program through your personnel office, and your financial aid package is a reality. You're on your way! Who cares if federal and state financial aid funds are scarce for adult students when you have an employer-sponsored financial aid package available to you?

Where Do You Find EAP Funding?

EAPs are more commonly found among sizable companies than at small firms. Among the companies that offer the most generous EAPs, according to an annual survey by the Chamber of Commerce of the United States, are those engaged in industries such as insurance, hospital care, and public utilities. Less than half of all retailers offer EAPs, and manufacturing plants aren't high on education benefits either.

Do You Pay Taxes on EAP Funds?

Two kinds of EAPs are typically offered by employers: those that are specifically job related and those that are for general self-improvement purposes.

Funds provided to employees for job-related education and training are tax free to employees and are tax deductible to employers.

Education for the general self-improvement of the employee is more ambiguous. For the past two decades, companies have been able to deduct their educational expenses from

Action Plan

Studies by the National Association of Independent Colleges and Universities show that, of employees who go to college on the employer's nickel, 33 percent pursue Associate (two-year) degrees, 23 percent pursue Bachelor's degrees, 22 percent pursue Master's degrees, and 13 percent pursue professional certificates.

their tax returns, and employees were not taxed on the educational assistance money they received. However, this has been a controversial issue in Congress, so make sure you know what the latest tax regulations are when you apply for EAP funds.

Do You Have to Pay Back EAPs?

Twenty years ago, employers weren't fussy if you didn't stick around after you completed your schooling. That's changed, says Cynthia Pintails, senior government relations associate for the American Society of Training and Development. "Increasingly, employers want to be sure they get a return on their educational investments." Don't be surprised if you're asked to sign an agreement stating that you'll repay the company if you depart the premises before a specific period of time.

Negotiate, Negotiate, and Negotiate Some More

What are your options if you work for a company that doesn't offer educational assistance for its employees? For starters, it doesn't hurt to ask for help anyway! Walk into your boss's office and simply ask him or her if there's any way the company can assist you in getting a college degree. The way you phrase the questions and your subsequent conversation will clearly have to depend on your position in the company.

It's time to negotiate! Suppose you're an accountant and you have a burning desire to get an advanced degree in accounting. You can remind your boss that if the company is willing to invest a few bucks in your education, with what you'll learn you'll be able to return a whole lot more to the company. You may get a very favorable response.

> **Action Plan**
>
> Most employers that do have educational reimbursement plans reimburse employees for tuition rather than paying the college outright. About half of them pay 100 percent of the tuition, and 30 percent pay below 50 percent. The other 20 percent pay somewhere between 50 and 90 percent. In almost all instances, you must get a C or higher before you can be reimbursed.

What If You Get a "No"?

Suppose you're working for a company that flat out rejects any notion of helping you or any other employee meet his or her respective educational expenses. Maybe it's time to look for an employer that offers a generous educational reimbursement plan to its employees. Here's a classic example of what we're talking about.

Dan was working for a company that we'll call XYZ Corporation. Although he liked his job and the people, he did not enjoy the fact that XYZ Corporation had limited employee benefits and no employee educational program. Dan believed that if he didn't get a college degree, he would be relegated to doing the same job for the rest of his life—not a very exciting option to him.

Dan started looking for other job opportunities and found a position with a company that was willing to offer him a salary that was $2,000 a year less than what he was currently earning, but their employee education program would pay him up to $6,000 a year for educational expenses. In effect, Dan was getting a $4,000 increase in salary ($6,000 – $2,000) because he intended to take full advantage of the company's educational program. He took the job.

Making It All Happen with an Action Plan

The key to going to college as an adult student, a graduate student, an international student, or any combination thereof is not necessarily having a lot of money. Most of us don't have a lot of money. What we need is a plan. Planning is the first step in taking control of your educational future. Your plan should be flexible but structured, and most important, you must decide to stick to it.

Planning for college is not difficult if you stick to the fundamentals, which are simple and obvious. Yet many adult students spend a disproportionate amount of time trying to find an easy way to get there by relying on others rather than on themselves. Had they done even some basic planning in the beginning, they could have been in great shape to enhance their educational objectives.

Action Plan

Collectively, the majority of American graduate and undergraduate students now fit nontraditional descriptions. They're not in the bloom of their youth and are not full-time students, according to the University of Phoenix, which caters strictly to nontraditional students. Over 74,000 students have attended this nationally based university.

Watch Your Pennies

Remember the old saying "Watch your pennies and the dollars will take care of themselves"? It's still true today. If you're like most people, you spend money on things you don't really need, and somehow the money you make is just enough to cover your expenses. Your first challenge will be to get control over your spending habits and establish a monthly budget. You'll be amazed at how it will help you save and how those little things add up to big dollars over a relatively short period of time.

Here's how you can do it. Let's say you get paid twice a month like most people. The first thing you do is run to the bank to deposit your paycheck so that you can start paying off all of those ugly bills. Before you pay off any bill, pay yourself first. Write a check for a hundred dollars, deposit it into a savings account, and then forget about it. Over a period of one year, you will have deposited $2,600 into your savings account and earned interest on top of that.

Set Priorities with a Spending Plan

If you want to get serious about going to college, you have to set priorities and recognize that you can't have everything right now.

A spending plan is an active strategy used to control your spending so you can afford to go to college. It starts with a commitment to yourself: "I want to save more of my money." Why? "Because I want to have enough money to go to college so that I can expand my career opportunities."

When you activate your plan, it will capture the cash that slips through your fingers every day unnoticed. It will help you discern the difference between what you need and what you want. Here are 10 reasons why you need a good spending plan:

1. You can use your plan to get out of debt. Without a spending plan, it'll never happen.

2. It helps you prepare for the really big expenses such as college.

3. You eliminate spending on frivolous things.

4. More money will go into your savings account for college every month.

5. You get used to living on what you make.

6. Money won't slip through your fingers anymore.

7. It sets the groundwork for developing a financial plan, your road map to financial independence.

Action Plan

Be sure to review the financial planning material in Chapter 8. It supplements the money-saving tips in this section.

8. You, your spouse, and your kids will be pulling in the same direction so that you can meet your goal of going to college.

9. You will have a clear vision about what you really want: a college degree, an advanced college degree, or an opportunity to study abroad.

Painless Money-Saving Tips

What you really need is a savings account that you can count on to pay for college. You can do this only if you're willing to pay yourself first:

♦ Make up a card or envelope labeled "savings bill" that you keep with your other monthly bills. When it comes time to pay the bills, make sure it's the first bill that gets paid in the form of a deposit to your college expenses savings account.

♦ Whenever you pay off all your bills and discover that you have some money left over, make another deposit to your savings account.

♦ Find out if your employer's payroll system allows you to make direct deposits into a savings account. If it does, sign up for this feature immediately. In a short period of time, you won't even miss the money that's deducted from your paycheck.

> **HELP!**
> If you're looking for more advice on how to save money, get a copy of Edward Romney's book *Living Well on Practically Nothing: Revised and Updated Edition* (Paladin Press, 2001). It's a collection of great money-saving articles and tips from a newsletter that Larry Roth publishes.

♦ When you get a raise, deposit the extra amount from the raise directly into your savings account so you won't miss it.

♦ Take lunches to work instead of eating out. You'll be amazed at how much you'll save.

♦ When you get your income tax refund, use it to pay off credit cards. Then cut up the cards and deposit the money you previously spent on monthly credit card payments into your savings account.

♦ Deposit all overtime and bonus checks into your savings account.

♦ When you get your college bills, you'll be glad you had an action plan and have money in the bank to pay them.

The Least You Need to Know

♦ If you're an adult, a pending graduate student, or a student who is interested in studying outside of the United States, you'll soon discover that financial aid funds are relatively scarce.

- International college co-op programs are one of the easiest ways to study abroad at discounted rates.

- The admissions officer of the college of your choice may be willing to help you create a financial aid program that benefits both you and the school.

- Try hitting up your employer for tuition assistance—whether the company has a formal program or not.

- To make it all happen, you must have an action plan to cut spending and increase savings earmarked for college expenses.

Chapter 15

The Inside Scoop on Student Loans

In This Chapter

- Learning about the various low-interest student loans that you can apply for
- Discovering how to find the best lender for you
- Learning how to compare different loan offers to pick the one that best meets your needs

A student loan is money you borrow to help meet the cost of your education. Applying for a loan, whether from government or private sources, is not something to be afraid of, and you should not let it prohibit you from going to the school of your choice. You should research all your options and clearly understand the terms of any loans you're considering.

Loans are part of the self-help portion of any financial aid award you might receive from a school. Several types of loan programs are available to you, including Federal Perkins Loans, subsidized Federal Stafford Loans, subsidized Federal Direct Loans, unsubsidized Federal Stafford Loans, and Direct Loans, to name a few.

Subsidized and Unsubsidized Loans

Subsidized student loans have lower interest rates than commercial or unsubsidized loans. Federal Perkins Loans, subsidized Federal Stafford Loans, and subsidized Federal Direct Loans are all need-based subsidized loans. No payments are made while a student is in school, but six months after leaving school, students must begin to make regular monthly payments.

> ⚠ **Warning**
>
> Before you sign any loan documents, ask the lender every question you can think of regarding your repayment options. If you don't get a clear answer, ask the same question again until you fully understand what all of your options are. Get it in writing.

Unsubsidized Federal Stafford Loans and Federal Direct Loans are awarded without regard to need. Interest payments begin immediately, and regular payments start six months after the borrower ceases to be at least a half-time student. The amount you can borrow is fixed and is dependent on your year in school.

Parent Loans

Federal Parent Loans for Undergraduate Students, also known as PLUS Loans, are for creditworthy parents. These loans have annually adjusted variable interest rates. Repayment begins within 60 days after the loan has been fully disbursed. Interest begins to accrue on the day the loan is disbursed. Parents can borrow up to all school costs not covered by estimated financial assistance. For help with loan application procedures, contact your high school's guidance counselor, the college's financial aid officer, or your congressional representative. Also see the federal financial aid listings in Appendix B and the listings of financial aid offices by state in Appendix C.

Stafford Loans

All Stafford Loans are either subsidized, which means the government pays the interest while you're in school, or unsubsidized, in which case you pay all the interest. If you pay the interest on an unsubsidized loan, you can have the payments deferred until after graduation.

To receive a subsidized Stafford Loan, you must be able to demonstrate financial need. With an unsubsidized Stafford Loan, you can defer the payments until after graduation by capitalizing the interest. Capitalizing means the interest payments are added to the loan balance, increasing the size and cost of the loan. All students, regardless of need, are eligible for the unsubsidized Stafford Loans.

Stafford Loans allow dependent undergraduates to borrow up to $2,625 for their freshman year, $3,500 for their sophomore year, and $5,500 for each remaining year. Independent students can borrow an additional unsubsidized $4,000 the first two years and $5,000 the remaining years for a total of up to $46,000 during their undergraduate career. Graduate students can borrow $18,500 per year, although only $8,500 of the loan is subsidized. Many students combine subsidized loans with unsubsidized loans to borrow the maximum amount permitted each year. Graduate students can borrow up to $138,000 total, which also includes any undergraduate loans they may have borrowed.

To apply for a Stafford Loan, you must submit the Free Application for Federal Student Aid (FAFSA) form. Even though the unsubsidized Stafford Loan is available to all students regardless of financial need, you must still submit the FAFSA to be eligible. You can receive a subsidized loan and an unsubsidized loan for the same period.

> **Action Plan**
>
> Commercial lenders offer varying loan policies. If possible, stick with one lender for all of your loans so that you have a single point of contact to simplify your life.

Perkins Loans

The Perkins Loan is the best student loan available. Perkins Loans are awarded to undergraduate and graduate students with exceptional financial need. This is a campus-based loan program in which the school acts as the lender using a limited pool of funds provided by the federal government. It's a subsidized loan, with the interest paid by the federal government during the in-school and nine-month grace periods. There are no origination or guarantee fees, and the interest rate is very competitive with other loan alternatives. There is a 10-year repayment period.

The amount of a Perkins Loan is determined by the financial aid office. The program limits are $4,000 per year for undergraduate students and $6,000 per year for graduate students, with cumulative limits of $20,000 for undergraduate loans and $40,000 for undergraduate and graduate loans combined.

Institutions participating in the Expanded Lending Option (ELO) may offer higher loan limits for the Perkins Loan. To participate in the ELO, a school must have a default rate no higher than 15 percent. The annual loan limits are increased by $1,000 each and the cumulative limits by $5,000 and $10,000, respectively. Perkins Loans offer better cancellation provisions than the Stafford or PLUS loans.

Signature Education Loans

Sallie Mae's Signature Education Loan Program offers all the money you need to pay for school through low-cost loan alternatives. The Sallie Mae (officially known as the Student Loan Marketing Association) program works hand in hand with federal loan programs such as the Federal Family Education Loan (FFEL) and Federal Direct Loan Program (FDLP) and helps with costs not covered by traditional programs, such as grants and scholarships. You can read more about Sallie Mae later in the chapter.

You may be eligible for a Signature Education Loan if you're an undergraduate or graduate student about to attend, or already attending, an eligible school at least half-time. Submit a FAFSA when you apply for this credit-based loan. Your credit history will be reviewed by the lender. The better your credit score or your coborrower's score (if you have one), the lower your interest rate, the lower the fees (generally), and the greater the possibility of loan approval.

HELP!
To order the Sallie Mae application by mail, call Sallie Mae at 1-800-543-7562. For more information, see the "Graduate and Professional Student Loans" section in Appendix B or visit the Sallie Mae website at www.salliemae.com.

Private Loans

Private loans, also known as alternative loans, help parents bridge the gap between the actual cost of their kids' education and the limited amount the government allows them to borrow in its loan programs.

Private loans are offered by private lenders, and there are no federal forms to complete. Some families turn to private loans when the federal loans don't provide enough money or when they need different repayment options. For example, a parent might want to defer repayment until the student graduates, an option that is not available from the government parent-loan program. Lenders provide different types of private loans, depending on the student's level of study.

Institutional Loans

An institutional loan means the school is the lender. Eligibility and loan characteristics will be different at each school you consider. Talk to someone in the financial aid office to find out whether your school offers these loans. If you pay on time or have your payments automatically deducted from your checking or savings account, you can receive interest-rate reductions worth hundreds or even thousands of dollars in savings over the life of your loan.

Sallie Mae Loans

Sallie Mae is one of the biggest student loan producers in the system. It is responsible for most student loans because it buys them back from banks and other financial institutions. A little background about Sallie Mae can help you understand how this all works.

Congress established Sallie Mae as a quasi-profit/nonprofit agency to buy student loan paper from lenders, thus replenishing the supply of money to make new student loans available.

Here's how the Sallie Mae program works. Suppose a bank starts out with $10 million to lend to students. The bank has the students sign all of the promissory notes and related statements, and then it sells the loan paper to Sallie Mae and gets another $10 million to circulate.

Sallie Mae, as well as all its commercial customers who lent the money in the first place, receives a cost allowance referred to as a special allowance. This fee adds up to substantial profits for the banks and other financial institutions.

Perhaps because the student loan-banking complex wants you to borrow, borrow, borrow, it's not surprising that neither Sallie Mae nor its participating lenders have developed a program for loan forgiveness. But other nonprofit entities, including government agencies, have discovered that it pays to reward graduates for putting their education to use to serve society by granting partial- to full-loan forgiveness.

> **Action Plan**
>
> Some programs provide partial or complete loan forgiveness for people who volunteer to help others or who work under special circumstances. AmeriCorps is a program of volunteer service in return for help with college tuition. Participating states have programs that reward 12 months' volunteer service with up to $7,400 in stipends plus $4,725 that can be used to pay college costs. See "Loan Consolidation and Forgiveness Programs" in Appendix B for more details.

Applying for a Loan

Although your financial aid package may indicate that you are eligible for an educational loan, you can't receive a loan without completing a loan application. Complete the FAFSA to determine the types of loans you might be eligible to receive.

The FAFSA form is required for all students who seek consideration for federal financial aid programs. Before completing the form, compile all tax information, both student's and parents'. For most federal student aid programs, the FAFSA is the only form you'll need to file. To receive a Federal Family Education Loan (FFEL), Stafford Loan, or an FFEL Plus Loan, you'll have to complete additional forms.

Check with your high school or your college's financial aid office for a loan application. You can also download one from the Internet at www.ed.gov.

Submit the forms in January. (Also see Chapter 2 for FAFSA information and Chapter 19 for line-by-line guidance in filling out the forms.)

Warning

Financial aid loan dollars are distributed on a first-come basis. If you're last on the list because you were late in filing your application, there may be no more funds available, and you'll be out of luck.

About a month after you submit your application, you'll receive your Student Aid Report (SAR), which you should check for accuracy. This report will identify the amount you're expected to contribute toward your education, called the expected family contribution (EFC). At about the same time, the school you plan to attend will send you a financial aid award letter summarizing the grants and loans you're eligible for. (See Chapter 2 for more information on the SAR and the EFC.)

What Happens When You Get a Loan?

When you take out a student loan, you have certain responsibilities. You're required to sign a promissory note, agreeing to repay the loan according to the terms of the note. The note is a binding legal document and states that you must repay the loan even if you don't complete your education, except in cases of discharge where your loan is forgiven (that is, you don't have to pay it back).

Loan funds are either distributed by check or sent electronically to your college in installments. The money is first applied to your college costs, and then you receive any remaining amount for additional expenses.

Think about what this obligation means before you take out a loan. If you don't repay your loan on time or according to the terms in your promissory note (that is, your promise to pay back a loan), you may go into *default*, which has very serious consequences. You must make payments on your loan even if you don't receive a bill or repayment notice. Billing statements or coupon books are sent to you as a convenience, but you're obligated to make payments even if you don't receive any reminders.

If you apply for a *deferment* or *forbearance* that allows you to delay payment, you must continue to make payments until you're notified that the request has been granted. If you don't continue, you may end up in default. You should keep a copy of any request form you submit, and you should document all contacts with the organization that holds your loan.

Getting Started

Default is a legal term that lending institutions use to declare that a borrower has failed to make payments on a loan in accordance with the loan's terms and conditions. It authorizes the lender to initiate aggressive collection procedures and to submit a "bad debt" report on the borrower's credit status. **Deferment** of a loan is a period of postponement during which repaying the loan principal is suspended because the borrower has met one or more of a number of deferment requirements established by law. **Forbearance** on a loan allows a temporary cessation of payments or a reduction of payment amounts for subsidized or unsubsidized federal loans.

If you find yourself in any of the following circumstances, you must notify the appropriate representative who manages your loan. Notify the loan representative when you …

- Graduate.

- Withdraw from school.

- Drop below half-time status.

- Change your name, address, or Social Security number.

- Transfer to another school.

How Are Loans Administered?

How your loan is administered depends on the type of loan it is.

- If you borrow a Perkins Loan, your loan will be managed by the school that lends you the money or by an agency that the school assigns to service the loan.

- If you borrow a direct loan, it will be managed by the Direct Loan Servicing Center.

◆ If you borrow a Federal Family Education Loan (FFEL), your lender or its servicing agent will manage it. During your loan counseling session, you'll be given the name of the representative who manages your loan.

Regardless of the type of loan, you must receive entrance counseling before you're given your first loan disbursement, and you must receive exit counseling before you leave school. These counseling sessions will be administered by your school and will explain important information about your loan. Your lender or the Direct Loan Servicing Center will provide you with additional information.

What Happens If You Default?

If you default on your loan, your school or the agency that holds your loan may take action to recover the money, including notifying national credit bureaus of your default. This may affect your credit rating for a long time. If that happens, you may find it very difficult to borrow from a bank to buy a car or a house.

In addition, if you default …

> **Warning**
>
> If loan defaults and poor payment records get on your credit report, you may find it difficult or impossible to get future loans unless you're willing to pay exorbitant loan fees and interest rates. Paying your debts and paying them on time, however, will help you build a solid credit record for the future.

◆ The agency holding your loan may ask your employer to deduct payments from your paycheck.

◆ You may be held liable for expenses incurred in collecting the loan.

◆ If you decide to return to school, you won't be entitled to receive any more federal student aid.

◆ The U.S. Department of Education may ask the Internal Revenue Service to withhold your income tax refund and apply it toward the amount you owe.

Loan Terms and Conditions

Whenever your school credits your account with funds from a Stafford Loan, PLUS Loan, or Perkins Loan, it must notify you or your parents in writing. This notification must be sent no earlier than 30 days before and no later than 30 days after the school credits your account. If you or your parents want to cancel all or a portion of a PLUS loan, you can do so by informing your school within 14 days after the date of the notification or by the first day of the payment period, whichever is later. Your school can tell you what the first day of your payment period is.

If you receive loan funds directly by check, you may refuse the funds simply by not depositing the check or by returning it with "cancel" written on the face of the check.

Before you graduate and leave school, you'll receive information about your loan from your school, lender, or the Direct Loan Servicing Center. For example, they'll tell you the amount of your total debt, including principal and the estimated interest payments over the term of the loan.

If you borrow a Federal Perkins Loan, your school will provide this same information to you.

If you borrow a Direct Loan or an FFEL Program Loan, the Direct Loan Servicing Center or your lender will provide this information to you as appropriate.

If you have Direct or FFEL Stafford loans, your school will provide you with a current description of your loans, including average monthly anticipated payments. You'll also get a description of applicable deferment, forbearance, and discharge provisions and repayment options.

Repayment Plans

When you contact a lending organization, you'll discover that it offers several types of loans and a number of options for reducing your monthly payments. Make sure you compare the options to see which ones best fit with both your short- and long-term career plans. Don't assume that you're doomed to giant payments for as far as the eye can see. Before you jump into repayment waves that may be over your head, test the water. If your income can support standard plan payments, you'll save interest over the term of the loan. Although a standard plan carries the highest monthly payment, you can overcome your debt faster and pay less in interest. You can pay a fixed amount for up to 10 years; payments on loans with variable interest rates may fluctuate.

The following sections describe the kinds of plans you may want to consider.

HELP! Check out the websites listed under "Lenders of College Loans (Websites)" in Appendix B to help you find a lender that can meet your exacting requirements.

Graduated Payment Plans

If your starting income is relatively low or next to zero, but is expected to increase on a regular basis as you get closer to graduating, then a graduated payment plan is a more graceful method that may ease your payment pangs. Payments start low and increase every 2 to 3 years for the next 10 to 30 years. Interest charges, which are based on the outstanding principal, will remain high for the first few years, so you'll pay more total interest over the life of your loan.

Federal education loans, including Stafford, SLS, PLUS, HEAL, and Federal Consolidation Loans, as well as some private loans, offer graduated repayment terms that can vary from lender to lender. Some lenders, including Sallie Mae, let you make interest-only payments for the first two to four years; after that period, you must pay principal and interest.

Long-Term Payment Plans

If all you can afford is a tiny monthly payment, an extended long-term repayment plan may be your best option. The feds and other lenders allow you to extend payments from 12 to 30 years and even offer plans that combine graduated repayments with an extended schedule. Although your monthly payments may be low, you could end up paying twice the original amount of your loan over the long term.

> **Getting Started**
>
> Six out of ten college students go to college on borrowed money. The average student will owe $20,000 when he or she graduates and will face monthly payments of $250 for 10 years thereafter.

As mentioned earlier in this chapter, AmeriCorps is a program of providing help with college tuition in return for volunteer service. Participating states have programs that reward 12 months' volunteer service with up to $7,400 in stipends plus $4,725 that can be used to pay off long-term loans.

Grace Periods

Students have the right to a grace period before their repayment period begins. Parents do not receive a grace period for a PLUS Loan. Your grace period begins when you leave school or drop below half-time status. During exit counseling, your school, lender, and/or the Direct Loan Servicing Center, as appropriate, must give you a loan repayment schedule that states when your first payment is due, the number and frequency of payments, and the amount of each payment.

If you or your parents borrow an FFEL Loan, you must be notified when the loan is sold if the results of the sale mean that you will be making payments to a new lender or agency. Both the old and new lenders or agencies must notify the borrower of the sale. Further, they must state the identity of the new lender or agency holding the loan, the address to which the borrower must make payments, and the telephone numbers of both the old and the new lenders or agencies.

Finding the Right Lender

Your neighborhood bank, savings and loan association, or credit union may offer special loan programs for college-bound students. Unless you, the student, have a record of regular income and a credit history, these financial institutions will examine your parents' ability to repay loans.

Although the rates offered on these loans may not be much different from those for any other form of commercial credit, the repayment schedules may be more liberal. We recommend that you apply for federally subsidized loans through your college financial aid office before pursuing other lenders.

Many student loan borrowers do not give much consideration to choosing a lender. They often rely totally on the lender list provided by the school, thinking that, because loan terms and benefits programs are very similar, the lender decision is not that important. There are, however, subtle differences, and they could save you time and money.

Some lenders may offer to simplify and shorten the application process. Don't underestimate what some lenders offer over the life of the loan. Since you're entering into a relationship with a lender that could last for many years, you should learn more about these differences. This section gives you the information you need to make a more informed decision.

Ask the financial aid office at your school for its list of preferred lenders for FFEL and private loan programs. Your school's preferred lender list should include lenders that are trustworthy and reliable, have proven track records, and offer attractive loan terms to borrowers.

Preferred lenders offer excellent service to the borrower. You don't have to pick a lender from the list, but it's a good idea to do so if

Action Plan

Consider all available financial loan options, including federal, state, and local loan programs, institutional loan plans, home equity loans, and any other loan program you can find to help you get through college. The money you spend today will reward you with big dividends in the future.

you want to ensure that your application is processed in a timely and accurate manner. Remember, you do not have a choice of lenders for loans under the FDLP and Federal Perkins Loan programs.

The services of some preferred lenders to consider are outlined in the following list. To learn more about any of them, visit their websites. See "Lenders of College Loans (Websites)," "Loan Programs," and also "Financial Aid Resources," all in Appendix B.

- **Chase Bank.** This site at www.chasestudentloans.com offers information about the financial aid process, a planning calendar for high school students, need-estimation and budgeting calculators, and an online application.

- **Academic Management Services.** Academic Management Services at www. amsweb.com makes education financing more manageable by coupling flexible payment options with innovative customer service. In addition to offering Stafford, PLUS, and private alternative loans, it is the nation's largest provider of monthly tuition payment plans.

- **Bank of America (BOA).** Bank of America offers Federal Stafford and PLUS loans, as well as a private loan program for students and their parents. The bank's Education Maximizer is an alternative source of funding that supplements federal loans at competitive rates. BOA also offers Guaranteed Access to Education (GATE) loans, home equity loans, and lines of credit. Visit www.bankofamerica. com/studentbanking.

Action Plan

Build a budget and stick to it! Using the budget calculator on the web, you can quickly get an overview of where your money goes. And you may be able to cut expenses or increase your income to avoid having to borrow. The site address is www.collegeanswer.com, listed under "Budgeting" and "Adult Financial Aid Programs," both in Appendix B.

- **Key Bank.** Key Bank has been helping families achieve their education goals for more than 40 years. Key provides students and parents with convenient access to quality educational finance products, payment plans, and support services. Key offers both federal and private loans for undergraduate students. Check them out at www.key.com.

- **PNC Bank.** PNC Bank's site at www.pncbank. com provides details about its financing options and scholarship program. It also includes several loan calculators.

Before you borrow, calculate how much you'll be expected to repay on education loans each month and how that amount compares with what you think you'll earn after graduation. What percentage of your monthly income is the monthly loan payment? If it's more than 10 percent, then either you've already borrowed too much or you're getting ready to!

Remember, even if you don't finish school or can't find a job, you'll still have to repay your loans with interest.

Comparing Loan Offers

It seems simple enough when your loan is approved. You borrow money, and as long as you repay it, everything is okay. But as you begin to read the fine print, you realize it's not so simple. There's lots of small print and it's confusing—and that's only for one loan. What happens when you have more than one loan to consider?

First of all, don't panic. The writing on each application or brochure may seem different, but all loans have the same basic characteristics. The following list will help you decide which loan is best for you.

Warning

Borrow only what you absolutely need to cover the cost of your education. Be conservative. If you have to borrow, accept only what's necessary to cover your college costs.

- ◆ **Compare interest rates and terms.** For federal programs, they're generally very similar. However, some lenders offer discounts for early payments. Private programs can vary significantly.

- ◆ **Compare borrower benefits,** including those for paying on time and for making loan payments electronically.

- ◆ **Compare repayment plans.**

- ◆ **Compare loan application processes.** Lenders are beginning to offer online applications and instant loan approvals.

- ◆ **Compare levels of customer service.**

Interest Rates and Fees

Some loans have a variable rate and an interest rate cap, which means that the cost of borrowing the money can fluctuate up to a specific percentage while you're repaying it. Your goal as you look at the various loans is to find the lowest interest rate with the lowest cap.

◆ Look for fixed interest rate loans where the payment amount will be constant. If the interest rate is variable, find out how often the rate could change.

◆ If the interest rate is variable, find out if the payments start low but balloon later to unmanageable monthly payments.

◆ Determine whether the rate is linked to a published rate, such as the prime rate. This could tell you how often it might change.

◆ Ask for estimates of total interest charges, and find out if there are any interest-free periods.

> **Warning** _____
>
> Restrict your use of credit cards, or they'll eat you up. Restrict yourself to one or two credit cards, because owning multiple cards will only compound your problem. Balancing your debt across many cards can lull you into believing that you don't have a problem because each card's balance looks small in comparison with the total debt.

Most private loans have a variety of fees associated with them. Fees for originating the loan and fees for insuring loans are the most common. Make sure you understand all of the fees; if you don't understand one, ask the lender to explain it.

◆ Ask how the fees are handled. Are they deducted from the amount you're borrowing, are they in addition to that amount, or are they "out of pocket"? If the fees are not "out of pocket," you'll probably have to pay interest on the fee amounts.

◆ Find out if the fees are based on a percentage of your loan or are flat fees regardless of the amount you're borrowing.

◆ Ask how late fees are assessed and whether there are any service charges that you're required to pay over the life of the loan.

Loan Terms

Each private loan may give you a different length of time, or term, in which to repay the loan. Understand that you'll pay more in interest on a longer-term loan. A 20-year loan with low payments may look very enticing, but it will cost you much more over the long haul than the 10-year loan with slightly higher payments.

When you take out a student loan, you sign a promissory note. This is your promise to repay the loan with interest, on time, and in full. Responsible management of your student loans can be easy. It can help you establish a good credit rating and can protect you from experiencing the negative impact of too much debt. Even if you don't complete your education or are unsatisfied with your schooling, you still have to pay back your loan.

Failing to pay back a loan will put you in default, which can scar your credit rating for years. If you ever have trouble paying back a loan, call your lender or service right away. It can help you explore different repayment options that will work with your particular financial situation.

The Least You Need to Know

- Low-interest subsidized loans are need-based; unsubsidized loans are not, and interest payments begin while the student is still in school.

- You can balance your future with loan repayment plans that won't get in your way.

- Interpret and compare different loan terms and conditions to determine which loan is best for you.

Tax-Saving Strategies

In This Chapter

◆ Learning how to take advantage of savings plans that offer tax credits

◆ Discovering savings plans that earn tax-free interest if the money is used for your kid's education

◆ Finding out about college savings plans that let you have the money when you need it

Smart parents know how much a college degree can improve job and income prospects, so they begin saving up for their kids' education while the kids are still young. Like most college-minded families, they're planning how they're going to pay for it! What will college cost when your kids are ready? How much should you start saving and when? Where's the money going to come from?

Most families' answers lie in long-term savings; they start socking away money in stocks and bonds even before their children utter their first words. Financial wizards call this long-term planning. They also recommend all kinds of detailed financial asset reshuffling about two years before anyone goes to college; they call this short-term planning.

College costs are high enough to discourage most parents before they even begin the long run. Use the tips in this chapter to start a fund for your kids' education. There are several ways to save money to pay for college, and some programs include tax-deferred or even tax-free incentives. Be sure to explore all of the options in this chapter and start saving today. Remember, it's never too late to start!

Tax Credits

A tax credit is an amount you can subtract from your federal income tax to reduce your taxable income. Tax credits can help finance school and offer a way to recover some of the costs of college expenses. For example, the HOPE scholarship and the Lifetime Learning Credit offer students and their families credit on their federal income tax bill for tuition and fees incurred at eligible schools.

HOPE Scholarship Tax Credits

Tax credits for the Helping Outstanding Pupils Educationally (HOPE) scholarship cover 100 percent of the first $1,000 in payments for qualified tuition and fees, and 50 percent of the second $1,000. Expenses that qualify for the HOPE scholarship include school tuition and required fees minus any tax-free grants or scholarships. The costs of books and supplies are usually not covered, but you should check with your school. This tax credit does not cover room and board, insurance, transportation, or medical fees.

(HELP!)
> If you need more information about HOPE scholarships, see the "Tax Deductions" section in Appendix B.

The HOPE scholarship provides a family with a maximum tax credit of $1,500 a year per student. You may claim it for two years if your kid is a freshman or sophomore and is enrolled in a program that leads to a degree, certificate, or other recognized educational credential. Students also must be taking at least half the normal full-time course load for their major, and they must be doing so for at least one academic period that begins during the calendar year. They must be free of any felony conviction for possessing or distributing a controlled substance. If you have questions, your school's financial aid office should be able to help you determine whether you meet the requirements.

Lifetime Learning Credits

Lifetime Learning Credits allow up to a $1,000 tax credit per family for postsecondary education courses. You may claim only one credit per tax year. To get this credit, parents have to file a tax return. They may claim the Lifetime Learning Credit if their kids are enrolled at eligible institutions. Lifetime credits are not based on the student's workload and are allowed for one or more courses. They are not limited to students in the first two years of postsecondary education and can be claimed for expenses for graduate-level degree work.

Lifetime credits have no limits on the number of years for which the credit can be claimed for each student and do not increase based on the number of students receiving qualified expenses.

Tax-Exempt Bonds

Tax-exempt bonds are basically IOUs that you purchase from local, state, or federal government agencies. Otherwise known as municipal bonds, government-issued bonds earn you tax-exempt interest. U.S. government-issued bonds or Treasury bonds are both state and federal tax-exempt investments and are relatively risk-free.

City, county, and state governments and agencies with a public purpose (such as funding public utility companies, hospitals, and schools) issue municipal bonds, which are often called munis. Interest rates are lower than for other investments because you don't have to pay taxes on the interest you make on your investment. Munis and tax-sheltered retirement accounts generally help parents in tax brackets higher than 30 percent to cover college expenses far better than bonds that require taxable interest. Interest is exempt from federal and state taxes. Munis are low risk as long as the credit rating on the bond is good. They are redeemable before their maturity date.

Although nothing is totally risk-free, most bonds are about as low risk as you can get. However, there are some high-risk government bonds that offer no guarantees that they'll grow or survive. Check with your broker or banker before you buy any bonds to find out the bond rating (that is, high-, medium-, or low-risk). All bonds normally pay more in returns than bank savings or money market mutual funds, but they tend to carry a greater risk. Consider the following college savings options.

U.S. Series EE Bonds

If you have little to invest, EE bonds may be your best strategy because they can cost as little as $25 or as much as $5,000 each. The most you can buy in any one year is $15,000 worth. U.S. bonds guarantee earnings with their fixed interest rate, but on the downside they return less than other savings tools. Nevertheless, U.S. savings bonds do have some advantages over other types of long-range savings.

◆ Bonds are purchased for half their worth. For example, if you want to buy a $1,000 savings bond, you'll pay $500 for it.

♦ Bonds can be redeemed after six months in return for the exact purchase price plus any interest earned. The coupon rate is reset every six months, resulting in little risk of losing interest and no risk of losing the capital investment.

♦ The original purchase price or capital outlay will never go down, and its interest will always be positive.

♦ Taxes on the interest earned are deferred until the bond is cashed, as long as the bond is held for a minimum of five years.

♦ If you cash in the bonds to pay for college fees and tuition, taxes on the interest earned are forgiven.

U.S. Treasury Bonds

Just as secure as savings bonds, U.S. Treasury bonds, or T-bills, require you to accept the feds' IOU for a longer period of time. But the longer you sit on T-bills, the more they're worth. Don't buy Treasury bonds that exceed five years because other investments will probably earn you more over the same period of time. To purchase Treasury bonds, contact your nearest Federal Reserve Bank branch or call 202-377-7715 for more information.

Warning

T-bills normally have lower returns than other investments, and there are limits on how much you can invest in them at any one time.

Although Treasury bonds may not be your lifelong best buddies, they have redeeming qualities worth considering for college financing:

♦ Earnings are exempt from state and local taxes.

♦ T-bills have virtually no credit risk. As long as the U.S. government is sound, these bills are sound.

♦ T-bills are more liquid than some other investments (such as CDs), and T-bills can be cashed in anytime after the maturity date without penalty.

♦ T-bills can be purchased with maturity dates that coincide with college bills. They can be withdrawn anytime before maturity to pay for college without penalty fees. However, if interest rates rise, you will get less money back if you sell before maturity.

State Tuition Bonds

More than 20 states sponsor programs modeled after Illinois' College Bonds to finance higher education. Parents can buy state-sponsored college bonds at extremely high discounts. Because the bonds serve as a college savings vehicle, they are sometimes referred to as baccalaureate bonds. States issue these bonds as a way for families to save for future education expenses. These instruments are known as zero-coupon bonds, and they allow you to buy a heavily discounted bond with high interest and begin collecting interest when the bond reaches maturity, instead of gradually collecting lower interest.

Like U.S. savings bonds, state-sponsored college (or baccalaureate) bonds sell for less than their face value and pay no interest until maturity. States use the proceeds from these bonds to meet the cost of their targeted building projects. State college savings bonds cost from $1,000 to $5,000, with maturities between 5 and 20 years. For college planning, bonds should mature the same year your kid goes to college.

Getting Started

Zero-coupon bonds are debt securities that are issued at substantial discounts from face value, offer no periodic interest payments, and pay the principal amount or face value at maturity. They may be obligations of the U.S. Treasury, governmental agencies, municipalities, or corporations. For example, on January 1, 2005, Mr. Smith purchased a $15,000, 8 percent, 5-year, zero-coupon bond issued by XYZ Company for $10,000. He will not receive any cash payments until December 31, 2010, when the bond matures and XYZ Company pays him $15,000.

In some states, college savings bonds can't be included in the college financial aid assessment (covered in Chapter 10). Although baccalaureate bonds are marketed as a means of saving for college, no requirements obligate you to use them for college tuition. You don't even have to designate a beneficiary, such as a college.

Although savings in the student's name typically subtract from financial aid eligibility, some tax breaks and earned interest plans may make up for the loss. For example, if the parent or grandparent deposits the money into a trust account for the student under the Uniform Gifts to Minors Act (UGMA) or the Uniform Transfers to Minors Act (UTMA), the IRS provides some tax breaks on the earned interest.

Some advantages of state college savings bonds include …

◆ The first $650 in earned interest is exempt from federal income tax.

♦ The second $650 in earned interest gets taxed at the student's tax rate, which could be next to nothing if the student earns nearly zilch.

♦ Earned interest above $1,300 gets taxed at the parents' rate until the student turns age 14.

♦ Funds can be withdrawn only for education-specific reasons until the student reaches an age between 18 and 21. (It varies with the state.)

♦ Interest earned is tax exempt from federal taxes and from state taxes for residents of the issuing state.

♦ Funds can be used at any time for any college expense, even out-of-state college expenses.

Some disadvantages of state tuition bonds include …

♦ Funds can be withdrawn for any use but only after the student reaches an age between 18 and 21, depending on the state.

♦ The money belongs to the student, and until the designated age, it can be used to cover only education costs, health, security, and welfare.

♦ The funds saved in your kid's name do subtract heavily (to the tune of 35 percent of the amount saved annually) from the student's financial aid eligibility.

♦ The minimum bond purchase amount is $1,000 at high-discount, low credit risk.

Action Plan

Bonds are rated on an alpha scale from AAA to EEE, where AAA is the highest rating that a bond can receive. It is an indication that the organization (government agency, corporation, or other issuer) that has issued the bonds is financially stable and will in all likelihood meet its bond debt obligations. The lowest rating (EEE) indicates doubt about the financial integrity of the issuer and its ability to meet its bond debt obligations. As a general rule, the lower the bond rating, the higher the interest that's paid on the bonds.

Tax-Exempt Trust Accounts

A *trust* is a legal instrument that holds and manages your real property as well as your tangible and intangible property. When you put assets into a trust, you're transferring them from your ownership to the ownership of the entity known as the trust. Sorry for the abbreviated legal explanation, but if you're a parent, it's important for you to know that certain types of trusts allow you to transfer a portion of your assets into a trust fund for your kid(s). Why would you want to do this? Because it may allow you to declare a lower asset base when you file for financial aid, and any income earned by income-producing assets in the trust avoids taxes until the money is withdrawn.

Charitable Remainder Trusts

A charitable remainder trust is useful for families with a lot of money. This planning vehicle allows parents to combine a charitable gift with a financing plan for their college-bound child. Parents can present a gift to a charitable institution with the provision that a certain amount of the gift be set aside for the kid's tuition account.

There are, however, tax consequences to a charitable trust investment. The interest earned is subject to federal, state, and local taxes. Further information on this type of trust may be obtained from a certified financial planner, banker, or accountant.

Clifford Trusts

Clifford trusts are legal arrangements transferring some type of property from one person to another. The properties are managed by a trustee for the benefit of the beneficiary. Anyone can be named the beneficiary of the trust, and there may be several beneficiaries. The trust can be funded for a kid after his or her fourteenth birthday.

Crummey Trusts

In Crummey trusts, parents name the student as the beneficiary. Under the terms of the agreement, parents may make annual tax-free gifts of up to $20,000 if they are married and $10,000 if they are single. Income can remain in this type of trust for an indefinite period of time. Parents should seek the advice of financial experts for more information on this type of trust arrangement.

Custodial Accounts

A custodial account is one way that parents can transfer some of their financial assets to their children. The Tax Reform Act of 1986, however, introduced the so-called "kiddie tax," which made custodial accounts less attractive financially than was previously the case.

For example, if a kid is under the age of 14, the first $650 of income is tax-free and the second $650 is taxed at the kid's rate, usually 15 percent. Anything over that amount is taxed at the parents' rate until the kid reaches age 14, when income is again taxed at the kid's rate. However, it's important to remember that students must contribute 35 percent of their assets, and parents are required to contribute only 5.6 percent of theirs.

College Sure CDs

College Sure certificates of deposit (CDs) are the only savings plan that are indexed on increased college costs. Other savings plans are tied to the *prime rate*, which is the rate at which the Federal Reserve System loans money to banks.

Introduced in 1987 to help parents meet new increases in education costs, College Sure CDs allow a variable rate of return based on the inflation of college costs. Each July, interest rates reset at 1.5 percent below the rate of annual inflation in college costs for the index.

Some of the advantages of College Sure CDs include …

 ◆ If tuition suddenly skyrockets, this CD could protect the long-range saver from the decreasing purchasing power resulting from inflation.

 ◆ The minimum deposit is only $1,000 per CD.

 ◆ They're insured by the Federal Deposit Insurance Corporation (FDIC) up to $100,000.

Some of the disadvantages of College Sure CDs include …

 ◆ Interest earned is taxable.

 ◆ College Sure CDs are less profitable when tuition inflation rates are low.

 ◆ CDs lack the significant long-term-growth potential of stocks and mutual funds.

Money Market Mutual Funds

Because college fees can sneak up on you very quickly, don't even think about investing money in any kind of unstable investment. Maybe you couldn't start a good savings plan 18 years ago. Perhaps you've already spent everything you'd saved because you didn't think your children wanted to go to college. Now your kids are telling you they want to go. *Money market mutual funds* allow you to set up a relatively short-term investment and make a reasonable return on your money before you'll need it for college.

Most money market mutual funds slot money into government and corporate bonds. You can collect a fair amount of interest from these shortest of short-term bonds. Although they're not insured by the FDIC, these funds provide low-risk investments with fairly high returns. They typically plug your investment money into low-risk government securities, commercial certificates from well-established corporations, and bank certificates.

> **Action Plan**
>
> A good money market mutual fund will provide higher yields than bank savings accounts and most CDs.

Coverdell Education Savings Account

The Coverdell Education Savings Account (or "Coverdell ESA") is another way to save for college. The federal government allows parents to contribute up to $2,000 per year to the education fund of each child under 18. The contributions are not tax-deductible, but earnings do accumulate tax-deferred. And better yet, as long as the monies are used to pay for education-related expenses (tuition, room and board, textbooks, and fees), they are not taxed at the time of withdrawal. Coverdell Education Savings Account are an option for single taxpayers earning less than $95,000 per year adjusted gross income (AGI) or married taxpayers filing jointly earning less than $150,000 per year of AGI. Before the named beneficiary turns 30, however, the IRA fund must be spent or transferred to another minor family member.

529 IRA Plans

The relatively new education IRA that was covered in the preceding section offers a puny $500 annual contribution. Most mutual-fund companies won't even open an account for $500. Even if they would, saving such a tiny sum each year wouldn't make a real dent in the cost of a college education anyway.

But a little-known 1997 piece of tax legislation has come to the rescue. Under section 529 of the tax code, state college plans now enjoy tax-deferred growth and estate tax advantages, and they are now referred to as 529 plans. As a result, more states are starting to offer college savings plans. This new breed of college plan is a major improvement over both the Uniform Gifts to Minors Act and the prepaid tuition plans that had been established by a number of states. These state savings plans are a great way for grandparents to help their grandchildren and lower estate taxes at the same time. If you want to learn more about the 529 plans, check out the website at www.savingforcollege.com.

College Savings Plans

College savings plans offer parents a way to save money for college expenses and get great tax benefits. These plans are more flexible than prepaid tuition plans since they do not dictate which institution your kid must attend.

You can participate in college savings plans with colleges inside or outside of your state, and the funds can be used for all kinds of college expenses, not just tuition and room and board.

Other features of the plans include tax-deferred earnings until your kid enters college. Withdrawals are taxed at the student's low tax bracket, not at the higher bracket of the contributor, who is usually the parent.

If you're worried about the rising cost of tuition, this type of college savings plan might be for you. In general, prepaid tuition plans allow families to prepay for college expenses at discounted rates. However, the plans vary from state to state, so be sure to investigate all of the details for this type of plan in your state. Some plans can be used at both public and private universities within your state, while others are more limit-ing. Check with your state's financial aid office, listed in Appendix C.

Some of the features of prepaid tuition plans are ...

- There are several types of payment options, such as one-time, lump-sum pay-ments or payment schedules that allow you to spread the payments over time.

- If the parents are the contributors, then they maintain control of the account.

- Income level is not a limiting factor, and you can contribute over $100,000 per year.

- If the intended beneficiary does not attend college, the funds can be transferred to another family member or refunded to you, minus a penalty fee.

For parents or students trying to meet the higher cost of education, tax-saving op-portunities have been limited. However, with the renewed national interest in educa-tion, things are beginning to change. Congress is becoming increasingly focused on education as a top national priority and on tax incentives to ease the cost burden of education.

The Least You Need to Know

♦ If you're interested in saving money either tax-deferred or tax-exempt for college, you should know about the multitude of savings programs that are available to you for that purpose. However, you should research these programs before investing in them since, like other financial vehicles, they vary in the quality of their ratings.

♦ Education IRAs are a great way to save tax-deferred dollars for college.

♦ Opening up a trust account on behalf of your kid offers you a legal way to reduce your asset base and earn tax-deferred income on assets in the trust.

♦ The recently introduced 529 plan for college tax savings is an improved plan that gives you tax-deferred growth and new estate tax advantages.

Financial Aid Consulting Services

In This Chapter

- ◆ Learning what financial aid consultants do and what services they can offer you

- ◆ Discovering the advantages and disadvantages of using a financial aid consulting service

- ◆ Spotting an incompetent consultant before you've been had

- ◆ Getting tips on finding a qualified financial aid consulting service

The new arrival on the college scene is the college financial aid consultant, an expert who leads families through the financial aid process. The good ones know how to work with you to develop strategies that meet your family's objectives, and they can assist you in filling out forms to maximize your financial aid benefits. They can also work with you to appeal a rejected claim, negotiate a better aid offer, or compare financial aid offers to determine which one is the best for you.

How Much Do They Cost?

Good college financial aid consultants cost money but can save you more than their fees if you hire a competent one. Over a four-year period, expert planners can save you thousands of dollars. Their payment terms range from hourly charges as high as $125 or more, to package prices of $500 and up for a year's service. Their fees should depend on the level of service you need and not some arbitrary number.

HELP!
If you have the time to learn about the complete financial aid process, then you probably don't need to hire a financial aid consultant.

Warning
Anyone can hang out a financial aid shingle. No certification, degree, or license requirement exists for an individual to open a financial aid service and charge a fee for consulting. Like many other consultants, financial aid professionals come in two basic groups: experts and incompetents.

Suppose you only want your Free Application for Federal Student Aid (FAFSA) completed. Are your financial affairs simple or complex? If your money matters are uncomplicated and you hired a tax preparer to complete a short form 1040A or 1040EZ tax return, you probably paid about $50. Expect to pay approximately the same for your rudimentary FAFSA. If, however, your fiscal situation is complex enough to require a 1040 long form, you probably paid a tax preparer $300 or more to assist you. Expect to pay a financial aid consultant a fee in the same neighborhood for a comparable task.

Should you look for a good college financial consultant to begin with? Yes, if you're a middle-income family and need to learn about alternative loans, state residency requirements, institutional policies on award packaging, financial aid appeals processes, or future financial aid award structuring. Remember that, as each year goes by, it seems that financial aid applications and procedures get more and more complicated. In such a situation, it may be well worth investing as much as $300 to $500 per year with a college financial aid consultant.

How Much Is Too Much?

When are charges from a college financial aid planner higher than normal? Avoid planners who are charging over $1,000 per year. The more you pay for services does not mean the more you'll get in financial aid.

Action Plan

In one way or another, the real financial aid experts are deep inside the financial aid system.

Who Are the Experts?

Experts have special knowledge derived from training or experience. Many, perhaps even most, financial aid experts have worked as financial aid counselors on a college campus. Sometimes they later were hired by banks or loan agencies and delivered education loans to college students and their families. Many have professional degrees and have worked first at foundations or private financial aid family services. Experts have been in the field and know the process from the inside out:

◆ They know which regulations are changing and how your family will be affected by the changes.

◆ They have a client base across the United States that consistently feeds them information from the financial aid trenches.

◆ They're on call throughout the financial aid process to keep you informed about where you are in the process.

◆ They know which appeal letters work with which colleges, states, and federal agencies.

◆ They know which out-of-state public universities award only loans and jobs and no gift aid.

◆ They will certify on the FAFSA that they assisted in preparing the FAFSA, as required by federal regulation.

◆ They will be able to develop a four-year financial plan for you that accommodates the multitude of documents, regulations, and college inquiries, and the plan will be both legal and ethical.

Who Are the Incompetents?

Incompetents may have exhaustive knowledge of taxes or other financial planning strategies, but they lack detailed, up-to-date knowledge of local and state educational grants, specific scholarships, or effective ways to deal with the financial aid structure at various institutions. Incompetents usually have a superficial knowledge, if any, of the financial aid system, recommend unethical strategies, guarantee results, and overcharge. Stay clear of incompetents.

If a financial aid consultant does any of the following, you'd be wise to find someone else:

- **Promises to slip into a college's side door to intercede with the financial aid officer on your behalf.** The expert knows that the college's financial aid officer has high legal exposure if student confidentiality is breached. Influence peddling doesn't happen among reputable professionals. Watch out for the consultant who pretends to have connections and can make an award "a sure thing" for your kid.

- **Suggests that your assets be hidden.** An asset that's hidden on these forms may reappear when the college asks for additional information. It's also possible that the vehicle suggested to hide assets from the financial aid office will keep that money out of a family's hands for quite some time. If assets are frozen, a family might not be able to meet its expected contribution, which could mean that the student can't go to college after all.

- **Wants to be paid upfront for four years.** If you quit school before graduation, don't expect a refund. The expert charges either by the hour or by the year.

- **Is hesitant to sign legal documents.** Refuses to sign a FAFSA or other application that requests a signature from a financial consultant.

- **Offers something free of charge.** Some unscrupulous consultants will try to drum up business by offering a free "introductory seminar" for financial aid strategies.

- **Claims hidden knowledge.** No financial aid available to the public is kept hidden. Someone who makes the claim that he or she has "insider information" should be looked upon with suspicion.

Action Plan

When you're checking on the qualifications of a financial aid planner, referrals from satisfied clients work best. Also call your high school guidance counselor and the college's financial aid officer. The expert will be recommended; the incompetent will not.

Incompetents know that their reference base is thin, so they use smoke and mirrors to look reputable. They'll claim that they belong to the local Better Business Bureau, to a state professional financial aid association, or even to the National Association of Student Financial Aid Administrators. They may, in fact, be members. Anyone can become a member of these organizations by paying membership dues. Legitimate credentials of financial aid consultants may include a CPA or CFT.

The incompetent focuses on paying college costs for a single year, rarely on a comprehensive plan.

Incompetents have been known to direct parents to keep two sets of forms, one for the IRS and the other for the completion of the FAFSA. This duplicity may be discovered if a college asks for a signed waiver to obtain your tax records from the IRS. Another trick is the so-called Grannie Loan. Incompetents frequently tell families to lower their expected family contribution by claiming that family assets belong to others.

All in all, it's not a good idea to hire anyone who's intent on helping a family beat the system. The financial aid planner will collect a fee and not have any liability, but the family will be taking an enormous risk.

> **Warning**
>
> You may feel as though you are wasting your time applying for financial aid money. You feel as though you don't have two minutes to rub together when—bingo!—you spot an ad that jumps out at you: "Money for College—Results Guaranteed!" Such seductive ads are often run by firms that claim to tailor a computerized scholarship search to your individual needs for a fee. Watch out!

What to Expect from a Planning Meeting

To assist you in setting up a financial aid plan, experts will ask you to come to their office (which may be their residence) because that's where the professional resources are located. Of course, incompetents may also invite you to an office.

Before you go to that meeting, make sure you've asked for and investigated the consultant's references. Referrals from satisfied clients work best. Call your high school guidance counselor for recommendations.

An expert should be prepared to discuss with you topics such as the following:

♦ **Family structure.** Are you married, separated, thinking about separation, divorced, single, or widowed?

♦ **Home equity.** The family's equity in its primary home is important to anticipate possible effects on other forms of assets and documents required by a college.

♦ **Retirement accounts.** The history of retirement accounts is important since these funds must be reported on some college applications.

♦ **Employment history.** The parents' job record is important because some colleges require business and farm supplemental income documents.

The incompetent financial aid person probably won't know about these issues and is not likely to bring them up or answer your questions satisfactorily. Conversely, a competent consultant should be able to answer all of your questions to your satisfaction. He or she will offer you insights that could help improve your chances of getting a better financial aid offer.

Computer Search Services

Computer-based research companies that do the legwork for you at a modest price can save some time if you're in a time crunch for finding private scholarships. But only a few scholarship search firms provide serious, targeted returns. We identify some of the best of the breed in the "Scholarships, Grants, and Fellowships" section of Appendix B. The unhappy truth is that some computerized search firms have proven to be borderline fraud cases, and they taint the entire industry with a bad odor. Some were such rip-offs that in recent years the Federal Trade Commission, state attorneys general, and other government scam squads shut them down.

> **Action Plan**
>
> A good scholarship search firm allows you to pay as you go: one hour, one week, one month, or one year at a time.

> **HELP!**
>
> Your high school guidance office, college financial aid office, and local library offer materials to conduct searches for financial aid at no cost.

Computer-based scholarship search firms, however, continue to take advantage of time- and tuition-short students and their families. Some persuasive services claim that, for a one-time fee ranging from $300 to $1,000, they'll set up your financial aid research for the next four years. Many of these firms last only a few months before disappearing. Moreover, anyone familiar with college life knows that few students know how long they'll be in school. You're wiser to use the college financial aid office's free resources.

Free Scholarship Search Services

Some reputable search firms offer their search for free over the Internet. They can do so because the service is advertising driven. This means they sell your name and contact information to mailing list houses to use for direct mail promotions and telemarketing solicitations. Because schools don't monitor the quality of online financial aid searches, the results of your search may disappoint you. If privacy is a concern, ask if the service keeps your information confidential. A good scholarship search firm can be for a fee or for free, but it does not sell your name without your permission.

Database Quality

The quality of the scholarship database is all-important. You need accurate, current information that matches your criteria.

Scholarship criteria change from year to year. Researchers who know their business are knowledgeable enough to update their information only after the sponsor's board of directors has met to determine the ground rules for the following year's awards. Normally, the boards meet between March and August. To merely verify this info on an arbitrary date is useless; for instance, verifying in January results in simply getting last year's data. Experienced researchers know when the boards meet because it's their business to know—they ask and note the dates in their working files.

Some scholarship search firms advertise that they update every quarter. This claim is marketing hype. Scholarship rules don't change with the seasons—they change once a year. A good scholarship search firm maintains its own research staff and updates its database annually using savvy research methods.

Government legislation changes frequently. If a search firm does not keep up with the latest state and federal laws concerning financial aid, it is not doing its job.

Questions to Ask Search Services

Find out whether you'll be told about scholarships for which you're ineligible. A good scholarship search firm doesn't try to stick you with inapplicable scholarships, for example, ones that are specific to geographic regions or to colleges you're not considering, or scholarships for groups of people to which you don't belong. Here are two important questions to ask:

- **What percentage of the service's database consists of portable awards?** You want financial aid you can take to any college or to any group of colleges that participate in a specific scholarship award, such as the National Merit Scholarship Program.

- **How large is the database, and how much has it grown in the past two years?** A typical size is a couple of hundred thousand scholarship sources.

Action Plan

Don't mistakenly assume that any computer search, no matter how credible the firm or reliable the data, can do all the heavy lifting for maximizing your college money. Look at printed publications that list sources of financial aid.

Incompetents claim that their databases balloon by the hundreds per day or week; genuine services admit that although they constantly add new sources, outdated information keeps total tallies low.

A good scholarship search firm doesn't oversell the size of its database from year to year. A smaller database with high-quality scholarships can prove far more valuable than a large one with the kitchen sink thrown in. One search firm, for instance, will not include any scholarship in its database that awards less than $1,000 per student. Another search firm, however, incorporates scholarships as small as $50 book awards.

The Least You Need to Know

- The best way to find a competent financial aid consultant is to seek out one who is recommended to you by friends or your high school or college counselors.

- Find out if the consultant is competent by asking lots of appropriate questions when you meet.

- Raise a red flag if you run across a consultant who wants a large, upfront advance before agreeing to start working on your kid's application.

- Beware of unethical advice, which can get you, not the consultant, into hot water later on.

- If you decide to pay for computer search services, first review the information about them in this chapter so you'll know what questions to ask.

Part 4

From Applications to Offers

Most, if not all, of us hate filling out forms. Filling out financial aid forms is complicated and even unsettling for some. You're required to disclose all kinds of personal information that will be reviewed by some unknown processor. Do you have a choice about it? Not when you apply for FAFSA (federal) funds, which is the first step in getting any type of financial aid.

The chapters in this part show you how to fill out the forms correctly so you can avoid having them rejected. Make no mistake about it: if you don't complete the forms properly, your application for financial aid will be rejected. In these chapters, you'll also learn what a financial aid offer looks like, how to compare offers, how to negotiate for more funds, and what to do if your application for aid is rejected.

What's Inside a Financial Aid Package?

In This Chapter

- ◆ Finding out what's in a financial aid package and how to dissect its parts
- ◆ Learning how to avoid an automatic rejection by submitting a properly completed form
- ◆ Seeing what a winning essay looks like, if your college requires you to write one
- ◆ Mastering the process of evaluating and comparing aid packages

Financial aid is supposed to go to students who need it the most as well as to the type of student a college or university is trying to attract. In reality, most of the money goes to those who best understand how to find and apply for it. Unfortunately, the process has become more complicated over the years. At first glance, it seems simple enough. You fill out a financial aid application (a FAFSA, covered in Chapter 19) and e-mail it to a central processing office, where the computers figure out how much your family can afford to pay for college.

If your family's contribution is short of the mark, the government and the college are supposed to help pay the difference. That's how the system is supposed to work. In reality, applying for college aid is one of the most complex and difficult financial processes you'll ever experience. In this chapter, we demystify much of the mystique in the financial aid system. Read what's here and you'll have a good chance of getting your fair share of the pie.

What You Should Know

You should *always* apply for federal and state financial aid. Most colleges and universities cannot consider applicants for their own scholarship and loan programs until the applicants have been denied aid from federal and state sources. The amount of a family's expected contribution will be affected by the cost of the college and the school's financial aid policies, so it's possible to receive more aid by attending an expensive school.

Always ask questions such as these about the school's financial aid policies:

◆ Is it the school's policy to do its best to fully meet the financial needs of all aid recipients? Or does the school meet only a portion of their need? Is aid provided after the first year?

◆ What is the average indebtedness of recent graduates? The answer will give you clues about the school's awarding policy.

◆ Is the school meeting the full need of all its financial aid applicants with loans, work-study programs, grants, and gifts?

Most colleges and universities offer their students money from institutional funds. Some awards are based on financial need and others on merit. Schools may offer special scholarships or grants to students with particular talents in, for example, music, drama, or journalism. Find out about the criteria the college uses to make these awards and the average amount awarded.

Action Plan

Apply for aid as early as possible. Deadlines vary, but your application for federal student aid can be sent anytime after January 1. An early application will help you get the best financial aid package possible.

When students submit aid applications, many colleges and universities will provide estimates of what their financial aid will be. Always ask for an estimate; having one means you won't have to guess at how much money you'll need from your own resources to finance your college education.

Your Expected Contribution

The school to which you're applying will prepare a financial aid package to help you meet your financial need. Financial need is the difference between your cost of attending school, including living expenses, and what you'll be expected to pay. Your aid package cannot exceed your financial need, but some forms of self-help assistance may be used to meet your expected family contribution (EFC).

The school will notify you of your aid package by sending you an award letter. You must maintain eligibility for the aid programs at the time your kid begins his first day of school in order to receive the awards. If you're selected for the verification process, you may be required to submit certain documentation, such as a copy of your family's IRS tax forms, prior to receiving any aid.

Shop Before You Buy

Once a college acknowledges a family's or student's "need," it's more than likely that its financial aid office will prepare a plan for meeting the cost of college. It may include a combination of grants, loans, scholarships, work-study, and payment programs. This "financial aid package" is designed in accordance with federal and college regulations.

The financial aid package may come in one of three forms: a firm offer or a plan subject to change based on additional information from the family, or one subject to changes in the college's financial aid program funding levels, which are dependent on institutional investments, donations, and gifts.

Shopping for a financial aid package and a college to attend should go hand in hand. Beginning early in your junior year of high school, start exploring which schools you would like to attend, and sign up for and take the standardized tests (the SAT, for example) required by most colleges for admission.

 Action Plan

Who's providing financial aid? Public institutions (26 percent), nonprofit institutions (35 percent), and profit institutions (39 percent).

Review as many college catalogues as possible. These catalogues are useful sources of information. Look at the course offerings, speak to counselors about specific programs offered in the areas you're interested in, check out the overall environment of the campus, and if at all possible, talk to graduates or to students attending those colleges.

Look closely at tuition and other related costs, but do not rule out a school because the price seems too high. More expensive schools often offer larger financial aid opportunities. The bottom line is not the total amount of aid, but the amount you will have to pay (or repay in the form of loans).

Take Care of the Paperwork

College catalogues will tell you how to apply for admission and financial aid. Each school will likely have a different application process, so follow the directions carefully when filling out the many forms. Many schools these days allow applicants to fill out their entire application package online. If that is the case and you choose to do so, make sure you have sufficient computer literacy to fill in the electronic forms accurately and to submit them accurately. It would be very distressing to learn from an institution that the application you "knew" had been electronically submitted was never received.

Action Plan

Your financial aid package is likely to include funds from the U.S. Department of Education, which provides 70 percent of all student financial assistance.

Most colleges will want to know about the student's and the family's financial background. This family financial statement will include questions about the family's annual income, debts, mortgage, financial holdings, and investments. Be prepared to answer very specific and personal questions. If you have a problem or question, contact the college's admissions or financial aid office.

When applying for financial aid, your kid may be expected to file as your dependent. If he or she has been employed, filed federal tax returns for two years, and had income of at least $4,000 a year, your son or daughter may be able to file as an independent student. If so, you cannot claim your student as a dependent on your tax return. By filing as an independent, however, your kid may become eligible for far more funds, in terms of grants and scholarships, than those you save by claiming him or her as a dependent.

Applicants who are 24 or older or who meet special circumstances may be expected to file as independents. It's important to note that students who try to apply as independents but who do not in fact meet the requirements are in violation of federal laws and may be subject to a fine. The forms that you fill out, at this point, represent the beginning of the process of determining whether your kid is eligible for financial aid. Get an early start.

Forms should be completed and submitted to the college as early as January of your kid's senior year in high school. Most schools reply in about one month, giving an analysis of your financial position and of what the school interprets as your "need." The initial reply may also include an offer of financial aid. The filing of these initial forms might not constitute an application for grants, scholarships, loans, or other forms of financial aid. Read the instructions carefully to see if there are further steps you must take.

What If They Require an Essay?

Some colleges require that the student submit an essay when applying for financial aid. Each college has different requirements, which will be spelled out in the application.

Writing the college application essay can be one of the most daunting parts of applying for financial aid. Both *what* you say and *how* you say it are important. You should expect to devote about one to two weeks to simply brainstorming ideas. Depending on your personality, brainstorming with friends can be helpful. However, only you can determine your best strategy. Here's an example of a winning essay:

Hiking to Understanding

Surrounded by thousands of stars, complete silence, and spectacular mountains, I stood atop New Hampshire's Presidential Range awestruck by nature's beauty. Immediately, I realized that I must dedicate my life to understanding the causes of the universe's beauty. In addition, the hike taught me several valuable lessons that will allow me to increase my understanding through scientific research.

Although the first few miles of the hike up Mt. Madison did not offer fantastic views, the vistas became spectacular once I climbed above the tree line. Immediately, I sensed that understanding the natural world parallels climbing a mountain. To reach my goal of total comprehension of natural phenomena, I realized that I must begin with knowledge that may be uninteresting by itself. However, this knowledge will form the foundation of an accurate view of the universe. Much like every step while hiking leads the hiker nearer the mountain peak, all knowledge leads the scientist nearer total understanding.

Above the tree line, the barrenness and silence of the hike taught me that individuals must have their own direction. All hikers know that they must carry complete maps to reach their destinations; they do not allow others to hold their maps for them. Similarly, surrounded only by mountaintops, sky, and silence, I recognized the need to remain individually focused on my life's goal of understanding the physical universe.

At the summit, the view of the surrounding mountain range was spectacular. The panorama offered a view of hills and smaller mountains. Some people during their lives climb many small hills. However, to have the most accurate view of the world, I must be dedicated to climbing the biggest mountains I can find. Too often people simply hike across a flat valley without ascending because they content themselves with the scenery. The mountain showed me that I cannot content myself with the scenery.

When night fell upon the summit, I stared at the slowly appearing stars until they completely filled the night sky. Despite the windy conditions and below-freezing temperatures, I could not tear myself away from the awe-inspiring beauty of the cosmos. Similarly, despite the frustration and difficulties inherent in scientific study, I cannot retreat from my goal of universal understanding.

When observing Saturn's rising, the Milky Way cloud, and the Presidio meteor shower, I simultaneously felt a great sense of insignificance and purpose. Obviously, earthly concerns are insignificant to the rest of the universe. However, I experienced the overriding need to understand the origins and causes of these phenomena. The hike also strengthened my resolve to climb the mountain of knowledge while still taking time to gaze at the wondrous scenery. Only then can the beauty of the universe and the study of science be purposefully united. Attaining this union is my lifelong goal.

What makes this a good essay? In the opening paragraph, the student who wrote the essay vividly captures the way in which the experience with nature drives his or her desire to learn more through scientific research. In the next two paragraphs, the student dynamically shows how the hike helped to focus his or her life goals of "understanding the physical universe." The rest of the essay reinforces the student's focused direction. If you were considering this student for admittance into your college based on the words in the essay, you could conclude that this person has a clear and definite sense of what he or she wants to achieve in life and will know how to get there.

HELP!
Refer to the "Scholarships, Grants, and Fellowships" section in Appendix B for more information on how to write an essay.

When Do You Get the Package?

Congratulations! You've taken the first step in the financial aid process, assuming you've completed and submitted a FAFSA form.

It will take three to four weeks for the feds to process your form before you'll receive a Student Aid Report (SAR) by mail. Keep these things in mind regarding the SAR:

HELP! If you're wondering, "Why do they ask that question?" see the "FAFSA Online" and "FAFSA Form" sections in Appendix B. The FAFSA site at www.FAFSA.gov answers questions and discusses how personal information should be reported.

- ◆ Your SAR will summarize the data that you reported on your application. Check the information carefully to make sure that it's accurate.

- ◆ Make sure that you keep a copy of the report and note the data release number (DRN) in the upper-right corner of the first page. You'll need it if you decide to apply for additional aid.

- ◆ If the information is complete, an expected family contribution (EFC) will be printed next to the DRN. The EFC is based on the income and expense information that you provide on the FAFSA, and your school will use it to award your financial aid.

The Award Letter

When your college has all the information it needs, it puts together an aid package that will probably include a combination of grants, loans, and work-study employment. Your award letter notifies you of what your aid package contains and gives you an idea of your probable cost of attendance. The letter also tells you how your need was determined, what your need turned out to be, and the composition of your financial aid package. If you're satisfied with the aid package, you sign the documents that come with the letter and return them to the school.

Even if you haven't decided which school to attend, you should keep your options open. If you're offered several aid packages, after you've evaluated them, move quickly to accept the best ones. Schools set response deadlines, and if you don't respond to your aid letter in time, you could miss out on the funds that have been offered to you.

Before you accept any award, read everything in the aid package carefully and compare what's being offered with other offers you've received. Some award statements may have special codes and terminology that are difficult for the layperson to discern. Make sure you understand the aid package clearly. If you find anything confusing or ambiguous, don't hesitate to call the financial aid office.

Consider the following as you evaluate the offer:

- ◆ Don't be fooled by big numbers. Pay special attention to how much of the offer is made up of grants versus loans.

- ◆ Note which schools are tossing in special awards for academic or athletic merit.

- ◆ If scholarships are offered, are they renewable? Or are they one-shot deals that go away at the end of the year?

- ◆ Break out your calculator and compare the loan interest rates offered by different lending institutions. Check out whether the loan payment requirements are especially onerous.

- ◆ If you're offered a work-study program, will you be able to juggle your study and school schedule with work so that your grades won't be affected?

Important: You may accept part of the award and reserve the right to appeal any objectionable parts.

Action Plan

Accepting an aid package does not obligate you to attend the school. This isn't to say that you should keep 10 colleges on a string—make your choices as quickly as possible so that the schools you don't choose can distribute the money to other students.

Eligibility

Eligibility for all federal grants, subsidized loans, and work-study programs is based on a need analysis. When you send your FAFSA to the feds for processing, they will determine your family's expected family contribution (EFC) and mail you a Student Aid Report (SAR) containing the results of their determination.

The Offer

The college financial aid need (level of eligibility) in this model is under $6,500 and may include self-help funds (from loans and/or work) and some gift money in the form of a grant or scholarship. The formula for calculating your need is as follows:

Example:

Total estimated cost of one year of college:	$12,000
Minus expected family contribution (EFC):	$7,000
Amount of demonstrated financial need:	**$5,000**

You don't have to wait for your Student Aid Report form or the even more elusive response from your chosen college. You can easily estimate your EFC ahead of time on the web at finaid.org.

After you know how much money colleges will expect you to shell out, you can start scrimping—or not scrimping. Simply enter your financial data next to the mathematical symbols in each box. Using the symbols, calculate figures until you reach the final boxes, which estimate the student's and parents' contributions (divided by the number of family members in college).

If you believe you have special circumstances that should be taken into account, such as a significant change in income from one year to the next, you should contact the financial aid administrator at the school(s) you're applying to. Sometimes emergencies arise that change one's ability to contribute to college expenses. Should this occur, notify the institution immediately. If the circumstances warrant it, the aid administrator has the authority to change your dependency status or to adjust the data used to calculate your EFC. Please note that the aid administrator's decision is final and cannot be appealed to the U.S. Department of Education.

> **Warning**
> Don't turn down an award just because there's something in it you don't like. You have the right to appeal any aspect of it that you object to.

The Least You Need to Know

- The financial aid package that you receive after you've filed the FAFSA discloses the amount of aid you qualify for.

- College catalogues explain any special requirements they might have for financial aid requests (such as essays).

- The dependent versus independent tax status of college-bound students will affect the amount of aid they're eligible to receive.

- Read and carefully compare all aid offers before you decide which ones to accept.

- You can accept part of an award and appeal any parts you find unacceptable.

Decoding the Forms

In This Chapter

- ◆ Finding out where you can get help completing the FAFSA form
- ◆ Learning how to complete many of the forms online to save time
- ◆ Knowing how to avoid making the most common mistakes when completing a FAFSA
- ◆ Getting line-by-line guidance on filling out the FAFSA

There are a number of ways to apply for federal financial aid, but it all starts with the Free Application for Federal Student Aid (FAFSA). This federal form is required for anyone applying for federal funds for college and is used by many institutions, but some schools require additional forms, so check with your school to determine exactly which forms it will want from you.

You can file electronically through your school, or you can use the Department of Education's FAFSA Express software. It runs on computers that use the Windows operating system and have a modem. Computers with the program set up and running can be found at many high schools, public libraries, and educational opportunity centers. You can download a copy yourself from the Department of Education's website at www.fafsa.ed.gov, or you can order the software on CD by calling 1-800-801-0576.

If you want to forego technology altogether, you can get a form that comes on old-fashioned paper by writing to:

Federal Student Aid Information Center
P.O. Box 84
Washington, D.C. 20044

Completing the FAFSA on the Web

The FAFSA is available online. While this offers an alternative to the paper application, students will need to sign and submit an original signature to fully complete the application process. If the student has a printer available, the software will print a copy of the applicant data and the signature page.

HELP!

For more information about the FAFSA form, which is used to apply for federal aid and public funds such as Pell Grants and Stafford or Perkins Loans, call 1-800-4-FEDAID (1-800-433-3243).

After receiving the student's FAFSA, the U.S. Department of Education (DOE) allows 14 days for the student's signature page to arrive. If the student does not send in a valid signature page within 14 days, the DOE will print a Student Aid Report (SAR) and request that the student and parent sign it and return it to the FAFSA processor. Once all appropriate signatures are sent to the FAFSA processor, the DOE can calculate your expected family contribution (EFC).

Warning

Approximately 2 to 3 weeks after the FAFSA is submitted, you should receive an official summary of the application called a Student Aid Report or SAR. It is your acknowledgment that your application has been received by the Federal Student Aid Program. If you do not receive a SAR within 4 to 5 weeks, contact the Federal Student Aid Program to find out why there is a delay.

FAFSA Express

Another way to send your FAFSA electronically is to connect to the FAFSA website at www.fafsa.us. When the main menu appears, select "Submit your FAFSA via the Web NOW" option that is on the left side of the menu and follow the instructions.

> **HELP!**
> Apply electronically or get a paper FAFSA from your high school, college, or local public library. To receive a paper copy by mail, call the Federal Student Aid Information Center at 1-800-433-3243. If you're unable to dial the toll-free number from your area, an alternate number is 319-337-5665. Call 1-800-801-0576 if you have technical questions about submitting an electronic FAFSA.

Sending FAFSA to College

If you want your application information sent to schools that you might attend, you have to enter the federal school codes for those schools on the FAFSA. If you don't know your schools' codes, contact the schools directly or visit their websites to obtain this information. Or you can use the FAFSA search function on the web to locate school codes.

You don't need to put something in every search box. Provide only the information that you know is accurate. For example, if you enter "Tech" without quotes in the School Name search box and then click the Next button, the results page will list schools with the word "Technical" in their name as well as technology and polytechnic schools. Spell out words like "Saint" and "Mount" in the School Name box instead of using common abbreviations like "St." and "Mt." and omit quotes. State names retain their common abbreviated form but do not have periods, as in AZ for Arizona.

Getting Started

You'll be asked to create a personal identification number (PIN) when you begin to fill out the FAFSA online. Your PIN is the identifier that lets you access personal information in various U.S. Department of Education systems. You must have a PIN to file an **online** renewal FAFSA or to make online corrections to your FAFSA.

Mistakes You Don't Want to Make

Many of the questions on the FAFSA seem too easy. Just because the form asks for information you can recite in your sleep doesn't mean you should take the form lightly when you fill it out. You'll soon discover that there are myriad lines requesting numbers, and they may require some digging. Applicants often make mistakes out of pure carelessness, which can cost them a rejected application. As you and your folks complete the application, double-check every entry you make.

Even when well-meaning parents fill out the FAFSA, they sometimes make simple mistakes such as entering one of their own Social Security numbers on the line where the form requests their kid's. The same parents, with stunning consistency, often go on to enter their own birth date instead of their kid's. It can be dangerous: when the application reviewer looks at the age listed on the form, he or she will probably classify the applicant as an adult independent student.

If you're a student filling out the FAFSA, some of the questions you'll be asked are as follows:

◆ **The marital status of your parents.** Legal separation isn't required for this question. If your parents are living apart for the purpose of eventually becoming divorced, answer the question "separated." Complete the rest of the form using information about the parent you live with or who provided the most financial support during the last 12 months.

◆ **The number of people in your family who will be attending an eligible college program at least half-time while you're attending college.** The more family members you can claim are in college, the more financial aid you're eligible to receive. If your parents are attending college, make sure you include them, even if their employer is paying for their tuition. Who pays for the tuition expenses is not relevant to this question.

◆ **Tax figures that were reported on your parents' income tax return.** Most parents use the long form, also known as the 1040 form. But if your parents make less than $50,000, they'll be eligible for more aid if they file the short form (either the 1040A or 1040EZ form). If they use the short form and net less than $50,000, they don't need to complete Section G on the FAFSA, which requires them to list assets.

◆ **Disclosure of any assets that are owned under the student's name.** You can generally qualify for more financial aid if you have minimal assets. For example, if your parents opened a savings account on your behalf when you were young and started to make generous deposits into the account to help fund your education, it could reduce the amount of aid you'll receive. Students are penalized 35 cents on the dollar for their assets. Parents are better off keeping the money in their own account.

HELP!

Students and parents can receive assistance in completing the FAFSA on the web by calling 1-800-801-0576.

Checklist for Filing the FAFSA

In this section, we cover the steps that you will want to check when filling out the FAFSA. Any errors that you make on this form can decrease your chances of getting financial aid.

- Find out and note the federal deadline for submitting your FAFSA.

- Find out and note your college's deadline for financial aid applications.

- Obtain the FAFSA form at your high school or college's financial aid office or online.

- You can contact your financial aid office to request additional materials that may be required by the U.S. Department of Education.

- If you're already in college and are applying for financial aid for the first time, request that your financial aid transcripts be sent to the college you're attending. You must do the same thing if you transfer to another college.

- Complete your taxes or an estimation of your taxes as soon as possible.

- If you're a dependent, make sure you have copies of your parents' tax returns so that you can record their tax information on your FAFSA.

- Submit your FAFSA online or through the mail prior to the deadline.

- Complete and submit any additional materials required by your college's financial aid office by its deadline date.

This chapter offered tips on how to fill out the FAFSA form and pointed out common mistakes to avoid. The bottom line is that the form is relatively easy to complete if you take your time and carefully check it over before you send it in. It can get complicated if you make a dumb mistake like entering a wrong Social Security number or birth date. Going through the correction process is a pain in the neck and will cost you valuable time, so check and double-check the form before you send it in.

The Least You Need to Know

- If you're applying for any form of federal financial aid for college, you must submit a FAFSA.

◆ If you prepare your FAFSA online, you'll improve the turnaround process and benefit from some of the automated editor features that have been built into the online systems.

◆ Do it right the first time. Make sure your FAFSA is error-free before you send it to the Department of Education.

20

What Does an Offer Look Like?

In This Chapter

- ◆ Learning how financial aid offers work
- ◆ Finding out what to look for to determine the best deal for you
- ◆ Considering the advantages and disadvantages of accepting a deal that includes work-study
- ◆ Finding the errors in your Student Aid Report that could have caused your rejection
- ◆ Getting financial aid in your own state even if you get rejected by the feds

Aid from the student financial assistance programs will be paid to you through the school. Your aid awards will almost always be paid to you by the time of your college's semester or quarter enrollment period.

A college will first use the aid to pay any tuition, fees, and room-and-board charges owed to the school. The remainder will be paid to you for your other living expenses. Aid funds might not be credited for books, supplies, and other school expenses unless you have given the college written authorization.

When you receive an award letter, all you need to do is indicate that you are accepting for the mid-year term. If you wait until the fall to apply for the spring or mid-year, you'll probably get only federal loan money and perhaps a Pell Grant. You may not get money from your state, your college, or private scholarships. Remember: you cannot apply for financial aid until after January 1 of the year of enrollment. Award letters are usually received four to six weeks from the date your application is received by the processor.

Figuring Out Your Best Deal

Celebrate when your award letters begin to arrive, but then be critical. Analyze each letter you receive and figure out what it's offering. Is it a good deal for you? Don't take the words in any award letter personally, because they usually aren't. Award letters are kicked out by computers programmed with specific criteria, and most college financial aid counselors don't have the time to review each letter before it's mailed. Also see Chapter 18 for more on award letters.

Because the letters are computer generated, you should go over yours with a fine-toothed comb.

◆ Look for your best deal among the various awards, and keep an eye out for reasons to appeal for even more aid.

> ### Warning
> Never burn your bridge with any college by not responding to their reward offerings. It could eliminate your chances of applying for financial aid with them in the future.

◆ To keep your options open, immediately accept each award by signing and returning each college's acceptance form, which will be attached to its award letter. Even if you later turn down a particular school and its award, you want to be sure that the school doesn't give your aid to someone else while you're making up your mind. Don't forget to date your letter. Something as simple as a missing date can delay the acceptance process.

◆ Compare competing offers, and when you finally decide which school and aid offer to accept, notify the financial aid offices of the rejected schools as quickly as possible. Your thoughtfulness allows them to offer the vacated admission seat to another student.

What if the offer you finally select contains a job or a college work-study position, and you don't want to be employed during your first year when you're uncertain how much time you'll need for studies? Can you turn down work opportunities and accept only the gift aid? Will you make a big mistake if you do?

Consider these factors:

- Employers hiring new graduates consistently favor applicants who gained work or internship experience during their college years.

- Although different institutions have varying policies about part-time employment while in college, conventional wisdom says that a job will not interfere with your college education as long as you don't toil beyond 14 hours a week.

- Working improves your time-management skills, which will prove to be a blessing throughout your entire life.

- If you're a marginal student who needs every free hour to study, perhaps you shouldn't work during your undergraduate years. But whether you're a marginal student or a good one, if you do decide to turn down the work portion of the award, the financial aid counselor may bounce the money-gap ball back into your court, leaving you on your own to solve the shortage of funds.

What Does an Award Letter Look Like?

The following letter is an example of a typical college's offer of a scholarship or gift aid. Note that the scholarship becomes part of a financial aid offer that will either come with the letter or follow at a later date. (See our example of the financial aid award offer following the letter.) The award becomes firm once you sign and return the obligatory paperwork.

Dear John Doe Student:

Congratulations on your acceptance to ABC College. We are delighted to inform you that you have been awarded a merit scholarship in recognition of your high school academic achievements. You will receive a $4,000 academic scholarship for the current academic year beginning September 15, 20XX.

This scholarship will automatically renew for an additional three years provided that you are a full-time student and maintain a 3.0 cumulative grade-point average. You are therefore eligible to receive a total award of $16,000 over the next four years. Since you have applied for financial assistance, we have attached a copy of your Financial Aid Award Offer to this letter.

If you have any questions, please feel free to contact our Financial Aid Office at your convenience. We look forward to meeting you at the college reception for new students in September.

Yours Truly,

Jane Doe, Ph.D.
President of ABC College

Financial Aid Award Offer

Estimated Expenses

Resident Tuition & Fees	$3,600
Room & Board	$5,400
Books & Supplies	$700
Estimated Personal Expenses	$2,100
Transportation	$850
Medical	$1,200
Total Estimated Expenses	$13,850

Financial Aid

Scholarships	$4,000
Pell Grant	$1,500
College Grant	$1,000
Parent PLUS Loan	$850
Subsidized Stafford Loan	$6,500
Total Financial Aid	**$13,850**

Many Americans believe that financing their children's education is beyond their ability and that the increasing cost of going to college will make higher education unafford-able for all but the wealthy. For most families, financing a college education is a major undertaking. However, as we hope you learn from this chapter, financial aid can be *the* major factor in helping your kid go to college.

What If Your Application Is Rejected?

When you receive your Student Aid Report (SAR), it will be accompanied by a letter explaining what you need to do to receive aid. However, the letter may say, "Based on the information you provided, it appears that you are not eligible to receive a Federal Pell Grant at this time," or some other qualifying statement. Unfortunately, many students interpret this to mean that they are not eligible for any financial aid, which may not be the case. This is not what the statement means.

The correct interpretation of the SAR statement used in this example is that you cannot receive aid out of the Federal Pell Grant money bucket. You may be eligible to receive aid from the state, the college you plan to attend, the federal government (in the form of a subsidized loan), or some other source. You just won't get money from the Pell program. Before you start looking for other sources, review every line on your SAR for errors that may have caused the rejection, such as a wrong birth date or Social Security number.

Check Your SAR

If your aid application is rejected, the first thing to do is go through the following steps to see if you made any errors on your SAR that may have been responsible for the rejection:

1. Start with your Social Security number. If it's wrong on your SAR, you'll be missing in action in a college's financial aid office because that's how they keep track of you. If the office can't find you on its computer, you don't exist. In addition, this could create suspicion among the college administrators since a Social Security number is an absolutely essential piece of information in the application process.

2. Make sure that all colleges you potentially want to attend are listed on your SAR. If a school is missing, call the Federal Student Aid Information Center (319-337-5665) to report the omission. The center will ask for your SAR's PIN number, so have it ready. If a school doesn't get your SAR, you won't be able to get any money from that school.

> **Warning**
>
> Whether you communicate in writing or by phone with federal, state, or private individuals about the status of your financial aid application, always have your PIN number available. This is the one number that they use to tie everything together on your behalf. If you don't have it, they won't know how to proceed.

3. Check to see how you answered this question on the SAR: "Do you have a Bachelor's degree?" Many students think that a high school diploma is a Bachelor's degree. If you already have a Bachelor's degree, you automatically become ineligible for Federal Pell Grants, Federal Supplemental Educational Opportunity Grants, and most state grants. That's a mistake you don't want to make!

Don't Lose Aid Because You Won't Respond

Colleges are required by federal laws to verify by random sample the eligibility of 30 percent of the students filing for aid. You may receive a standard verification form that requires you to verify things such as the number of family members listed as household residents on your FAFSA, to declare any untaxed income, and to submit copies of income tax returns and W-2 statements.

Many families have a problem with this process because they believe they are being audited in the same way that the IRS audits taxes. This is not so. A verification is not an audit. It's an effort by the college to verify the integrity of the financial aid process. If you did make an error when you completed your FAFSA, you could be eligible for more aid or less. You can't ignore a verification request; it's the law. If you do fail to respond to the verification request, you are no longer eligible for any kind of financial aid.

College financial aid offices can't award federal money to students who have previously attended a postsecondary institution until they receive a financial aid transcript (FAT) from the previous college(s). The FAT is required even if you never received financial aid in the past. Unfortunately, many students think they took care of this issue when they requested that academic transcripts be sent in. An academic transcript reports grades, whereas a financial aid transcript reports money or shows that you didn't get any money if that was the case. Your aid will be held up until your FAT(s) is received. Accepting or rejecting college offers is not as casual as accepting or rejecting social invitations.

Don't Get Rejected Because You Didn't Renew

Pick up financial aid packets from your college's financial aid office to continue or initiate awards for next year. Many colleges do initiate aid renewals automatically, but they are not responsible if your renewal slips through the cracks.

The federal government sends out renewal FAFSA forms to remind you that it's time to start the process all over again. Renewal FAFSA forms are available on the web. Just because you didn't get federal money or a state scholarship one year does not mean you'll be ineligible forever. Eligibility can boomerang as a result of changes in income, parents' marital status, revisions in assets and savings, fresh money in a college's resources, or changes in the federal budget.

Action Plan

In many respects, state financial aid agencies play a more significant role in the financial aid award process than the federal government does. That's because the feds collect most of the aid money through the country's tax system and then distribute the funds to the states for dispersal.

Ask Your State for Help

Don't forget to apply to your state for financial aid, even if your request for federal financial aid was denied. Some states are more generous than the federal government in determining whether you qualify. Federal awards are based on your adjusted gross income, which includes some notice of your assets. In contrast, some states award aid based solely on taxable income, without regard to your assets.

In some states you can own an estate, a condominium in Aspen, and several Ferrari sports cars, and still qualify for thousands of state aid dollars, as long as your taxable income falls within state limits. Many states award a full ride, including room and board, to in-state students who participate in the federal free-lunch program. State rules vary significantly from state to state.

Don't overlook inquiring about possible aid awards at your state's student financial aid agency. If the application forms for student aid aren't available at your high school or college financial aid office, contact your state's Department of Education. States vary in the information they need to decide whether you're eligible for aid. Some will use the data from the FAFSA; others require a supplemental aid form that is processed by the state's Department of Education.

Look to your state (and its financial aid office, listed in Appendix C) to play a substantial role in supporting your education. Tuition at state schools is much less costly when you're a state resident. The difference between being an in-state student and an out-of-state student can be as much as $10,000 or more per year.

Establishing State Residency

Although establishing residency in a state used to be fairly simple, rules have tightened over the years. Many states now require that parents pay state taxes and have a primary residence in the state. If you have your eye on another state's public university, find out what it takes to become a resident. It may be worth your while to drop out of college for a year, work in that state, and pay state taxes to establish residency. Make sure you know exactly what you must do to meet all the residency rules of the state.

Action Plan

If you snag aid from one state but attend school in another, you'll have to contact your state financial aid agency to learn the ropes. Addresses of all state aid offices are listed by state in Appendix C.

Residency requirements vary not only from state to state but often from school to school within a state. Don't count on starting school during the year that you're establishing your residency. Community colleges, which are usually under the jurisdiction of the county in which they're located, add another requirement for residency. Not only do you have to live in the state, you also have to live in the school's county to be eligible for its residency tuition.

When you contact a state's financial aid agency, don't expect the agency to know details about state residency requirements, which may change from year to year. Most will only know about their state's financial aid programs, but they should be able to tell you whom to contact to verify residency requirements. The most common answer will be the college's financial aid office.

Different institutions in a state require more or fewer years to establish residency. Always verify residency requirements with the college you hope to attend.

The Least You Need to Know

- Know how to compare the various offers you'll get to determine which offer is right for you.

- Understand how offers will be presented to you so that you'll know in advance what to expect.

- Always verify the accuracy of the information on your SAR. An error can prevent you from getting financial aid.

- Just because you got turned down for one type of aid doesn't mean you're ineligible for another type.

- Don't overlook applying for financial aid in your home state. States can be more generous than the feds.

Negotiating a Better Offer

In This Chapter

♦ Gaining a clear understanding of what you need to do to negotiate a better offer

♦ Knowing how to research information that will strengthen your negotiating position

♦ Learning how to write an appeal letter that will improve your negotiating position

It's the spring of your high school senior year, and you're looking forward to entering college next fall. You know you're about to embark on some of the best years of your life, but the next couple of months are pure torture as you await answers from the colleges you applied to for financial aid. You live from one mailbox visit to the next, ready for good news or, perish the thought, dreading bad news.

Suddenly, the envelopes start to arrive. At first glance, you're happy to see that they're all thick acceptance letters rather than thin rejection notes. Everything is going great until you get a reduced offer from your favorite college. Good grief, their financial aid award is $4,000 short of the amount you need to make it through the year. What went wrong, when all of the other colleges are meeting your financial needs? What are your options?

Before you think about giving up, don't give up. The $4,000 shortfall in this example doesn't spell doom for your chances of attending your preferred college. If you organize a good negotiation strategy, you may be able to get the college to come up with the additional $4,000 you need. We'll show you how to do it in this chapter.

Check Your Appeal Options

Most colleges have an appeals process if a student believes he or she has not received a fair financial aid package. If you're not sure about the process at the college you're interested in, call their financial aid office and ask. If the college doesn't offer an appeals process, then don't waste your time. They won't listen. If the school does have one, make sure you understand exactly what you need to do to submit an appeal. You're going to get only one shot at it.

> **Action Plan**
>
> If parents are paying most of a student's college expenses, then they're the ones who should conduct the negotiations.

One of the surest ways to mount and win an appeal is to provide a legitimate, sincere reason for needing additional aid. Base all of your negotiation on facts.

Call attention to information on your application that the aid counselor may have overlooked. Always remember that the amount you requested was based on the information provided in your application. If the facts haven't changed, you can conclude that the financial aid office's interpretation of the facts is different from yours. Try to get them to tell you why they arrived at a lower number than you requested. Is there something they may have overlooked?

How to Negotiate for More Aid

Parents more often than their kids conduct financial aid negotiations because they usually are more experienced with negotiating. Even though thousands of dollars may be at stake, in this chapter we address most of our suggestions to students rather than their parents since it is likely younger people need practice in the dynamics of negotiating.

Colleges usually state their appeals policies in their award letters. When you're in doubt about their negotiation policy, call the financial aid office and ask if the school has an award appeals process. There is no reason to provide them with your name at this point. You need to plan your strategy without wondering whether the institution is already researching your case. Colleges that suggest they have a "take it or leave it" policy tend to be elite, top-tier schools. They take a rigid stance because they can afford to. Institutions like Harvard enjoy a surplus of academically qualified applicants whose parents are able and willing to pay cash without a quibble.

Fortunately for most students, such schools are few. Most will be willing to consider negotiating an award offer. The great majority of colleges in the United States are pressured to enroll students at discounted tuitions in order to accommodate students' financial needs when possible. Most have estimated the size of the incoming freshman class and do not want to be shortchanged. If you provide good reasons for needing more aid, most colleges and universities will consider negotiating their financial aid award offers.

Remember: Base your negotiation on facts by presenting new information or by calling attention to factors that the financial aid counselor may have overlooked. It's the surest way to win an appeal. Be considerate and understanding. The world of academia does not operate flawlessly, and the counselor with whom you discuss the matter has an obligation to treat you fairly.

If new facts that warrant additional funding according to college policy can't be found, make an emotional appeal. Admit that you have a financial problem, and ask the counselor to help you find more aid. Make a supreme effort to make your appeal face to face. If that's not possible, write your appeal in a letter, being as specific and articulate as you can. Wait five business days and follow up with a telephone call if you have not heard from the office.

Negotiating Tactics

Initiating an award appeal that pays off is easier when you can bring up new or overlooked information.

As a negotiating strategy, mention a less pressing reason for seeking more aid. Save your major reasons for if the initial one does not work.

> **Warning**
>
> Determining whether or not a sudden change in your financial situation is a major or minor circumstance can be a subjective call. What you consider to be a minor financial circumstance may be considered major by government financial aid agencies. If you're not sure about how a change in your financial situation will affect your request for additional aid, seek out the advice of your high school counselor.

What would be considered a minor special circumstance? Childcare expenses or health insurance for students no longer covered by parental health plans are just two examples. A special circumstance you've forgotten to mention in your original aid request need not be earth-shattering in importance, just reasonable enough to give you a graceful entry into the appeals process.

Get Ready to Bargain

Colleges with large endowments have a better chance of meeting students' financial needs. They have more flexibility because they have more free money to work with. This is a well-kept secret within the collegiate financial aid industry but one you should know about.

A college's financial aid process doesn't always result in the best deal for every student. Often the first offer is less than you need and less than the college can deliver. It's not uncommon for colleges to submit their "low-ball" offer first, even though they know you're eligible for more. The rationale is that the offer can always be raised if that's what it takes to get you enrolled. If you bite and accept the initial offer, the college is richer and you are poorer.

Before you launch an appeal, it pays to determine the school's formulas in granting aid awards. A computer probably ground out your award letter with standard programming based on a specific blueprint. If you give financial aid counselors new information that makes the parameters inappropriate, the college routinely modifies awards.

Get the Facts

Anyone who has tried to get more of anything knows that detailed information is needed to negotiate a better deal. A look at the underlying factors and family complexities that impact the aid process can influence your request for more aid. However, your special circumstance will not be taken into consideration in your aid appeal if you fail to include documentation. Think of your appeal as a day in court. Your role is to present sufficient evidence to win your case. Here are some ideas that will help you get started:

- ◆ **Printed information.** The college's catalogue or letters to you are the first stops on your research trail. Make sure you understand exactly what they explain specifically and what are simply guidelines. If you try to ask for something they don't offer, you're wasting your time.

◆ **Personal inquiries.** Ask an admissions counselor at the college what percentage of demonstrated need the college has historically granted. Is your offer above or below their average offer? Admissions personnel should have this information because these numbers have to be reported to the federal government.

◆ **College websites.** The college's website may contain information not in its catalogue.

Action Plan

Learn all you can about the college financial aid system. Use that knowledge to prepare a plan for how you will pay for college. Simply demonstrating that you've done your homework may reflect positively on your appeal. However, if you don't know something, ask questions.

◆ **Network your friends.** Reaching out for information from your network of friends and acquaintances who currently attend or who have graduated from the college may provide data you need to pull the financial aid system's levers.

◆ **Discover trends.** Is their enrollment down? If it is, a college may be vulnerable. They need students. When a college is receiving a smaller-than-usual number of student applications, they may be frantic to add students, which will improve your odds of negotiating a better offer. Do not mention this to the college representative, however. It will suggest opportunism rather than a desire to get a good education.

◆ **Loss of job.** If you or your spouse lost your job after you applied for financial aid, you have a strong case for an appeal.

◆ **Diversion of income.** One of your parents is suddenly confined to a nursing home, and your family has to pay the extra expenses that are not covered by Medicare. That's the same money you planned to use for college.

Getting Started

All colleges and universities are required by state and federal laws to disclose an incredible amount of information about the disbursement of financial aid funds to their students. This is "public domain" information. If you run into an official who tries to tell you that the information is confidential, gently remind him or her of this fact. If the official still refuses to give you the information you desire, report the incident to someone with a higher level of authority.

♦ **Know the rules.** If something has changed in your family that can influence your eligibility for more aid, contact your financial aid counselor immediately.

♦ **Develop a winning strategy.** Always negotiate for a better financial aid offer in a professional, respectful manner.

Compare Tuition Costs

Check the college's fees against those of other comparable colleges. For example, if a school's tuition is 20 percent higher than at other institutions in the state, it may have room to offer you a lower tuition rate. Colleges with high tuition rates usually have more room to negotiate discounted tuitions. With the exception of elite colleges, colleges that charge high tuition generally have more room to negotiate than those with lower tuition rates.

Incorporate research into your appeal, noting that state colleges charge about a quarter of what it costs to go to private colleges. Ask whether there is possibly enough margin in the tuition structure to offer you more consideration. By researching tuition at somewhat similar colleges, you can refine your comparison even more by citing the tuition at "comparable private schools." Publications such as *The Chronicle of Higher Education* regularly publish charts that categorize comparable colleges. You can find copies of this journal (the bible of the workings of academia) at most public libraries.

Making Your Appeal

Does your research reveal that a large proportion of the college's student population is receiving financial aid? If so, the college's financial aid professionals are sensitive to the institution's high costs and the students' needs. This college is probably more student oriented than others with lower student-aid support. They should be receptive to aid appeals. Pull out all the stops with a factual and heartfelt appeal.

Competitive Offers

Although most colleges don't like to admit it, they are like any other business operating in a competitive world.

If you've received a better offer elsewhere, politely tell the financial aid officer about the other offer and ask whether it can be matched. This negotiating strategy assumes, of course, that all things being equal, you would rather go to this institution.

Let the financial aid officer know up front that you are set on attending his or her institution, not the one that made the better aid offer. This demonstrates that you're not playing the officer's college against another one.

When dealing with financial aid officers, be sensitive to how you leverage one financial aid offer against another. Always use tact and polite language, or the college representative will simply tell you to take the other offer. But if you're sincere and fair with them, they may come back and match, or even improve upon, a competing offer.

Warning

If a college refuses to increase its award offering, don't threaten to go elsewhere. Simply state that another college is one of your options, and you may have to call it to their attention. But do it in a professional manner. If your tone is threatening, you won't be given any options at all!

Do They Need Students?

All colleges desperately want to start off their school year at full enrollment. Anything less amounts to lost revenue that they can never recover. Find out from the admissions office what the enrollment figures have been over the past year. Then ask what their full enrollment figure is. If they're below the full enrollment figure, you might suggest to the aid officer that an enrolled student paying at a reduced rate is a lot better than not having that student at all. However, use this tactic with discretion. Don't raise this point if you think it will be insulting to the person with whom you're negotiating. Remember that he or she is supposed to be a professional and doesn't need a lecture about the economics of schooling.

Add Diversity

Whether you offer new facts or make a personal plea, when your research shows that your intended alma mater is blessed with endowment money, think diversity.

Emphasize your geographical desirability as an enrichment to other students on campus. For example, an East Coast campus may want to attract students from the West Coast who can share their experiences with the school's predominately East Coast student

Getting Started

Colleges are pressured by the feds, states, their alumni, faculty members, and even their students to increase minority student representation on campus. In the United States, a fourth of college students come from minority groups. We cover this subject in more detail in Chapter 13.

population. Liberally use the word "diversity" in your appeal. Say you can contribute to the cultural richness of the student body, but that you need help with the level of your financial aid.

If you're planning on attending an out-of-state college, you may have some additional room to negotiate. Most colleges actively recruit out-of-state students to add diversity. Some colleges even go so far as to embrace students from particular regions of the country. Check with the admissions office and see if you can find out what areas make them raise an eyebrow. Emphasize how you can contribute to the cultural richness of the student body.

Changes in Your Family

The amount of financial aid that you're offered is based on a standard formula that is applied to all families and is based on the FAFSA forms they've submitted. However, your family may be constructed in a way that is not covered in the standard formula. If so, bring up the issues when you start negotiating. Remember, however, that it's not enough to just mention special circumstances. You must be able to prove them.

- ◆ Is a new sibling coming on the scene? A central element in calculating your eligibility for aid is the number of household members. Count all your family's children who will receive more than half their support from your parents. Your appeal may be based on your mother being pregnant, which adds another mouth to feed during your school year.

- ◆ The college financial aid counselor has no way of knowing if one of your parents is planning to retire during your school year. If one is, explain the retirement benefits, which usually are lower than employment earnings. Ask the counselor to calculate a new aid base.

- ◆ If you and your parents are financially overextended, have a bad credit history, or for other reasons can't borrow more college money, share that fact with your financial aid counselor. The counselor may be sympathetic and award you more aid funds.

- ◆ Do other members of your family have uncommon costs that take away from your family's ability to pay the assessed expected family contribution? Perhaps a brother or sister is required to attend a private school because of learning disabilities, for example. The FAFSA form has no place to record such information.

Loss of Income

Social Security benefits for children are reduced at age 18 or on the last day of high school attendance, whichever date comes last. Usually this occurs after the FAFSA documents are filed, which means that the college's financial aid counselor has no way of knowing that your Social Security benefits are lower and your family will have fewer dollars for college.

Another income cut that your financial aid officer won't know about unless you announce it during your appeal occurs when parents split up. Most noncustodial divorced or separated parents are not obligated to contribute child support after the child's eighteenth birthday. If your parents get divorced or separated after you've submitted your financial aid form, all income and asset information must be corrected. Tell your financial aid counselor how much child support and home maintenance support your custodial parent expects to receive from the other.

In any event, your expected family contribution is likely to be lower under the new arrangement. The divorce or separation must have legally taken place. It can't be an action that may happen in the future. If the parent who was a wage earner during the base year of income is no longer able to contribute, your income drops and aid rises.

If your aid package requires you to complete an internship, co-op education assignment, or other program that requires an automobile for transportation, ask for additional aid funding to cover the related expenses. If you're enrolled in college for credit and must complete a study-abroad program to fulfill curriculum requirements, you may be able to get more money for transportation and living expenses abroad.

> **Action Plan**
>
> Don't be afraid to confide in financial aid officers. Their official mission in life is to help you get the aid you deserve. Ask them what steps you and/or your family need to take to increase your eligibility for financial aid. They'll give you an honest answer.

Prove Everything on Your Appeals Claim

Prove everything you are claiming by supplying documents such as retirement letters, canceled checks, medical bills, divorce papers, employment termination notices, and Social Security notifications. Many parents are caught in the "sandwich" generation, providing for their children and for their own aged parents. Costs of providing parent care in a home or a nursing facility can be overwhelming. Use such expenses in an appeal because the higher the expense, the greater your demonstrated need will be.

Example of an Appeal Letter

Many avenues for appeal are open once you begin to think through the college's issues and your family's fiscal fitness. Learn to write a good appeal letter. Even when you plan a face-to-face encounter in the financial aid office, take with you a letter stating the facts and give it to the financial aid officer at the beginning of the conversation so that he or she will have an official letter documenting your position.

Here is a sample letter written by a mother on behalf of her son:

> To: Office of Student Financial Aid
> Subject: Letter of Appeal, Loss of Income
> Re: John Doe (Student) SSN 000-000-000
>
> This is to inform you of my loss of income for the current year. I understand that students' financial aid is based on their demonstrated need, which involves the parents' and students' income and assets for the calendar base year.
>
> My income has been reduced significantly. I have enclosed a copy of a letter from the International Medical Group that confirms that my service agreement with them will not be renewed. On my current income tax return, I listed the income from this contract at $21,000. My income, however, will consist only of my full-time job, which pays me a salary of $58,000. This is a tremendous decrease from the original $79,000.
>
> I hope you can consider this new and disheartening information in a reevaluation of my son's financial need. John and I would greatly appreciate it.
>
> Thank you for what you have already done for John; our family would treasure any additional assistance toward John's education as he pays his own way at Adelphi University.
>
> Sincerely yours,
> (Mother of Student)

Negotiating is an important skill to learn because a college financial aid counselor has the authority to use professional judgment on a case-by-case basis. Third-party scholarships prove the point. The average award package is made up of 60 percent self-help funds from loans and/or jobs and 40 percent gift funds. When you receive an outside (third-party) scholarship, some colleges want to take back their gift aid in like proportion, leaving you with the same amount of debt. Good negotiation may modify that disappointment by persuading the college to reduce each type of assistance in the award letter by 50 percent of the outside award.

For example, suppose you win an outside scholarship of $2,000, and your award letter specifies a $3,500 loan and a $2,000 grant. You want your loan reduced by $1,000 and your grant reduced by $1,000. You don't want your grant reduced by $2,000, leaving you with $3,500 to pay off. If you don't fully understand the financial aid formulas and

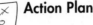

Action Plan

A special circumstance you forgot to mention in your original financial aid request need not be earth-shattering as long as it is true and can help you negotiate more aid.

don't know what's going on, you're going to pay thousands of dollars more than you really have to. In any industry—and education is, among other things, an industry—business managers try to get you to pay as much as possible, while you try to pay as little as possible.

After you've gathered all of your facts and made your appeal, ask whether it isn't better to have a student paying at a reduced rate than to have an empty seat in the classroom or an empty bed in the dorm. You need not mention an anemic enrollment, because school managers are well aware of the problem.

The Least You Need to Know

- Before you negotiate for more aid, first get all the facts about the colleges you're interested in.

- To negotiate a better financial aid option for yourself, support your position with adequate documentation.

- Consider every possible basis for making an appeal for more aid.

Part 5

Okay, You're Accepted and You Have Aid: Now What?

These chapters are full of advice for students who are about to begin a very challenging and exciting period of their lives. We give you ideas on how to earn while you learn and how to find work that can be a learning experience as well as a way to pay for some of your college expenses. We also give you tips and strategies for how to cut your living costs, and we tell you about the many innovative tuition plans that can trim your college bills.

22

Opportunities Are Everywhere

In This Chapter

◆ Learning how to make your own breaks by searching for money in the right places

◆ Discovering ways to grow your own opportunities by promoting your-self

◆ If you have to work, getting a job where you can learn and get a head start in your chosen field

This chapter focuses on individual actions you can take and choices you can make to ensure you'll continue to get financial aid. Perhaps none of our suggestions is startling news, but consider them timely reminders to act now to increase your chances for success in the future. Always remember that a good education and money go hand in hand. Unless you're one of the select few who win an all-expenses-paid four-year tour, you will need to pay for your own education.

Maintain Good Grades

Granted, other criteria can win you college funds, but a stellar grade-point average can make you eligible for many financial aid programs. If you're not the type to blank out under pressure, test your mettle for money in academic competitions. Many merit-based scholarships consider test scores.

Look for Contest Money

You'd never guess that acting in school plays, painting still-life oils, or other hobbies could be a cash cow in your future. The interests you develop during your high school years can indicate potential that may lead to scholarship dollars. Millions of contest dollars go out sponsors' doors each year to students who have honed their hobbies, activities, and talents to a competitive level. For example:

♦ **Communicative arts scholarships.** Sponsored by the Educational Theater Association/International Thespian Society, these scholarships require a 2.7 or better GPA to enter the competition. However, your academic record doesn't count in the judging; your high school activities do. Selection criteria include, for example, an acting award you received for your performance in a high school play, and how well you do in an interview with the judges. Each year about 10 scholarships worth $1,000 each are awarded.

> **Action Plan**
>
> Like it or not, getting good grades is the single best way to qualify for all kinds of financial aid programs that simply are not available to students who have poor grades.

♦ **Graphic arts scholarships.** The National Scholarship Trust Fund offers this award program to high school and college undergraduate students who wish to pursue a career in graphic communications. Finalists are selected based on SAT/PSAT scores, transcripts, recommendation letters, and their demonstrated ability to apply graphic arts. Over 160 awards ranging between $500 and $4,000 go to winners annually.

♦ *Guideposts* **Youth Writing Contest.** *Guideposts* magazine sponsors this nonfiction contest, which pays better than what many professional writers earn for similar work. High school juniors and seniors are invited to write about their most memorable and inspiring true experience. The judges assess the originality of the writing, the sincerity of the author, and the values of kindness, spirituality, fairness, and morality expressed in the essay. Over 30 students annually win between $1,000 and $4,000.

Community Service Payoffs

While you are doing good works through volunteering in community service activities, you can simultaneously build career skills and leadership experience. Not only that, many community service organizations return the favor with scholarships toward your education.

For example:

♦ **Soroptimist Foundation's Regional Youth Citizenship Awards.** Scholarships are given on the basis of service, dependability, leadership, and sense of purpose. Academic criteria (grades, test scores) aren't considered. The foundation gives over 50 scholarships annually worth several hundred dollars each, plus one $2,000 scholarship to study abroad.

♦ **The Tylenol Scholarship Fund.** These scholarships recognize students who provide leadership in community and school activities. What counts? School awards, academic record, activities, and honors are considered. Each year, 500 scholarships worth $1,000 each and 10 awards of $10,000 each are passed to upstanding students.

♦ **The U.S. Senate Youth Program.** Sponsored by the William Randolph Hearst Foundation, this program acknowledges students who have been elected to leadership offices in their high school student governments. It distributes over 100 scholarships annually.

♦ **The Toyota Community Scholars Program.** Each year 100 students who show dedication to community service as well as academic leadership receive these awards. The program was launched in 1997 with a bang of big bucks: the four-year awards range from $10,000 to $20,000. To be considered, you must have initiated, or been actively involved in, a service program that addresses a school or community need.

These and other lesser-known opportunities can be researched at your local library. Ask the librarian for a directory that provides information for individual grants or scholarships, and note the ones you may qualify for.

Get an Inside Job

A part-time student assistant job in the college's financial aid office can expose you to knowledge about how awards are determined and how students win them. By working in this office, you can pick up valuable information you may otherwise miss. Your close contact with the office's inner workings can unveil the perfect financial aid for you.

> **Action Plan**
>
> Have you ever heard the expression "It's *who* you know, not *what* you know"? This trite but true statement reflects reality. If you can land a job in an influential office on campus, you'll have access to important decision makers who can offer you all kinds of assistance, both during and after your college years.

Working in the alumni office offers you opportunities to find out which alumni are helping financially strapped students complete their education. As an added benefit, if you can get to know the alums who do the talent scouting for their companies, they may offer you summertime work or even a job after you graduate. Many alumni have emotional attachments to their alma mater and are quite eager to help out students. It often gives them a sense of satisfaction and maintains a psychological relationship to the institution. Think of older people when they recall their college years. They often talk about them with great fondness. For some, college was a highlight in their life. By helping an eager student, it helps reconnect alumni to something they have felt passionate about.

Find a Sponsor

Are you a pleasant, sincere, hardworking, and deserving person? If so, you may be able to find a sponsor who will pay part or all of your way through college. If you think such generosity doesn't happen, it does: multimillionaire Eugene Lang is well known for backing not just a single student but entire groups of students with his "I Have a Dream Project." Lang began with sixth-grade students at a Harlem school in New York City, promising that he'd pay for their college education if they graduated from high school. His program has since expanded into 20 cities. A practical and generous man, when he speaks in front of audiences about the need to help the younger generation achieve its educational goals, he usually ends his presentation with the words, "Keep your applause. Just send us money for our deserving students."

If you want to find your own sponsor, you can't be shy about asking teachers, friends, professionals, and community leaders to recommend potential sponsors. Ask whether they'll introduce you to people who might undertake a sponsorship. An Arizona State University student turned his sponsor search into an art by passing out self-marketing packets containing his transcript, personal profile, and recommendation letters to potential sponsors. As a result of his effort, he received several private scholarships. If you're lucky enough to find a sponsor, be sure to keep in touch with him or her, always say "thank you," and send him or her any positive notices about you in the college paper or any honors you may garner during your college career.

Market Yourself

Are you as good as you say you are? Well, of course you are. Many organizations are willing to sponsor a deserving student if the idea is properly presented to them. You might ask the question, "Why would they be willing to do that?" Most if not all organizations are keenly interested in maintaining an excellent public relations image. It's good for business. Offering a deserving student a scholarship is a great way to build their public profile through media coverage. They'll get free press releases, radio and local television exposure, plus lots of other free publicity that money can't buy.

You can't be shy when you start looking for a sponsor:

1. Start by asking your friends and teachers for names of business and community leaders whom you might talk to.

2. Call every major business that is, say, within a 25-mile radius of where you live and ask to speak to their public relations officer. Most public corporations have one. Smaller organizations may not have a public relations department, but they will usually have someone in their marketing department covering that function.

3. Many sponsor prospects will ask you to send a letter to formalize your request. Prepare a dynamite one-page letter that states what you're looking for (college sponsors, for example) and why you need the money (to pay for college tuition, for example) and gives a brief summary of your qualifications. Before you send out the letter, show it to as many friends and associates as you can to get their opinions and ideas for improvement. Ask your high school English teacher to proofread it. See if your local newspaper will help you find sponsors or maybe even publish the letter in one of its daily editions.

4. Sponsors enjoy learning about the success of young people. They take personal pride in knowing that someone they had faith in contributed something positive to their institution. Such things are very important and indeed are things that "money can't buy."

Employment Program Opportunities

One way to reduce college costs is by working. Several studies indicate that most students who work between 10 and 20 hours a week actually do better academically. It is not unrealistic for a student to expect to earn between $2,000 and $4,000 during the school year. Summer employment can easily add $2,000 or more to your college funds. If you multiply that sum by the four years you'll spend in college, you can make a substantial contribution to your school expenses. That's money you will not have to borrow and your parents will not have to find.

Action Plan

Your school's financial aid director, career counselor, and placement officer can all help you find the right job. Seek assistance and advice from the counselors in these offices and use the resources they can provide.

When you think of working while you're going to college, look at it not only as an opportunity to earn a portion of your college expenses, but also as an integral part of your long-term career plan and a way of becoming educated in the ways of the world. Your college employment can be career-related or even lead to a job after graduation.

Federal, state, institutional, and private work programs are available to college students both on and off campus. Investigate all sources covered in this section. Some work arrangements offer free room and board in exchange for household help. Ask your school counselor whether this type of arrangement is available. Try to find part-time employment that is career related; it will add to your job credentials when you graduate. You'll gain valuable experience and earn money at the same time.

Work Experience Programs

Some colleges and universities award credits based on work experience, thereby reducing the number of courses and credits you're normally required to take to graduate. Other institutions provide "co-op" programs in which a student receives coursework credit by being an intern in a "real-life" environment (see the section later in this chapter for more information). Check with your college's admissions office for further information on what you need to qualify. If you qualify, not only will you save on college fees, but by graduating early, you'll start earning money faster than you had originally planned.

Federal Work-Study Program

One of the most popular work programs is the Federal Work-Study Program (FWS), which provides employment on and off campus for students in postsecondary institutions. Although the subject has been discussed throughout the book, it is worthy of additional coverage because, quite frankly, it's a great program.

Work-study is a need-based program that's administered through colleges' financial aid offices. The federal government pays 50 percent of the student's wage for private sector jobs and 70 percent if the student is employed on campus. Jobs are available to undergraduate, vocational, and graduate students. The dollar-earning amount allocated to students may vary from year to year based on funding levels. It is also limited by the students' financial needs, based on the amount of their allocations as determined by their financial aid directors.

Federal work-study funds are awarded along with other financial aid. To be considered for this program, students must be U.S. citizens or permanent residents and must be enrolled or accepted for enrollment at an eligible institution. They must also maintain satisfactory academic progress to stay in the program.

Such programs need not be dull. Some work-study positions have included working as a cameraperson, carpenter, writer, designer, and interviewer.

Student Educational Employment Program (SEEP)

The federal government's Student Educational Employment Program (SEEP) employs students through its internship and fellowship programs. Opportunities are available at both the high school and college levels.

High school students should seek the advice of their guidance counselors about employment opportunities under the Junior Fellowship Program (described later in this chapter).

College students may obtain information about SEEP federal internship opportunities from their school's financial aid office or employment office.

Action Plan

When you make your rounds of the various offices on campus looking for a part-time job, always ask the person you are talking to if he or she knows of any job opportunities in other campus offices. Make sure you get the name of the person you should talk to.

Institutional Employment Programs

Many schools have placement offices that help students find employment. Almost all schools have personnel offices that hire students to work on campus. These institutional employment programs are not need-based. Check with your college's personnel director for more information.

Most colleges and universities offer tuition reduction or waiver programs to their employees. Under this plan, school employees and their dependents receive either full tuition remission or partial reductions in tuition costs. These programs are not need-based and provide an excellent opportunity to attend college at practically no cost.

Private Sector Employment Programs

In private sector employment programs, local businesses hire students. Check with your school's placement office for a list of off-campus employment opportunities. Try to find a job in your major field of interest. You may be able to turn part-time student work into a full-time job after graduation.

Resident Adviser (RA) Program

A resident adviser program provides financial assistance to students in the form of reduced tuition or room and board costs in exchange for working in residence halls. The RA may live in the dorm and be responsible for students on his or her floor. Interested students should contact the dean of students on their campus for further information and eligibility requirements.

State Work-Study Programs

Many states provide employment to residents under state-sponsored work-study programs. These employment programs are administered by state organizations and follow most of the federal eligibility requirements. Check with your school's financial aid office or state Department of Education (see Appendix C) for further details.

Employer Tuition Plans

Employer tuition plans are the great unclaimed area of financial aid, with billions of dollars available to millions of employees. Unfortunately, many companies won't hire you for a good position until you have your college degree. But if you're willing to attend college part-time and start in a low-paying position, you'll find many companies that will pay for your higher education. Although directories of employers who have such programs are commercially available, they tend to be expensive; however, you can find these sources in the public library or through your school library or guidance counselor. When you consider how high college expenses can be, an employer that is willing to pay you a salary *and* help pay for college is offering you a great deal!

Companies that pay employees' education bills want to make sure they'll get their money's worth, so tuition plans generally come with a hitch or two. The most important hitch: You have to make the grade—that means a B or better. This is the way it works:

◆ In reimbursement plans, you put up the tuition money and get the money back only when you've successfully completed the course—in some programs, "successfully" means a grade of B or better.

◆ In other programs the company pays up front, but if you drop out or flunk you have to reimburse your employer.

◆ You may have to prove that the courses you're taking are somehow related to your work. Still, an understanding boss can help you to frame your educational needs in such a way that they fit in nicely with company objectives.

Cooperative Education

Each year over 250,000 college students work at "co-op" jobs. Over 1,000 colleges and universities participate in cooperative education.

In co-op education, you combine your time in the classroom with practical experience on the job. It's something for everyone: You the student get a job, and the employer gets a highly motivated workforce. Co-op programs not only put money in your pocket, they also provide you with job contacts for the future. You get an opportunity to work in your chosen profession to make sure you're on the right career track. There's another significant advantage to consider. The firm for which you're working will often offer you a job after you graduate.

Getting Started

According to the U.S. Department of Education, 40 percent of co-op students continue working for their co-op employer after graduation. Another 40 percent find work in fields directly related to their co-op assignments. Add up those percentages, and it's pretty easy to see that working as a co-op employee can help you get the job you want after you graduate.

How Does the Co-Op Program Work?

Cooperative education programs allow students to alternate between working full- or part-time and studying full- or part-time. If you're in the program, it generally takes five years to complete a four-year Bachelor's degree. Although the federal government remains the largest employer, many businesses participate in cooperative education programs. These programs are not based on financial need and are available to undergraduate and graduate students, and students seeking professional degrees. The most important and attractive feature of employment programs is matching the students' future career plans with relevant employment.

HELP!

For further information about cooperative programs, call or write the National Commission for Cooperative Education, 360 Huntington Ave. 384 CP, Boston, MA 02115-5096 or call 617-373-3770.

Who's in the Program?

Roughly 1,000 colleges have cooperative programs of some kind or another; in some schools, virtually all the students are in cooperative education programs. Some 50,000 employers hire on the co-op plan, including the largest provider of co-op jobs, the federal government, which hires nearly 12,000 students each year.

The Program Takes Time

Co-oping takes time. Whether you alternate semesters of work and study or work part time while attending school, the programs usually require five years. Still, 200,000 students each year seem to feel the time is worth spending.

Get Help from Associates

If you've decided on a career to pursue, you may be eligible for aid from the professional association that specializes in your career field. If you want to get financial aid in your chosen career field and want to get a head start, you should consider attending a college that has a cooperative education program. But if your school doesn't provide such programs, you might be able to get help from the appropriate professional association.

There is an industry group for almost every trade and profession, from dental hygienists to hotel managers to wine experts. Most of this money gravitates toward schools that have well-regarded programs in that particular field (engineering at MIT, for example).

For suggestions on the strongest schools in your career area, you should consult guides such as *Rugg's Recommendations on the Colleges*. Still, many professional groups offer "portable" scholarships that are not tied to a particular school.

> **Action Plan**
>
> There are literally thousands of professional and trade associations worldwide, and we could not include all of them in Appendix B. Associations are easy to find in reference books such as *Gale's Encyclopedia of Associations*. The book is available at the research desks of most libraries and provides descriptions, addresses, and telephone numbers of national and international associations. Once you have the addresses, write and request their scholarship information. Include a stamped, self-addressed envelope to ensure a prompt response. If you learn who the appropriate contact person is, call a week or so after you send your letter. A personal touch is often a great motivator in our high-tech world that often cuts down on personal interaction.

Junior Fellowship Program

The Junior Fellowship Program resembles cooperative education but has some important differences. For one, your boss is the federal government. For another, you join the program in high school, but you don't begin working until you're in college, when you work during term breaks. You apply to the program through your high school guidance counselor. If your high school guidance counselor doesn't have information on the Junior Fellowship Program, write to: Director, Office of Personnel Management, 1900 E St. NW, Washington, D.C. 20415. Unlike cooperative education, which is offered only through certain schools, junior fellows can attend any college of their choice.

To qualify for a Junior Fellowship, you must have very good grades and prove financial need. Although the program is limited to 5,000 participants at a time, it historically has had vacancies. What a great opportunity!

Other Sources of Aid

Many organizations provide scholarships, though the amounts are usually small. If you've already received all you're going to get from the major sources of financial aid—federal government, state government, and college programs—you may be able to get additional money from sources you haven't considered previously.

Your Local Government

Your city, county, or even school district may have scholarship money or other special programs for you to consider. Although many of these programs amount to only a few hundred dollars, some do offer significant funds, possibly even in the thousands. Finding them involves investigative work on your part since relatively few of them make their way into the big scholarship databases. But you can find them: your high school or college financial aid officer should have some information about local government programs. Your local chamber of commerce may have leads as well. Watch for scholarships in the news section of your local newspaper or in a national newspaper such as *USA Today*.

Unions

Many unions offer college grants for the education of their members' children. Information about some of these programs can be found in the scholarship roster or listing that you can get by contacting the union's business office. However, for more specific information, contact the union's main office. Union programs are offered by both the national organization and the local chapters.

HELP!

You can get some college aid information from local unions. To get the fullest picture, write for the comprehensive AFL-CIO guide, which is free to members: *AFL-CIO Guide to Union Sponsored Scholarships, Awards, and Student Financial Aid*; Department of Publications, AFL-CIO; 815 16th St. NW; Washington, D.C. 20006; or call 202-637-5000.

Community Organizations

Don't forget to check into scholarship programs available from community organizations. An example is the American Legion, which offers a multitude of awards, including a $2,000 scholarship at the national level called the American Legion Auxiliary National President's Scholarship for children of veterans. It also sponsors a National High School Oratorical Contest with a grand prize of $16,000, plus many $1,000 scholarships. The American Legion is most valuable to students who are the children of veterans, but any student can apply.

(HELP!) For the most up-to-date listing of the American Legion's programs and contests, you should send $3 to get a copy of Need a Lift? Write to: The American Legion National Emblem Sales, P.O. Box 1050, Indianapolis, IN 46206; or call 317-630-1200.

Religious Organizations

Churches and religious organizations also grant money to college-bound students. Groups like the Aid Association for Lutherans host contests and offer scholarships and loans. Find these groups through your church's business office. You can find the addresses and telephone numbers of most religious organizations listed in *Gale Encyclopedia of Associations*.

You may run into a few restrictions, however, including a requirement of religious study or attendance at a church-sponsored school.

The Least You Need to Know

♦ Maintaining good grades is a prerequisite to getting ahead.

♦ Contest money is everywhere if you know where to find it—and it's fun to go after!

♦ Employer tuition plans are plentiful and a great way to mix learning with earning.

♦ Community service programs and part-time jobs can give you an early start on your career, along with making you some extra money.

Cost-Cutting Strategies

In This Chapter

- ◆ Discovering how to cram four years of college into three and save a bundle
- ◆ Finding out how you can get a head start by taking college classes while you're still in high school
- ◆ Knowing why you should consider two-year colleges first before you leap into a four-year institution
- ◆ Uncovering innovative tuition plans you never knew existed
- ◆ Learning how to cut unnecessary expenditures

If you're looking for ways to reduce the costs of going to college, then this chapter was written for you. We identify a variety of approaches that you can try to substantially reduce college expenses. Some of these strategies require a financial or academic about-face, whereas others call for minor changes in lifestyle.

The Three-Year Program

Most students finish college in four or five years, but a lot of students are now graduating in three years. How? In a three-year program, you carry 20 hours per semester and attend college in the summer to pick up the extra credits you need.

Even though you'll have extra bills for summer tuition, your total tab will fall well below what you'd pay over four years. You'll also enter the job market ahead of your class, which gives you an extra year of income and seniority over your classmates. That might even be enough to get that sports car you've always wanted!

However, a three-year program is not for everyone, and the decision to enter one has nothing to do with intelligence or even motivation. Often it just boils down to the personal "style" of the individual. If you're thinking about a three-year program, ask friends and counselors whether they think it's the right way to go for you.

Action Plan

Although colleges don't like to talk about it, most of them can offer you a three-year degree program if you'll just ask. Their three-year programs are not widely publicized because colleges would rather collect tuition and fees from you for four years. You owe it to yourself to ask the admissions office what you would need to do to graduate in three years, even if you plan to graduate in four. You'll at least know what your options are if you need to reduce costs.

Think of how much money you could save if you graduated in three years instead of the normal four. For example, if you're spending $12,000 a year for college, you could potentially save $12,000 by cutting a year out of the program. How do you do that? A typical full-time student must earn 15 credits per semester, or 120 total semester credits, to graduate in four years. To complete 120 credits in three years, you would need to earn 20 credits per semester (120 ÷ 6 semesters). That's a heavy load, and not all students would be able to accommodate it. However, if you're willing to go to summer school, you can earn the additional 10 credits you need without changing your 15-credit workload.

Take College Classes in High School

Another way to decrease college costs, if your high school allows it, is to attend a nearby college and take up to 12 semester hours of college-level courses before you graduate from high school. You may have to meet certain selection criteria, and your options may be few because your hours of attendance would be limited, but you'd have a head start on college.

Getting Started _____

The International Baccalaureate (IB) Program offers college preparatory courses at some high schools in the United States and abroad. If you are interested in participating in the program, visit its website at www.ibo.org.

Advanced Programs

The College Board has agreements with more than half of the nation's colleges to honor its Advanced Placement (AP) exams, which give credit to students who take AP classes and pass the exams. More than 150,000 students take AP exams annually, and two-thirds of them pass. Needless to say, if you pass an AP exam, you save on tuition by not having to take that course. More than 10,000 students last year tested out of all freshman year courses.

The College Board offers over 20 tests covering English, calculus, American history, European history, biology, chemistry, physics, computer science, art, music, and many languages.

HELP! _____

You can take the AP tests through your school for a fee of $50 per test. Some high schools will subsidize the costs of the tests for students. Contact the College Board, 45 Columbus Ave., New York, NY 10023 for more information. If you want a free booklet explaining testing-out procedures, order _Information for Candidates_ from College-Level Examination Programs, The College Board, Box 886, New York, NY 10101.

Go to a Community College First

Two-year community colleges are among the best buys in higher education. Their courses cost about half of those at four-year institutions, and the first two years of general education courses are roughly the same, no matter where you attend college. When money's a problem, beginning your studies at a community college is your best solution.

Action Plan _____

Magazines such as _Money_ and _US News & World Report_ annually publish reports on bargain schools where tuitions are modestly priced and the educational standards are high.

Warning

If you take courses at a community or junior college, make sure in advance that the four-year college(s) of your choice will allow you to transfer every credit you earn. The college admissions office can provide you with this information.

In addition, when you transfer to a four-year institution and eventually graduate with your Bachelor's degree, your diploma will bear the name of the more prestigious four-year college.

If you can manage to afford doubling up on your community college classes and going to summer school, you could be out in a little over a year. When you join a four-year institution as a junior, you'll be a half-year ahead of the game and will have saved a bundle on tuition.

Most community colleges coordinate their curricula with four-year institutions, so check that your four-year college or university will accept the credits you earn at a two-year institution before you sign up for specific classes. Contact an admissions counselor at the four-year institution you plan to attend and ask which community college courses will transfer for full credit. Get the counselor to sign the agreed-upon list of transferable courses for your records. Don't accept an oral agreement that certain courses will transfer for credit; you could find out when the time comes that the college won't give you the credits and the college official you talked to has no recollection of the conversation.

Co-Op Your Way Through

Wouldn't you like to gain some hands-on experience so that, upon graduation, you won't be considered a rookie when you enter the job market? Cooperative education programs allow you to gain "real-world" experience as you complete your education. You study some and work some throughout your college years, earning money as you go. Over a thousand colleges operate cooperative education programs in which students typically take about five years to complete an undergraduate degree.

One of the problems that new college graduates face when they search for a job is their lack of work-related experience. The first question a potential employer is likely to ask is, "Do you have any experience that will qualify you for this job?" Wouldn't it be great to answer with a resounding "Yes!" You could do that if you become a co-op student, alternating semesters of study with work for a company in your chosen field—and you get paid for it!

The potential downside is that you will probably take longer to graduate because of your work schedule, but at least you'll have some money to help pay for college. Many students earn enough money through cooperative programs to pay for all of their college expenses. When you graduate, you may even have an opportunity to go to work full-time for the company that you've been working for. You'll get to know each other, and after you graduate, if there's a job in your field, you could be in.

HELP!

If you need more information about cooperative education programs, you can order a free copy of *A College Guide to Cooperative Education* from the National Commission for College Education, 360 Huntington Ave., Boston, MA 02115. You can also check out work-study programs at www.collegefundingonline.com.

Earn While You Learn

Yet another moneysaving option is to work, either part-time or full-time, while taking a partial or full load of classes. Granted, working part-time and attending college full-time can take all your energy and time, but more students than ever have to double up on work and school to pay for everything. And literally thousands of students, many of them parents, do it the other way around: They hold full-time jobs and attend school part-time. The University of Phoenix is exclusively a night program school—with many course offerings provided online—and has over 50,000 students enrolled.

Challenge Classes

Many colleges will release you from having to take required course work if you can prove you know the material well enough not to need the course. It's known as taking challenge classes. Ask at your college admissions office about obtaining credits for passing tests without taking courses or about receiving credits by providing relevant proof of life experience. For example, let's say you have worked with computers either in a job or in the military. You could escape a required $600 computer competency course, or you could take the school's computer competency exam. If you pass (test out), that's one less course you'll have to take.

Innovative Tuition Plans

Most colleges and universities increase their tuition fees annually, and because they are the benevolent souls they are, they're always looking for ways to take the sting out of paying tuition. Most offer programs that allow you to pay on monthly plans rather than having to pay in one or two annual lump sums. There are as many programs as there are colleges, and programs at different schools that sound similar may have significant differences between them.

Colleges are also getting smarter about giving students and their families more ways to pay for college. Many schools now allow tuition to be paid through regular electronic fund transfers from bank accounts or through credit cards.

Installment Plans

More colleges now allow students to pay tuition on an installment plan. Installment plans can run monthly, two payments per semester, or they can be stretched out over several years. Check with your school for more details.

Banks and private companies are also working with colleges to create installment-plan tuition programs. Many colleges manage their own installment plans, while others have private companies run them. Contact your state's guaranty agency (listed in Appendix B) for more information on college installment plans.

Prepayment Discounts

Schools like having money in the bank, and the sooner they get it the better. They can earn interest on it and invest it, which is why they're willing to make attractive offers to you in return for getting money quickly.

Many colleges offer prepayment discounts on tuition for students who pay their entire tuition in a single upfront payment. It can save you in excess of 10 percent. Contact your state's guaranty agency (see Appendix B) for more information about advanced tuition plans.

HELP!

There's no substitute for getting the full description of all of your school's programs from the school itself. However, if you need a broad survey of programs available at different schools, you can order a chart-filled paperback from College Check Mate, Octameron Associates, P.O. Box 2748, Alexandria, VA 22301.

Leadership Programs

Some schools offer tuition breaks for students who are willing to take leadership roles in student organizations, such as student government. Participation in student referral programs and a variety of other programs may also produce discounts. Check to see whether the college you want to attend offers any of the programs in the following sections.

Legacy Programs

Some schools reduce tuition for children of alumni in programs referred to as legacy programs. Many schools now offer discounts for referring other family members to their "sacred halls." They may also give a tuition discount for convincing a friend to attend.

Test-the-Waters Programs

Some colleges are letting prospective students test the waters during their first semester by attending at a discount to see whether they like the place.

Tuition-Matching Programs

Some private schools now offer tuition-matching programs in which they match the tuition of local public schools to stay competitive. Many states offer scholarship programs to equalize tuition rates between public and private schools.

Moral Obligation Scholarships

Moral obligation scholarships are gifts from the school to you that are granted with a "moral obligation" to pay back the money after graduation. These programs pack a potent tax benefit. Since the payback is technically construed to be a gift to the school, the student gets a tax deduction. Colleges are constantly thinking up new, headline-grabbing alternatives. Keep an eye on the media for gift programs that pop up unexpectedly.

You can expect moral obligation scholarships to be scrutinized by the IRS. In fact, any program that promises to help people save money for college at low tax rates will attract the attention of the IRS. So it's important to check with the school to see whether the IRS has ruled that the school's "too good to be true" program really is too good to be true.

> **Warning**
>
> It's a fact of life! Many of the great college tuition plans end up running afoul of the IRS sooner or later. One previously popular method of saving for college—shifting assets to children in order to take advantage of lower taxation rates for parents—has been all but eliminated by changes in the tax laws. The IRS is already taking a hard look at long-term tuition prepayment plans.

Wait Before You Buy Anything

College students tend to use shopping sprees to escape from study sessions. Somehow they get their parents to spring for new wardrobes and dorm supplies, forgetting that materialistic trappings rarely improve higher learning. As a rule of thumb, don't buy anything until you know you really need it.

Before you buy any clothes, first see what your classmates are wearing. A surprising amount of money is wasted on new clothes that never leave a student's closet. The best wardrobe investments you'll make during college will be the cap and gown you'll wear during the graduation ceremony and the suits you'll need for job interviews.

Watch for student discounts on everything you buy. Put every practical need—like clothes, bookshelves, and computer equipment—on a wish list. Share it with relatives near major holidays.

> **Action Plan**
>
> Watch for student discounts. When you walk into any store, automatically ask, "Do you offer student discounts?" If the answer is yes, just take out your college ID card when you are ready to make your purchases. Many stores don't advertise their student rates. Others may offer you a one-time discount. You can also ask when items you're interested in buying will be going on sale.
>
> Schedule your travel well in advance. That's when you'll find the discounted tickets, not two days before Thanksgiving.

If you're as preoccupied as most students, you may think that take-out food costs the same as grocery store food. Those $5 fast-food meals twice a day add up to $300 per month!

If you buy food items, buy in bulk whenever it makes sense. Bulk items are typically 25 percent cheaper per weight of measure than their smaller counterpart packages. Use an electric frying pan to fix your own meals. Save your money and get a small refrigerator that will fit under your desk; then you can buy soft drinks and healthy snacks in larger quantities from a supermarket and store them in the fridge, or split bulk purchases between your friends.

Buy Used Books

Try not to choke when you discover what it costs to buy a single textbook these days. Some of the ways you can cut textbook costs are ...

- ◆ Always buy used books if you can; this can save you as much as 50 to 75 percent of the new-book price. Look for bookstores on or off campus that sell used books. If the store wants you to buy the "new" book because it has just been "revised," ask your instructor whether the revisions are significant enough to warrant buying new as opposed to used.

- ◆ Check with your friends who are taking the same classes you'll be taking next semester. They might be interested in selling or trading their books when they've finished their courses.

- ◆ College bookstores often have exclusives on assigned textbooks, so try to buy their used ones. They can cost half of what you'd pay for a comparable new textbook.

- ◆ Don't automatically believe the book list you're told to get for your classes. Talk to your instructor before the first day of class and find out which books you should have first, then take it from there. You may not really need all the books on the instructor's list. If you do, you may have plenty of extra time to shop for a good used one.

- ◆ If a course requires an especially pricey book and you don't expect to ever read it again after the final, see whether you can check it out of the library.

- ◆ Sell or trade any textbooks you don't plan to use again.

- ◆ Concerned about the rising cost of college textbooks, some states have enacted legislation to assure that students get the best deals. Virginia, for example, passed a state law requiring teachers to announce their textbook titles no later than one month before classes start. This gives students time to shop around for the best deals.

Travel Smart

Some college towns are so well designed that you won't need a car most of the time. A friend's car, a bus, a subway, or a taxi can come in handy occasionally (and there's always walking), but the expense of purchasing, maintaining, parking, fueling, and paying insurance on your own car can eat up sparse dollars. Consider saving your money for your dream car after you graduate. Schedule your trips home when a friend is driving to your area so that you can share expenses.

Other Cost-Cutting, Moneymaking Strategies

Allow your mind to wander as you think about all of the possible ways you can save money or even make money when you go to college. We cover some ideas for you to think about in this section.

Live at Home

Some families save money by having their kid live at home. This option saves dorm or apartment rental costs and looks very attractive on the surface. Yet there are a number of hidden costs to staying at home, one of which is losing out on a major part of the college social experience by not being at the center of things. Another is commuting costs, which can cut into the money that living at home saves.

Another reason why staying at home is more expensive than it looks is food. Students who live at home won't be able to eat all their meals at home because of the odd hours they keep. They'll spend more money in campus-area eateries, while students in dorms buy a relatively inexpensive meal plan or keep small refrigerators stocked. Meal plans may be available for nondormers and are worth looking into.

Barter for Deals

Some colleges will make a deal with parents to exchange a wide range of gifts for tuition. Almost any type of property can be swapped under such a program. Even if the college can't use what you have to offer, it might resell it; this occurs often when corporations make odd gifts to schools, such as yachts, for tax purposes. Ask about a barter program at the college.

Find Your Own Deal

Instead of relying on your college for a moderate- to low-paying work-study job, why not strike out on your own? If you have an entrepreneurial flair, you might find that a little investment of time and effort can provide you with a comfortable living while you're in school and after. Michael Dell began selling computers while he was in college—now his company sells millions of dollars worth of computers each year under the Dell Computer logo.

Become a Part-Time Salesperson

You might find plenty of sales opportunities among your fellow students. Students know students. Find an item that they need, buy it in bulk and offer it to others at a profitable price. This same strategy is responsible for the proliferation of student-run services that offer discounts on everything from computer diskettes to lecture notes.

Learn to think like an entrepreneur, and you'll come up with all kinds of creative ways to finance your college education.

The clearinghouse for information on entrepreneurship in college is the Association of College Entrepreneurs, a group founded by college students in 1983 that now numbers more than 4,500 members. It's based in Wichita, Kansas, but has local chapters nationwide. Even your own campus business department might have people who can give you pointers: more than 600 schools across the nation have entrepreneurship courses.

In conclusion, I sincerely hope that my book lived up to your expectations. It should be clear to you by now that there are literally thousands of financial aid opportunities out there for you and your kids to explore. And, with the current political environment favoring enhanced educational programs, you can look forward to increased funding for all financial aid programs.

The trick is to know how to find and apply for financial aid. If you check out the comprehensive appendixes in this book, they'll help you seek out and find the opportunities that are right for you. There are also hundreds of websites that cover every aspect of the financial aid process. All of the major ones are listed in Appendix B. I wish you the best of luck in your search for the financial aid your family deserves.

The Least You Need to Know

◆ There are all kinds of ways to graduate from college in three years instead of four.

◆ Working part-time while you're in school offers you an opportunity to gain "real world" working experience and earn some money at the same time.

◆ The myriad innovative tuition plans are well worth looking into.

◆ If you watch how you spend your money, you can save a bundle.

Glossary of Financial Aid Terms

AA   An Associate of Arts degree. Can be earned at most two-year colleges.

AAMC   American Association of Medical Colleges.

AAS   An Associate of Applied Science degree. Can be earned at some two-year colleges.

academic year   A measure of academic work to be accomplished by a student. A school defines its own academic year, but federal statutes and regulations set minimum standards to determine federal financial aid awards.

accounting period   The time period for which financial records are maintained and at the end of which financial statements are prepared.

accrual basis   Type of accounting under which income is recorded when earned.

accrued interest   Interest on a loan that is not paid during the period of the loan but accumulates and is paid in installments at a later time.

achievement tests   Tests required by some colleges to measure student achievement in specific areas of study, such as English, math, or science.

ACT test   Published by American College Testing to measure a student's ability in math, verbal comprehension, and problem solving. Usually taken by students during their junior or senior year of high school.

adjusted gross income (AGI)   Taxable income after all allowable tax deductions are made.

advanced placement (AP) test   Test used to earn credit for college subjects studied in high school and scored on a scale from 1 to 5 (the best possible score).

aid package   A combination of financial aid (scholarships, grants, loans, and/or work-study) determined by the financial aid office of a college or university. See also *award letter*.

Alternative Loan Program (ALP)   Used to supplement the funds students need to attend college.

amortization   The process of gradually repaying a loan over an extended period of time through periodic installments of principal and interest.

annual percentage rate (APR)   The total annual cost of a loan, including all fees and interest.

Armed Services Vocational Aptitude Battery (ASVAB)   A test designed to measure aptitude in 10 different career-related skills.

asset protection   A sum subtracted from a family's total assets when determining the expected family contribution to college costs.

assets   The amount a family has in savings and investments. This includes savings and checking accounts, a business, a farm or other real estate, and stocks, bonds, and trust funds.

award   A specific amount of financial assistance to pay for education costs, offered to a student through one or more financial aid programs.

award adjustment or revision   An action by a financial aid office resulting in an increase, decrease, program-source substitution, or cancellation of a student's financial aid award.

award letter   An official document issued by a financial aid office listing all the financial aid awarded to the student. See also *aid package*.

award year   An award year begins on July 1 of one year and extends to June 30 of the next year.

BA and BS   Bachelor of Arts degree and Bachelor of Science degree, respectively.

base year   For need-analysis purposes, the base year is the calendar year preceding the award year.

borrower   Anyone who obtains money from a lender. The borrower signs a promissory note, which serves as the formal promise to repay the loan.

business office   The school office responsible for an institution's financial accounting, including Title IV aid program activity. The office disburses financial aid award payments to students.

campus-based programs   Financial aid programs administered by the university. The federal government provides the university with a fixed annual allocation.

cancellation of a loan   Nullifying the borrower's obligation to repay all or a designated portion of the principal and interest on a student loan upon the condition that the borrower has met specific requirements. It may also be referred to as *discharge*.

CASHE   See *College Aid Sources for Higher Education*.

certificate   Award granted for the successful completion of a sub-baccalaureate program of studies.

citizen eligibility requirements   To be eligible for federal student aid, the borrower must be either a U.S. citizen, a U.S. national (including natives of American Samoa or Swain's Island), or a U.S. permanent resident (who has an I-151, I-551, or I-551C [Alien Registration Card]).

claim   An application made to a guarantor for payment of an insured student loan because of loss of payment due to borrower's death, total and permanent disability, bankruptcy, default, or school closure.

COA   See *cost of attendance*.

coborrower   A person who signs a promissory note in addition to the borrower and is responsible for the obligation if the borrower does not pay.

collateral   Something of value pledged as security for a loan. Banks do not require collateral for all loans.

college   A postsecondary school that offers general or liberal arts education, usually leading to an Associate's, Bachelor's, Master's, Doctor's, or first professional degree. Junior colleges and community colleges are included under this terminology.

College Aid Sources for Higher Education (CASHE)   A free financial aid service offered by Sallie Mae.

College Board   A nonprofit membership organization of colleges, secondary schools, and education associations that administers the SATs and runs the College Scholarship Service.

College Scholarship Service   An arm of the College Board and one of the agencies that processes financial aid information and applications.

commercial bank   An institution whose primary function is making loans to businesses.

consolidation loan   Combines several loans into one loan. This sometimes results in a lower interest rate, for example when a consumer loan is used to pay off high-interest credit card balances.

cosigner   A second creditworthy party who signs a promissory note with a borrower who does not have collateral or a good credit history.

cost of attendance (COA)   The total cost of attending a postsecondary institution for one academic year.

data release number (DRN)   A number appearing on the Student Aid Report (SAR) in the upper-right corner of the first page (next to the printed EFC). It is needed to identify the appropriate FAFSA data for release to schools beyond the six (maximum) listed by the student in the original FAFSA submission.

default   Failure to repay a loan in accordance with the terms of the promissory note. Default can also occur if a student fails to submit a request for deferment or discharge (cancellation) in a timely manner.

deferment of a loan   A period of postponement during which the repayment of loan principal is suspended because the borrower meets one or more deferment requirements established by law.

deferred interest   Interest payments that are delayed while a borrower is not gainfully employed.

delinquency   You are delinquent if your payment is not received by the due date. Delinquencies greater than 30 days are reported to national credit bureaus.

dependency status   The degree to which the student is expected to have access to parental financial resources. An independent student is one who is 24 years old.

dependent student   A student who, under federal criteria, is considered to be financially dependent on his or her parents or guardians. Most full-time students are considered dependent until they are 24 years old.

Direct Loan   See *Federal Direct Loan Program*.

disbursement   The release of loan funds to a school for delivery to the borrower. Disbursements are usually made in equal multiple installments copayable to the borrower and the school.

discharge   The release of a borrower from the obligation to repay his or her loan.

disclosure statement   A statement of the total cost and amount of a loan, including the interest rate and any additional finance charges.

Doctor's degree   An earned degree carrying the title of "Doctor." The Doctor of Philosophy degree (Ph.D.) is the highest academic degree and requires mastery within a field of knowledge and demonstrated ability to perform scholarly research. Other doctorates are awarded for fulfilling specialized requirements in professional fields such as education (Ed.D.), musical arts (D.M.A.), business administration (D.B.A.), and engineering (D.Eng. or D.E.S.).

DRN   See *data release number*.

due diligence   The requirement by the federal government that a lender, holder, or servicer exercise reasonable care and diligence in the making, servicing, and collection of insured federal student loans in order to retain the insurance (against default claims) of the loans.

early action   A college admissions program that consists of earlier deadlines and notification dates than for the regular admissions process, but it does not require a binding commitment from the student to enroll if admission is offered.

early decision   A college admissions program that consists of earlier deadlines and notification dates than for the regular admissions process, and it requires a student's binding commitment to enroll if admission is offered.

education IRA   A tax-deferred savings and investment account for educational expenses. Parents are allowed to put away $500 a year for each child or grandchild under the age of 18. Contributions aren't tax-deductible, but withdrawals are tax-free. The money must be used by the time the student turns 30.

Educational Testing Service (ETS)   The company that produces and administers the SAT and other educational achievement tests.

EFC   See *expected family contribution*.

eligible institution   A public or private nonprofit institution of higher education, a postsecondary vocational school, or a proprietary institution of higher education that meets all the criteria to participate in Title IV student financial aid programs.

eligible program   A course of study that requires a certain minimum number of hours of instruction and period of time and that leads to a degree or certificate.

endowment   Funds owned by an institution and invested to produce income to support the operation of the institution.

enrollment status   An indication of whether you are a full-time or part-time student. Generally you must be enrolled at least half-time (and in some cases full-time) to qualify for financial aid.

entitlement counseling   Students with federal educational loans are required to receive counseling before they receive their first loan disbursement. The borrower's rights and responsibilities and the loan terms and conditions are reviewed with the student.

exit counseling   Students with federal educational loans are required to receive counseling before they graduate or withdraw (leave school), during which the borrower's rights and responsibilities and loan terms and conditions are reviewed with the student.

expected family contribution (EFC)   The amount a family is expected to contribute to a student's education based on family earnings, net assets, savings, size of family, and number of siblings in college.

extended repayment plan   A recent addition to repayment options for the federal loan programs, it extends the repayment terms on federally sponsored loans.

FAA   See *financial aid administrator*.

FAFSA   See *Free Application for Federal Student Aid*.

FAT   See *financial aid transcript*.

Federal Direct Consolidated Loan   A loan arranged through the U.S. Department of Education's Direct Loan Servicing Center. The loan is designed to combine Title IV education loans (including non–Direct Loans) into a single loan with one monthly repayment.

Federal Direct Education Loan (FDEL) Program   A group of federal education loans that includes Federal Stafford Loans (both subsidized and unsubsidized), Federal PLUS (parent) Loans, and Federal Consolidation Loans. All of these are long-term loans insured by state or private nonprofit guaranty agencies that are reimbursed by the federal government for all or part of the insurance claims paid to lenders.

Federal Direct Loan Program   A program of four types of education loans to student and parent borrowers: Federal Direct Stafford/Ford Loan, Federal Direct Unsubsidized Stafford/Ford Loan, Federal Direct PLUS Loan, and Federal Direct Consolidation Loan.

Federal Direct Stafford Loan   Federally financed low-interest loan that is government subsidized only when based on student financial need.

Federal Family Education Loan (FFEL) Program   Stafford and PLUS loans, which are financed by private lenders and guaranteed by the federal government.

Federal Methodology   The formula used to determine an expected family contribution (EFC) for Pell Grants, campus-based programs, FFEL programs, and Direct Loan programs.

Federal Pell Grant payment and disbursement schedules   Charts published annually by the U.S. Secretary of Education. They determine the dollar value of student Federal Pell Grant awards on the basis of schools' costs of attendance (COA) and students' expected family contributions (EFC).

Federal Pell Grant Program   A need-based grant program for undergraduate students who have not completed a first baccalaureate degree.

Federal Perkins Loan (FPL) Program   A campus-based loan program providing low-interest student loans to undergraduate and graduate students with financial need.

Federal PLUS Loan   Loans for parents borrowing for the education of their dependent children.

Federal Processor   The organization that processes the information submitted on the FAFSA and uses it to compute eligibility for federal student aid.

Federal Register   A government publication published each weekday that prints regulations, regulatory amendments, notices, and proposed regulatory changes for all federal executive agencies.

Federal Student Aid Information Center (FSAIC)   The office associated with the Department of Education that assists students and families in applying for financial aid from the federal government.

Federal Student Financial Aid Handbook   The Department of Education publication that explains procedures that schools should follow in administering federal Student Financial Aid (SFA) programs.

Federal Supplemental Educational Opportunity Grant (FSEOG) Program   A campus-based and need-based aid program that provides grant assistance to students in undergraduate programs who have not earned a Bachelor's degree or first professional degree.

Federal Work-Study Program   A program providing part-time jobs for undergraduate and graduate students with financial need.

fellowship   A form of aid given primarily to graduate students to help support their education.

financial aid   Financial assistance in the form of scholarships, grants, work-study, and loans for education.

financial aid administrator (FAA)   A college or university employee involved in administering financial aid. Also known as a financial aid advisor, officer, or counselor.

financial aid award   The total amount of financial aid (federal and nonfederal) in scholarships, grants, loans, and/or work-study that a student has been awarded. Also called a financial aid package.

financial aid officer   See *financial aid administrator.*

financial aid package   See *financial aid award.*

financial aid transcript   A record of all federal aid received by students at each school attended.

financial need   The difference between the cost of attendance at a college and the expected family contribution (EFC). Also known as financial aid eligibility.

financial responsibility   An institution's demonstrated ability to responsibly participate in federal Title IV student aid programs.

forbearance on a loan   A temporary cessation or reduction of payment amounts allowed by an FFEL lender (or the U.S. Department of Education for Direct Loans) for subsidized or unsubsidized Federal Stafford, Federal PLUS, Federal Perkins, or Federal Direct Loans.

Free Application for Federal Student Aid (FAFSA)   The form that must be completed by students and parents when applying for federal Title IV student aid.

General Educational Development (GED) Test   A test administered by the American Council on Education as the basis for awarding high school equivalency certification.

gift aid   Financial aid, generally in the form of a grant or scholarship, that a student is not required to repay or earn through employment.

grace period   The time period beginning the day after a loan recipient ceases to be enrolled at least half-time and ending the day before the loan repayment period starts.

Graduate Record Examination (GRE)   Multiple-choice examination administered by the Educational Testing Service (ETS) and taken by applicants who plan to attend certain graduate schools.

graduate student   A student in a postsecondary institution who is enrolled in a Master's or higher-level degree program.

graduated repayment   A repayment schedule in which the monthly payments are smaller at the start of the repayment period and become larger later on.

grants   Financial aid awards that do not have to be repaid. Grants are available through the federal government, state agencies, and colleges.

gross income   Income before taxes, deductions, and allowances have been subtracted.

guaranty agency   A state agency or private nonprofit institution that insures student loans for lenders and helps administer the federal loan programs.

holder   The institution that owns a loan.

home equity line of credit   A variation of the home equity loan that allows a homeowner to draw money (write checks) against his or her home's equity on an ongoing basis.

HOPE scholarship   Provides a family with a tax credit of up to $1,500 maximum per year for two years for each dependent student.

independent student   A student who is either married, 24 years of age or older, enrolled in a graduate or professional education program, has legal dependents other than a spouse, is an orphan or ward of the court, or is a veteran of the U.S. armed forces.

individual retirement account (IRA)   An individual tax-deferred savings and investment account meant to accumulate funds for retirement.

information review form   A document associated with the Student Aid Report (SAR) on which the borrower can correct any incorrect information on the SAR.

institutional loan   A loan specific to a college, university, or other postsecondary educational institution.

Institutional Methodology   A specific formula used by a college or university to determine financial need for allocation of the school's own financial aid funds.

institutional student information record   A report about a student sent by the Department of Education to the student's chosen schools after the student's application for federal aid has been received via the FAFSA.

insurance   An agreement between the guaranty agency and the lender in which the guaranty agency agrees to reimburse the lender for its losses on claims.

insurance fee   A fee charged by guaranty agencies that is deducted from loan proceeds and used to insure against defaulted loans.

interest subsidy   Interest the federal government pays on certain loans during authorized deferment or grace periods or while borrowers are in school.

interest-only payment   Payment that covers only accrued interest owed on a loan but that does not prohibit borrowers from making additional or larger payments at any time.

international student   A student who is not a citizen or resident of the United States and intends to attend, or is attending, a college, university, or other postsecondary educational institution in the United States.

internship   A type of part-time job in which a student receives supervised learning and work experience during the academic year or the summer months.

Leveraging Educational Assistance Partnership (LEAP) Program   A program that provides grant aid for education costs to postsecondary students with substantial financial need through matching formula grants to the states.

Lifetime Learning Credit   A tax credit of up to $1,000 per family per tax year for postsecondary education courses. Claimant must file a tax credit and owe taxes for that tax year.

loan counseling   Students with federal educational loans are required to receive counseling before they receive their first loan disbursement.

loan disclosure statement   A statement sent to a loan borrower by the lender before or at the time a loan is disbursed and before the start of the repayment period.

master promissory note   The note a student signs when taking out a Stafford Loan (subsidized or unsubsidized).

National Merit Scholastic Qualifying Test (NMSQT)   A test given during the junior year of high school in the form of the Preliminary Scholastic Assessment Test (PSAT). Sometimes abbreviated as PSAT/NMSQT. See also *PSAT.*

National Service Trust   A U.S. national community service program. If you participate in this program before attending college, its funds may be used to pay your educational expenses.

National Student Loan Clearinghouse   A central repository for the collection of postsecondary enrollment status and related information.

need-based analysis   The formula used to determine a student's need for financial assistance for college expenses. It determines the family's ability to contribute to the student's cost of attendance.

net income   Income after taxes, deductions, and allowances have been subtracted.

Office of Student Financial Assistance (OSFA)   The office of the U.S. Department of Education that is responsible for administering federal student financial aid programs and for developing aid policies and procedures.

origination   The process whereby the lender, or a servicing agent on behalf of the lender, handles the initial application processing and disbursement of loan proceeds.

origination fee   An upfront charge deducted from a loan to pay part of the loan's administrative costs.

over award   The amount of loan proceeds that exceed the borrower's educational need.

Parent Loans for Undergraduate Students (PLUS)   Federally insured loans for parents of dependent students. The amount of the loan is generally limited to the actual cost of attendance minus any financial aid already received.

parents' contribution   As determined by the Federal Methodology, the expected contribution by parents to the yearly cost of their children's education.

part-time enrollment   The number of students enrolled in higher education courses with a total credit load less than 75 percent of the normal full-time load.

payment period   A school-defined length of time for which financial aid funds are paid to a student.

payment reimbursement method   A method certain schools must use to request federal financial aid funds from the Department of Education.

payoff balance   The amount you would pay if you were to pay off your loan today. It includes the outstanding principal plus any unpaid accrued interest.

Pell Grants   Grants generally awarded to undergraduates based on need and family income qualifications. The maximum award for the 2006–2007 award year was $4,310.

period of enrollment   The time period during which aid is granted. It coincides with the school's academic terms such as the academic year, semester, and so on.

Perkins Loan Program   Federally insured low-interest loans repayable over an extended period. Funded by the federal government and awarded by the school.

personal income   Current income received by persons from all sources.

PLUS Loan   See *Parent Loans for Undergraduate Students.*

postsecondary   A term meaning "after high school." It refers to all programs for high school graduates, including programs at two- and four-year colleges and at vocational and technical schools.

Preliminary Scholastic Assessment Test (PSAT)   The test that helps prepare high school students for the SAT. If taken during the junior year, it is one of the qualifying criteria for the National Merit Scholarship Program. It is usually taken during the sophomore year or early in the junior year. Sometimes abbreviated as PSAT/NMSQT. See *National Merit Scholastic Qualifying Test.*

prepaid tuition plan   A college savings plan guaranteed to increase in value at the same rate as college tuition.

prime rate   A fluctuating interest rate that banks charge for short-term loans to corporations or individuals whose credit standing is excellent.

principal   The amount borrowed, which may increase as a result of interest capitalization. Also, the amount on which interest is calculated. Also known as principal balance.

private school   A school or institution that is controlled by an individual, agency, or board rather than by the government. It is usually not supported primarily by public funds or operated by publicly elected or appointed officials.

professional judgment   The financial aid administrator's ability to make changes to a student's financial aid package based on extenuating circumstances.

Profile   Sometimes referred to as the College Scholarship Services Profile, this is the customized financial aid application form required at certain colleges to determine eligibility for institutional aid.

promissory note   The contract between a borrower and a lender that includes all the terms and conditions under which the borrower promises to repay the loan.

proprietary school   A postsecondary school that is private and legally permitted to make a profit. Most offer technical and vocational courses.

PSAT   See *Preliminary Scholastic Assessment Test.*

racial/ethnic group   Classification indicating general racial or ethnic heritage based on self-identification (as in data collected by the Bureau of the Census) or on observer identification (as in data collected by the Office for Civil Rights). These categories are in accordance with the Office of Management and Budget standard classification scheme.

renewal FAFSA   Version of the FAFSA that students may use if they applied for federal financial aid the previous award year.

repayment period   The time during which a borrower actively pays back an education loan.

repayment policy   An institutionally established policy that determines the amount of education-related expenses (noninstitutional costs) reasonably incurred during a student's actual period of attendance.

repayment schedule   A specific timetable detailing the amount of principal and interest in a borrower's installment payments and the number of payments required to pay off the loan.

Reserve Officers Training Corps (ROTC)   Programs that combine military education with baccalaureate degree study, often with financial support and required commitment to future service in the armed services. Scholarship recipients participate in summer training while in college and meet a service commitment after college.

resources   As defined in federal regulations for campus-based programs, other student aid that must be taken into account to prevent an over award in the campus-based programs.

SAP   See *satisfactory academic progress.*

SAR   See *Student Aid Report.*

SASE   Self-addressed, stamped envelope.

SAT I   The Scholastic Aptitude Test, which is used to measure a student's ability in math, verbal comprehension, and problem solving. SATs are administered during the junior and senior years in high school.

SAT II Subject Test   A test offered in many areas of study, including English, mathematics, many sciences, history, and foreign languages. Some colleges require students to take one or more SAT II tests when they apply for admission.

satisfactory academic progress (SAP)   To be eligible to receive federal student aid, a student must maintain, based on the school's written standard, satisfactory academic progress toward a degree or certificate.

scholarships   Funds used to pay for higher education that do not have to be repaid. Scholarships may be awarded based on any number of criteria such as academics, achievements, hobbies, talents, affiliations with various groups, or career aspirations.

Scholastic Aptitude Test   See *SAT I.*

secondary market   Institutions that buy student loans from the institutions that originated or owned them.

Selective Service   Registration for the military draft. If required by law, you must register, or arrange to register, with the Selective Service to receive federal student aid.

self-help aid   Financial aid in the form of student loans or student employment.

servicer   An organization that administers and collects loan payments.

simplified needs test   The basis on which only the first part of the FAFSA form is required. Asset information is not required if the parents of a dependent student have income of less than $50,000 and the relevant family members were non–tax filers or were eligible to use a 1040A or a 1040EZ to file their taxes.

Stafford Loans   Subsidized (need-based) and unsubsidized (non-need-based) loans guaranteed by the federal government and available to students to fund their education.

Statement of Educational Purpose   A legal document in which the student agrees to use his or her financial aid for educational expenses only.

Student Aid Report (SAR)   A report sent to a student by the federal government summarizing financial and other information reported on the FAFSA. The student's financial aid need or eligibility is indicated by the expected family contribution (EFC), which is printed on the document.

Student Financial Aid (SFA) Programs   The programs administered by the Office of Student Financial Assistance Programs within the U.S. Department of Education. These include Federal Pell Grants, Federal Supplemental Educational Opportunity Grants, Federal Work-Study, Federal Perkins Loans, Federal Direct Stafford/Ford Loans, Federal Direct PLUS Loans, Federal Stafford Loans, Federal PLUS Loans, and State Student Incentive Grants.

subsidized Stafford Loans   These are awarded to students based on financial need. Interest is subsidized by the Department of Education while borrowers are enrolled in school at least half-time and during grace and deferment periods.

Supplemental Educational Opportunity Grant (SEOG) Program   Federal grant funds made available through some schools to a limited number of undergraduate students with financial need.

tax credit   The amount subtracted from your federal income taxes dollar-for-dollar for the cost of education. Taxes must be owed for the given tax year, and a tax return must be filed to receive any tax credit.

teaching assistantship (TA)   A form of financial aid that is given to graduate students and that usually provides them with a waiver of all or part of tuition, plus a small stipend for living expenses.

transcript   A list of all the courses a student has taken in high school or college and the grades received.

tuition and fees   Payment or charges for instruction or compensation for services, privileges, or the use of equipment, books, or other goods.

undergraduate student   A degree-seeking student at a college or university who has not earned a first Bachelor's degree.

Uniform Gifts to Minors Act (UGMA)   Legislation that introduced a tax-effective manner of transferring property to minors without the complications of trusts or guardianship restrictions.

university   An institution of higher education that consists of a liberal arts college, a diverse graduate program, and usually two or more professional schools or faculties and that is empowered to confer degrees in various fields of study.

U.S. Department of Education (DOE)   The government agency that administers several federal student financial aid programs, including the Federal Pell Grant, the Federal Work-Study Program, the Federal Perkins Loan, the FFELP, and the FDLP. Also known as the ED.

U.S. Department of Health and Human Services (DHHS or HHS)   The government agency that administers several federal health education loan programs, including the HEAL, HPSL, and NSL loan programs.

variable interest   Interest rates for the Federal Stafford Loans (subsidized and unsubsidized) are set by the government each year and therefore vary from year to year.

verification   A procedure by which a school checks the information a student reported on the FAFSA, usually by requesting a copy of the student's signed federal tax returns.

vocational education   Organized educational programs, services, and activities that are directly related to the preparation of individuals for paid or unpaid employment or for additional preparation for a career.

work-study   A generic term for programs designed to provide part-time employment as a source of funds to pay for postsecondary education, and for a federal program that is administered through postsecondary institutions.

Directory of General Financial Aid Resources

In many respects, Appendix B is one of the more exciting parts of this book. How in the world can an appendix be exciting? Well, for starters, it offers a comprehensive index of where you can go to find any additional information you may need on financial aid. You'll also discover financial aid sources that you may not have considered previously. For even more information and listings, Appendix C contains addresses and other useful resources listed by state.

The table of contents shown here will help you locate the topic you're looking for:

Appendix B Contents

Associations Related to Financial Aid

There are literally hundreds of associations that are directly or indirectly associated with the financial aid process. Here's a partial listing of the major associations that you may want to contact. For state-by-state alphabetical listings of financial aid resources, see Appendix C.

American Association of University Women (AAUW)   The Educational Foundation of the association is dedicated to improving women's access to the education system. Call 319-337-1716 for more information.

Association of Fundraising Professionals (AFP)   AFP is a major professional organization that lists educational opportunities and other services. Visit its website for more information: www.afpnet.org.

Council of Better Business Bureaus   The council is dedicated to ensuring fair and legitimate practices within the financial aid process. Call 703-276-0100 for more information.

Higher Education Washington, Inc.   This is an information resources company serving the student financial aid administrator community. Resources include publications and conferences. Visit the company's website if you need more information: www.hewi.net.

Institute of International Education   The institute helps students gain access to international colleges and universities. Call 212-883-8200 for more information.

National Association for College Admissions Counseling (NACAC)   NACAC is an education association of secondary school counselors, college admissions officers and counselors, and related individuals who work with students as they make the transition from high school to postsecondary education. Members of NACAC join together because they recognize that, for students and their families, a real choice demands information and communication. School admissions counselors are often the primary sources of information about the transition process and are uniquely aware of the concerns held by the people they serve. Call 703-836-2222 or visit the association's website if you need more information: www. nacacnet.org.

HELP! **Americorp National and Community Service Program**   Americorp is an excellent source for scholarships, work-study, and community service programs. Call 1-800-942-2677 for more information.

National Association of Student Financial Aid Administrators   These are the people who decide how much you get. They've assembled a nice collection of basic information for parents and students, including an online version of the popular brochure "Cash for College." Visit the association's website if you need more information: www.nasfaa.org.

Northwest Education Loan Association   Information on student loans, financial aid, and college planning for students and families in the Pacific Northwest is available through this association: www.nela.net.

Pennsylvania Higher Education Assistance Agency (PHEAA)   This is a full-service student financial aid organization and a national leader in providing affordable and efficient access to higher education. Visit the agency's website for more information: www.pheaa.org.

Western Interstate Commission for Higher Education (WICHE)   WICHE offers exchange programs among member colleges in the western states. Eligible students get a reduction in tuition. Call 303-541-0210 for more information.

Adult Financial Aid Programs

As more and more adults attend college on a part-time basis, there's renewed interest in the development of financial aid programs for the adult population. The following are several programs to consider:

Distance learning programs   If you're thinking about school, Peterson's excellent website offers information about distance learning programs, as well as a discussion area for graduate students. Visit its website for more information: www.petersons.com/graduate/indexfa.html.

The University Alliance   The alliance offers news resources for nontraditional education and options for adult re-entry into the higher education system. Get the inside scoop on financial aid, distance education, graduate school, employment, internships, and educational trends. Visit the alliance's website for more information: www.back2college.com.

Virtual College   This guidebook by Pam Dixon shows how to use distance learning in your career plan. If you are interested in ordering the book, visit www.amazon.com or your local bookstore or call Peterson's at 1-800-338-3282.

Athletic Scholarships

Athletic scholarship programs are very competitive, but if you know where and how to look for them, you can dramatically improve your odds of getting one.

College/University Volleyball Scholarships   This website specializes in helping students get volleyball scholarships. Visit the site for more information: www.volleyball.org/college/index.html.

CSA College Recruiting   Collegiate Sports of America (CSA) offers information updated daily on the nation's top high-school athletes. Visit its website for more information: www.csasports.com.

Florida Bluechip Report   At this website covering the state of Florida, recruiters can browse through over 275 Florida high school prospects for college football. Features include a variety of ways to mine and sort the data, as well as ways of checking updated news for each profile. For more information or to file your profile, visit www.floridabluechips.com.

PrepStar College Recruiting   PrepStar offers information updated daily on the nation's top football and basketball prospects. Since 1982, PrepStar has helped thousands of qualified and deserving student-athletes in all sports obtain athletic scholarships and financial aid for college. Its online recruiting center is used by thousands of college coaches nationwide as a vital tool for recruiting efforts. Visit its website for more information: www.prepstar.com.

Rivals 100   Famed analyst Bobby Burton covers the college football recruiting scene and ranks the top 100 prep players in the country. Visit his site for more information: rivals100.rivals.com.

Budget Planning

If you go to college without first setting up a budget, you'll have little or no idea where your money is being spent, and you'll miss opportunities to save money on key items in your budget.

BACK calculators   This website offers an entire set of specialized calculators to complete every aspect of the budget process. Visit the site for more information: www.statesavingsbank.com/calculators.html.

Career Guidance

Many freshmen enter college with no idea of what subject they want to major in. Somewhere in their sophomore year, they'll decide on a major, only to find out that many of the courses they've already taken can't be credited toward their selected major. To take the additional required courses, many of these students have to spend another semester in college—and that's an expensive proposition that might have been avoided if they'd sought career advice from organizations such as the following:

Career and Guidance Foundation   This website lists over 8,100 college catalogs online! Visit the site for more information: www.cgf.org/home.asp.

The Coalition of Colleges and Universities   This group has assembled advice for students and their parents on preparing for college, choosing the right school, and finding ways to pay for it. Its website includes recommendations on which middle school and high school courses to take and offers many good Internet links. Visit the site for more information: www.collegeispossible.org.

Major databases   Major databases provide information for specific majors or career interests such as art, computer science, journalism, and nursing. FinAid's website describes scholarships and other forms of aid available. Visit its website for more information: www.finaid.org/otheraid/majors.phtml.

Mapping Your Future   At this site, you'll find information to help you plan your career, select a school, and pay for your education. This site is sponsored by guaranty agencies that participate in the Federal Family Education Loan (FFEL) program and are committed to providing information about higher education and career opportunities. Visit the site for more information: mapping-your-future.org.

College Admissions Requirements

Before you apply to a college, make sure you understand its admissions requirements. If you can't meet the admissions requirements, don't waste your time applying unless you have talked to someone in the admissions office who has told you that you might have a chance of being admitted.

Common Application   The recommended application form for admission to undergraduate programs at many independent colleges and universities is known as the Common Application. It was developed to simplify the college application process.

Students complete the form and send copies to any of the participating colleges to which they wish to apply. Paper and disk copies of the Common Application are available at most high schools. The form can also be downloaded or completed online at www.commonapp.org.

My College Guide   My College Guide is a service that allows you to order admissions information for almost any college or university through its website. Visit the site for more information: mycollegeguide.org.

College Financial Aid Directory

Virtually every college in the country offers financial aid of some sort, and the types of aid programs offered vary. If you want to get the inside story on what's available at the colleges you're interested in, contact their financial aid offices.

College Information   Choosing the right school is difficult. Even narrowing your choices to a few likely candidates can be an exercise in frustration. With thousands of schools in the United States, how will you ever find the right one for you? College Information's website provides you with selection criteria that are important to you and that help you narrow your list. Visit the site for more information: www. collegeinfo.com.

Community Colleges

Community colleges offer students an opportunity to complete the first two years of college for significantly less than what it would cost at a four-year institution.

The Community College Web   This site contains a searchable index to the websites for community colleges in the United States, Canada, and elsewhere in the world. The interface allows you to search alphabetically, geographically, or by location, web address, or keywords in the college name. Visit the site for more information: www.mcli.dist.maricopa.edu/cc/index.html.

Two-year college directory   If you're interested in attending a two-year college, this online directory will provide you with the names, addresses, and telephone numbers of junior colleges throughout the country. Visit the website for more information: cset.sp.utoledo.edu/twoyrcol.html.

Consulting Services

If you're a busy parent without the time to check out all of your financial aid options, you may want to consider hiring a financial aid consultant to do it for you. Here's how to find a good one:

Ask the experts   Sixty financial aid administrators and financial aid professionals have graciously volunteered to answer questions submitted via this forum. Visit the website for more information: www.finaid.org/questions.

(HELP!)

College Information   This website offers information about every major college in the country and allows side-by-side comparisons of information. Other features include practice SAT and ACT tests, a personal organizer, and downloadable financial aid forms. Free registration required. Visit the website for more information: www. collegeinfo.com.

Directory of Colleges and Universities

If you don't know the addresses or websites of the colleges you're interested in attending, or if you need more detailed information to narrow your list, you can assess your options by using the following websites:

College admissions   This website details what colleges look for and how they make admissions decisions. Visit the site for more information: www.collegeapps.about.com.

College resources   This college and career resource from *U.S. News & World Report* includes a searchable directory of colleges, a yearly ranking of colleges, information on financial aid, and more. It features a special section on over 1,200 community colleges. Visit the website for more information: www.usnews.com/sections/education/index.html.

FAFSA Form

Filling out a FAFSA application is the first step in applying for student aid. Line-by-line instructions for completing the form can be found in Chapter 19.

> **HELP!** **Peterson's Education Center**   Peterson's is famous for having one of the best web-
> sites about financial aid. It features extensive financial aid info for beginners and
> experts alike. The site also provides an admissions calendar so you can synchronize
> your schedule with the rest of the financial aid world. Visit the site for more information:
> www.petersons.com.

FAFSA Online

You have the option of completing the FAFSA online. This section tells you how to get answers to the most commonly asked questions about the FAFSA form and gives instructions for completing it.

FAFSA on the web   Completing the FAFSA on the web is the fastest way to apply for student financial aid. Students who applied for aid last year can also complete a renewal FAFSA application online at www.fafsa.ed.gov.

Federal Financial Aid

The U.S. Department of Education disburses financial aid money to the states and is fairly lenient in how it allows the different states to distribute the money. Make sure you contact the Department of Education in the state(s) where you plan to attend college to find out how their programs work. They are all different. See Appendix C for state-by-state listings of state Departments of Education.

Department of Education's Student Guide   This online guide provides information about financial aid from the U.S. Department of Education. Visit its website at www.ed.gov and enter the words "Financial Aid" in the advance search box that appears in the main menu.

FinAid   This website is one of the most comprehensive resources for objective and unbiased information about student financial aid. Visit the site for more information: www.finaid.org.

Federal Financial Aid Regional Offices and Related Sites

The country is divided up into 10 financial aid regional offices, which are listed in this section. Related sites follow. (You can find any state's Department of Education listing and listings for other state offices compiled by state in Appendix C.)

Region I (Connecticut, Maine, Massachusetts, New Hampshire, Rhode Island, Vermont)
U.S. Department of Education
Student Financial Assistance Programs
J.W. McCormack Post Office and Courthouse, Room 502
Boston, MA 02109
617-223-9338

Region II (New Jersey, New York, Puerto Rico, Virgin Islands, Panama Canal Zone)
U.S. Department of Education
Student Financial Assistance Programs
75 Park Pl., Room 1206
New York, NY 10007
212-264-4022

Region III (Delaware, District of Columbia, Maryland, Pennsylvania, Virginia, West Virginia)
U.S. Department of Education
Student Financial Assistance Programs
3535 Market St., Room 16200
Philadelphia, PA 19104
215-596-0247

Region IV (Alabama, Florida, Georgia, Kentucky, Mississippi, North Carolina, South Carolina, Tennessee)
U.S. Department of Education
Office of Student Financial Assistance
101 Marietta Tower, Suite 2203
Atlanta, GA 30323
1-800-433-3243

Region V (Illinois, Indiana, Michigan, Minnesota, Ohio, Wisconsin)
U.S. Department of Education
Office of Student Financial Assistance
111 North Canal St., Room 830
Chicago, IL 60605
1-800-433-3243

Regions VI and VII (Arkansas, Iowa, Kansas, Louisiana, Missouri, Nebraska, New Mexico, Oklahoma, Texas)
U.S. Department of Education
Student Financial Assistance Programs
1200 Main Tower, Room 2150
Dallas, TX 75202
214-767-3811

Region VIII (Colorado, Montana, North Dakota, South Dakota, Utah, Wyoming)
U.S. Department of Education
Office of Student Financial Assistance Programs
1391 North Speer Blvd., Suite 8
Denver, CO 80204-2512
303-844-3676

Region IX (Arizona, California, Hawaii, Nevada, American Samoa, Guam, Federated States of Micronesia, Marshall Islands, Republic of Palau, Wake Island)
U.S. Department of Education
Office of Student Financial Assistance
50 United Nations Plaza
San Francisco, CA 94102
415-437-8293

Region X (Alaska, Idaho, Oregon, Washington)
U.S. Department of Education
Office of Student Financial Assistance Programs
1000 Second Ave., Suite 1200
Seattle, WA 98104-1023
206-287-1770

Related Sites

National Council of Education Opportunity Association   This program is designed to encourage undergraduate students from low-income families and from underrepresented minority groups to pursue doctoral degrees and careers in college teaching. It represents the largest and best pipeline in the nation for potential graduate students from these groups. Call 202-347-7430.

National Council of Higher Education Loan Programs Inc. (NCHELP)
NCHELP represents a nationwide network of guaranty agencies, secondary markets,
lenders, loan servicers, collection agencies, schools, and other organizations involved
in the administration of the Federal Family Education Loan (FFEL) program.
Contact the NCHELP at 1100 Connecticut Ave. NW, 12th Floor, Washington, D.C.
20036 or call 1-202-822-2106.

National representatives   This website will show you how to contact your congressperson. Visit the site for more information: www.visi.com/juan/congress.

Financial Aid Resources

There are literally hundreds of resources out there that you can use to find all types
of financial aid. This section lists the primary ones to help you get started.

> **HELP!**
>
> **Fast Web**   Fast Web is the largest and most comprehensive scholarship search
> engine on the Internet. It provides access to a searchable database of more than
> 400,000 private sector scholarships, fellowships, grants, and loans available to students.
> Visit the site for more information: www.fastweb.com.

College Edge to College Finder   This website includes advice from the experts on
choosing a college. Visit the site if you need more information: www.collegeedge.com.

College Opportunities Online   This website links to over 9,000 colleges and
universities in the United States. If you're thinking about a large university, a small
liberal arts college, a specialized college, a community college, a career or technical college, or a trade school, you can find it here. College Opportunities Online is
brought to you by the National Center for Education Statistics in the U.S. Department of Education. Visit the site for more information: nces.ed.gov/ipeds/cool.

Federal Student Aid Hotline   This hotline is a toll-free number that you can call if
you have any questions regarding the financial aid process. Call 1-800-433-3243.

Financial Aid   This site is a major financial aid information page on the Internet.
No other site even comes close to having the massive amount of guidance that this
site provides. You can use its financial aid calculators, look up laws, locate lenders,
find specialized scholarships, or browse top-drawer links to other great sites. Visit the
site for more information: www.finaid.com.

Financial aid links   At About.com, you'll find a fairly comprehensive list of links about college financial aid. Visit the website for more information: collegeapps. about.com.

Funding services   College funding and financial aid sources, including scholarships, grants, loans, private sources, and work-study programs, are covered by the Funding Service Center. Coming up with all of the money you need to attend college can be a challenge. In reality, your college funds will probably be made up of a combination of funds from financial aid sources, private sources, and your own money. Visit the website for more information: www.collegefundingonline.com.

Pennsylvania Higher Education Assistance Agency (PHEAA)   This is a collaborative effort to use cutting-edge technology and business processes to dramatically transform the administration of student financial aid and improve both funding for education beyond high school and customer access to information. Visit the website for more information: www.pheaa.org.

Student loans   This website includes excellent student loan counseling and interactive tools to plan your loan requirements. Visit the site for more information: mapping-your-future.org.

Yahoo's Financial Aid Search   This website allows you to locate online financial aid and provides Internet links to college financial aid offices, listed alphabetically by college. Visit the site for more information: www.yahoo.com and enter "financial aid" in the search screen.

Financial Planning

Without a financial plan for college, you can't know for sure whether you can afford the school of your choice. The following listings can help you get started on a financial plan.

Academic Management Services   Academic Management Services offers a website to help families plan and finance their kids' education. Visit the site for more information: www.amsweb.com.

Financial Aid Calculators   These financial aid calculators were implemented by Mark Kantrowitz. They are free, accurate, and completely confidential. Playing "what-if" games with these calculators can provide you with a better understanding of college education financing and help you plan for the future. Visit this site for more information: www.finaid.org/calculators.

Frauds and Scams

Fortunately, financial aid frauds and scams seldom occur, but they are out there. Before hiring a consulting service or taking a too-good-to-be-true deal, make sure you check it out first.

Hotline   If you're suspicious about a financial aid "deal," call the U.S. Department of Education, Inspector General's Hotline at 1-800-647-8733.

Reporting fraud   You can report any financial aid fraud situation to the Council of Better Business Bureaus by calling 703-276-0100.

Scholarship scams   Learn how to recognize and protect yourself from financial aid scams. If you must pay money to get money, it might be a scam. Visit this website for more information: www.finaid.org/scholarships/scams.phtml.

Graduate and Professional Student Loans

Less than half of all graduate students and students seeking professional degrees (lawyers, medical doctors, etc.) receive any financial aid. Here are several sources to check out if you are a postgraduate student seeking financial aid.

Achiever Loan   The Knight College Resource Group offers loans to graduate students in any discipline. Write to the group at 855 Boylston St., Boston, MA 02116 or call 1-800-225-6783.

Business Access Loan Program   This program is for business graduate students only. Write to the Access Group, P.O. Box 7430, Wilmington, DE 19803-0430 or call 1-800-282-1550.

CitiAssist   Graduate students in any discipline may apply for a loan. Write to Citibank Student Loan Corporation, 99 Garnsey Rd., Pittsford, NY 14534 or call 716-248-7672 or 1-800-692-8200.

ENGLoans   Loans for engineering students only are available from United Student Aid Group. Write to the group at P.O. Box 6182, Indianapolis, IN 46206 or call 1-800-255-8374.

Federal Stafford and Direct Student Loans   These loans are available to graduate students in any discipline. Write to the U.S. Department of Education, Federal Student Aid Information Center, P.O. Box 84, Washington, D.C. 20044-0084, call 1-800-433-3243, or visit www.ed.gov.

GradSHARE   These loans are for graduate students in any discipline. Write to the New England Loan Marketing Association, Nellie Mae, 50 Braintree Hill Park, Suite 300, Braintree, MA 02184 or call 1-800-634-9308.

Graduate Access Loans   Graduate students in any discipline may apply for these loans. Write to the Access Group, P.O. Box 7430, Wilmington, DE 19803-0430 or call 1-800-282-1550.

Health Education Assistance Loan (HEAL)   These loans are limited to medical students only. Write to the Division of Student Assistance HEAL Branch, Parklawn Building, Room 8–37, 5600 Fishers Ln., Rockville, MD 20857 or call 301-443-1540.

Law Access Loan   These loans are for law students. Write to the Access Group, P.O. Box 7430, Wilmington, DE 19803-0430 or call 1-800-282-1550.

LawLoans   Law students only may apply for these loans. Write to Sallie Mae, P.O. Box 59023, Panama City, FL 32402-9023 or call 1-800-282-1550.

LawSHARE   Only law students may apply for these loans. Write to the New England Loan Marketing Association, Nellie Mae, 50 Braintree Hill Park, Suite 300, Braintree, MA 02184 or call 1-800-634-9308.

MBASHARE   Business students may apply for these loans. Write to the New England Loan Marketing Association, Nellie Mae, 50 Braintree Hill Park, Suite 300, Braintree, MA 02184 or call 1-800-634-9308.

Medical Access Loans   These loans are for medical students. Write to the Access Group, P.O. Box 7430, Wilmington, DE 19803-0430 or call 1-800-282-1550.

MEDLOANS and Alternative Loan Program (ALP)   Medical students may apply for these loans. Write to the Association of American Medical Colleges, 2450 N St. NW, Washington, D.C. 20037 or call 202-828-0400.

MEDSHARE   These loans are limited to medical and dental students. Write to the New England Loan Marketing Association, Nellie Mae, 50 Braintree Hill Park, Suite 300, Braintree, MA 02184 or call 1-800-634-9308.

Option 4 Loan Program   This loan program focuses on graduate students in any discipline. Write to USAFunds, P.O. Box 6198, Indianapolis, IN 46206-6198 or call 1-800-635-3785.

PLATO   Graduate students in any discipline may apply for these loans. Write to the Classic Student Loan, 205 Van Buren St., Suite 200, Herndon, VA 20170-5336, call 1-800-467-5286, or fax 703-709-8609.

Professional Education Plan   Applicants must be graduate and professional students, including but not limited to students in the chiropractic, osteopathic, optometric, veterinary, physical therapy, physician's assistant, nursing, or occupational therapy fields. Write to the Education Resources Institute, 330 Stuart St., Suite 500, Boston, MA 02116-5237 or call 1-800-243-8886.

Signature Health Loan   These loans are designed for students in allopathic medicine, dentistry, optometry, osteopathic medicine, pharmacy, podiatry, and veterinary medicine only. Write to Sallie Mae, 1050 Thomas Jefferson St. NW, Washington, D.C. 20007-3871 or call 1-888-888-3461.

Graduate Study Financial Aid Programs

Graduate students can acquire financial aid from many of the same sources that undergraduate students do. In addition, many colleges award money to graduate students for fellowships and teaching assistant positions.

Distance learning programs   If you're thinking about graduate school, Peterson's excellent website offers information about distance learning programs, as well as a discussion area for graduate students. Visit the site for more information: www.petersons.com/graduate/indexfa.html.

Graduate Tests (GMAT, GRE, LSAT, MCAT)

If you decide that you want to go to graduate school, you'll probably have to take one of the following tests.

Graduate Management Assessment Test (GMAT)

This is used by graduate schools of business to assess the qualifications of applicants to graduate management programs. The GMAT is available only as a computer-adaptive test (CAT), in which questions are displayed on a computer terminal and answers are entered directly into the computer.

GMAT Practice Test   The website www.petersons.com includes "hot tips" on how to take the test as well as other information. Just visit the website and type in "GMAT" in the window marked "Select Test."

GMAT Information and Registration
Sylvan Learning Systems International Ltd.
P.O. Box 38502
Baltimore, MD 21231-8502
Telephone: 410-843-8160
Fax: 410-843-8S69

Graduate Record Examination (GRE)

This is a multiple-choice and writing test that most graduate schools use for admission into their graduate programs. The GRE is available only as a computer-adaptive test (CAT), in which questions are displayed on a computer terminal and answers are entered directly into the computer.

GRE Information and Registration   For information, go to the Educational Testing Service Network website at www.ets.org or write to Graduate Record Examination Educational Testing Service, P.O. Box 6000, Princeton, NJ 08541 or call 609-771-7670.

HELP!
The GRE program provides practice tests, publications, and services. Visit its website at www.gre.org to learn more.

Getting Started

Peterson's is a recognized name and publisher of a wide variety of student test materials. It offers GRE practice tests that include "hot tips" on how to take the test. Visit the website at www.petersons.com and click the Select a Test option that appears on the left side of the main menu.

Law School Admission Test (LSAT)

The current fee for this test is $123.00. The LSAT is administered by the Law School Admissions Council. For information and registration, call the council at 215-968-1001 or visit its website at www.lsac.org.

Medical College Admissions Test (MCAT)

Almost all U.S. medical schools require applicants to submit MCAT scores. Medical college admission committees consider MCAT scores as part of their admission decision process.

Information and registration   For information or to register, write to MCAT Registration, The American College Testing Program, P.O. Box 414, Iowa City, IA 52243.

   4Tests.com offers a number of practice tests for college entrance exams, including one for the MCAT. Visit its website at www.4tests.com.

Handicapped Students Assistance Programs

The following section lists private organizations that offer assistance to handicapped persons. Also see Appendix C for the office that administers rehabilitation services in your state, where you can get information on special programs available in your area.

Alexander Graham Bell Association for the Deaf   This association awards several outstanding scholarships annually to deaf students. For information write to 3417 Volta Pl. NW, Washington, D.C. 20007.

American Council of the Blind   This nonprofit organization works with colleges and universities throughout the country to provide the latest tools and technology to assist blind students in obtaining college degrees. The council also awards several scholarships each year to qualified blind students. For more information write to 1010 Vermont Ave., Washington, D.C. 20005.

Deafness and Communicative Disorders Branch   This national institute on deafness and other communication disorders offers several scholarship programs. To learn more about the programs, visit its website at www.nidcd.nih.gov or write to Switzer Building, M/S 3228, 330 C St. SW, Washington, D.C. 20202-2736.

Epilepsy Foundation   The Epilepsy Foundation is a national charitable organization founded in 1968 as the Epilepsy Foundation of America. It is the only such organization wholly dedicated to the welfare of people with epilepsy. To learn more about its scholarship programs, visit the website at www.epilepsyfoundation.org or write to 4251 Garden City Dr., Landover, MD 20785.

Gallaudet University   The mission of Gallaudet University is to serve as a comprehensive, multipurpose institution of higher education for deaf and hard-of-hearing citizens of the United States and the world. In addition to its undergraduate and graduate academic programs, the university also offers national demonstration elementary and secondary education programs. To learn more about its scholarship programs, visit the university's website at www.gallaudet.edu or write to 800 Florida Ave. NE, Washington, D.C. 20002.

Health Resources and Services Administration (HRSA)   The HRSA directs national health programs that improve the nation's health by ensuring equitable access to comprehensive, quality health care for all. The HRSA works to improve and extend life for people living with HIV/AIDS, provide primary health care for medically underserved people, serve women and children through state programs, and train a health workforce that is both diverse and motivated to work in underserved areas. To learn more about its scholarship programs, visit the website at www.hrsa.gov or write to One Dupont Circle NW, Washington, D.C. 20036-1193.

Helen Keller National Center   Since the launch of the Interpreters' Network in September 1996, this website has been visited more than 60,000 times. It is rapidly becoming "information central" for interpreters whose working languages include a signed language. The site has been reviewed by Magellan and given a three-star rating, and also has been reviewed by Look Smart; their banners are proudly displayed on the front page of the site. To learn more about the center's scholarship programs, visit www.hknc.org or write to 111 Middle Neck Rd., Sands Point, NY 11050.

Immune Deficiency Foundation   This national nonprofit health organization is dedicated to improving the diagnosis and treatment of primary immune deficiency diseases through research. To learn more about the foundation's scholarship programs, visit its website at www.primaryimmune.org or write to 25 W. Chesapeake Ave., Suite 206, Towson, MD 21204, 410-321-6647.

National Technical Institute for the Deaf (NTID)   The NTID is the world's largest technical college for deaf students. To learn more about its scholarship programs, visit the website at www.ntid.rit.edu or write to Office of the Dean, 52 Lomb Memorial Dr., Rochester, NY 14623.

Recording for the Blind and Dyslexic   This nonprofit organization provides textbooks on cassette and computer disk to blind and visually impaired students. To learn more about the group's programs, visit its website at www.rfbdnj.org or write to 20 Roszel Rd., Princeton, NJ 08540.

International Financial Aid Directory

Unfortunately, there are not a lot of financial aid sources for study abroad. However, we have listed several major points of contact in this section to help you get started.

American Institute for Foreign Study   This organization arranges cultural exchange and study-abroad programs throughout the world for more than 40,000 students each year. For more information, write to 102 Greenwich Ave., Greenwich, CT 06830 or call 1-800-727-2437.

Canadian opportunities   This completely Canadian website is chock-full of scholarships, grants, and bursaries available to Canadian students. For more information, visit www.studentawards.com.

Council on International Educational Exchange   The council offers a variety of programs, domestic and overseas, for U.S. faculty and administrators, focusing on global issues and regions of the world. Visit the council's website at www.ciee.org or write to 205 E. 42nd St., New York, NY 10017, 212-822-2600.

Institute for International Education   The institute provides detailed descriptions of its 250 grant programs, including the prestigious Fulbright Program. For more information, visit its website at www.iie.org or write to 809 United Nations Plaza, New York, NY 10017, 212-883-8200.

Major Fellowship Opportunities and Aid to Advanced Education for Foreign Nationals

This section offers several websites and addresses for organizations that foreign students can contact for financial aid.

Dan Cassidy's Worldwide College Scholarship Directory   This directory offers a complete listing of financial aid resources from Australia to Zanzibar. To order, contact the National Scholarship Research Service at 1-800-432-7827 or 707-546-6781.

Financial Resources for International Study   This is a listing of funding sources for U.S. students seeking support for study abroad. For more information, contact the Institute for International Education, IIE Books, P.O. Box 371, Annapolis Junction, MA 20701 or call 1-800-445-0443.

International Student Guide   This guide discusses many topics of interest to international students, including financial aid for specific colleges. To order the guide, contact College Board Publications, 2 College Way, Forrester Center, WV 25438 or call 1-800-323-7155.

Loan Consolidation and Forgiveness Programs

The following organizations can help you consolidate your loans into one manageable monthly payment. They can also provide you with information on loan forgiveness program options.

The National College Scholarship Foundation (NCSF)   You can find out about loan forgiveness programs by calling 301-548-9423.

Nellie Mae   Federal and private education loans for undergraduate and graduate students are processed through a program known as Nellie Mae. To learn more about the program, call 1-800-634-9308 or visit its website at www.nelliemae.com.

Pennsylvania Higher Education Assistance Agency (PHEAA)   This agency is a full-service student financial aid organization and a national leader in educational assistance. To learn more about the program, call 1-800-692-7392 or visit its website at www.pheaa.org.

Sallie Mae Educational Loan Center   Sallie Mae provides student loans and other financial aid services to make paying for a college education more affordable for students and their families. To learn more, call 1-800-524-9100 or visit its website at www. salliemae.com.

Loan Programs

There is a wealth of information out there to help you determine whether a student loan is right for you. Here are several sources to contact:

KeyBank   For more information about Key education resources, call 1-1-800-KEY-LEND (539-5363) or visit the bank's website at www.key.com.

Parent or PLUS loans   This website explains what PLUS loans are, who is eligible, and how you apply for a loan. Visit the website for more information: www.finaid. org/loans/parentloan.phtml.

Private or alternative loans   This website explains what private or alternative loans are all about and how you apply for a loan. Visit the site for more information: www. finaid.org/loans/privateloan.phtml.

Stafford and Perkins Loans   At this website, you'll learn what Stafford and Perkins Loans are all about, who is eligible, and how you apply for a loan. Visit the site for more information: www.finaid.org/loans/studentloan.phtml.

Military and Veterans Programs

The military and veterans organizations offer exciting scholarship opportunities that you may want to check out. Veterans Administration centers are listed by state in Appendix C.

GI Bill   This website explains the GI Bill and also covers military scholarships, education benefits, and school rankings, all from a military perspective. Visit the site for more information: gibill.va.gov.

Minority Programs

The following is just a partial list of contacts for more information about some of the excellent financial aid programs available for minorities.

American Institute of Certified Public Accountants   This organization offers financial assistance to qualified minority students. For more information, write to the Manager, Minority Recruitment, American Institute of Certified Public Accountants, 1211 Avenue of the Americas, New York, NY 10036-3775. Application deadlines are July 1 and December 1.

Bureau of Indian Affairs   This program provides financial aid to eligible Native American students. The awards are based on financial need. For further information, write to the Bureau of Indian Affairs Higher Education Grant Program, Bureau of Indian Affairs, 18th and C St. NW, Washington, D.C. 20245.

Congressional Hispanic Caucus   This organization provides fellowships to qualified Hispanic students to work with members of Congress. The fellowships are for one academic term. For further information on this program, contact the Congressional Hispanic Caucus, 504 C St. NE, Washington, D.C. 20002.

General Motors   The GM Corporation provides scholarship assistance to qualified minority undergraduate students through several colleges and universities in the United States. For more information, write to the General Motors Scholarship Program, General Motors Corporation, 8–163 General Motors Building, Detroit, MI 48202.

National Action Council for Minorities in Engineering (NACME)   This organization provides financial assistance to qualified undergraduate minority students pursuing degrees in engineering. The major funding is directed through corporate scholarships that are administered by NACME. For more information, write to the

National Action Council for Minorities in Engineering, 3 W. 35th St., New York, NY 10001, call 212-279-2644, or fax 212-629-5178.

Office of Indian Education Programs   These scholarship awards are based on financial need. For further information, write to Indian Fellowship Program, Office of Indian Education Programs, 1849 C St. NW, MS-Room 3525, Washington, D.C. 20242.

United Methodist Church   The Board of Higher Education and Ministry awards scholarships to qualified undergraduate and graduate minority students. Applicants must be U.S. citizens or permanent residents; must be Hispanic, Asian, or Native American; and must be active members of the Methodist Church. The United Methodist Church also sponsors several scholarship and loan programs for graduate students. A church-sponsored loan program is available to undergraduate as well as graduate students. For additional information, write to the United Methodist Church, Board of Higher Education and Ministry, Box 871, Nashville, TN 37202.

United Negro College Fund   This organization awards over a thousand scholarships a year to students attending United Negro College Fund schools. The awards are based on financial need and academic merit. For more information, write to the United Negro College Fund, 8260 Willow Oaks Corporate Dr., Fairfax, VA 22031. For a list of United Negro College Fund schools, see Chapter 13.

Prepaid Tuition Plans

Prepaid tuition plans are usually operated statewide and permit families to lock in a tuition rate years in advance of when their kids will be ready for college. The money you deposit is set aside in a state account. For more information, see the following list of phone numbers for states whose college institutions participate in prepaid tuition plans. If your state is not listed, call your state Department of Education (listed under your state in Appendix C) and ask whether it plans to offer a prepaid tuition plan in the near future. It may have added the program after this book was printed.

Alabama, 1-800-252-7228
Alaska, 907-474-7469
Colorado, 1-800-478-5651
Florida, 1-800-552-4723
Indiana, 317-232-6386
Kentucky, 1-800-928-8926
Louisiana, 1-800-259-5626, ext. 1012

Maryland, 1-800-903-7875

Massachusetts, 1-800-449-6332, option 1

Michigan, 1-800-243-2847

Mississippi, 1-800-987-4450

Ohio, 1-800-589-6882 or 1-800-233-6734

Pennsylvania, 1-800-440-4000

Tennessee, 1-888-486-2378

Texas, 1-800-445-4723

Virginia, 1-888-567-0540

Wisconsin, 888-338-3789

Private Tuition Payment Plans

Academic Management Services (AMS)   This company offers innovative educational payment programs for college students. It also offers loan origination, including federal loan programs. To learn more about AMS, call 1-800-635-0120 or visit its website at www.amsweb.com.

FACTS Tuition Management System   This company provides tuition management services to colleges and universities throughout the country. To learn more about FACTS, call 1-800-624-7092 or visit its website at www.factsmgt.com.

Key Education Resources and Knight College Resources Group   Key offers a range of education planning and financing products that can help you meet your education goals. For more information, call 1-800-225-6783.

Reference Books, Periodicals, and News Sources

This section has a list of excellent books, periodicals, and news sources that will help you learn more about the financial aid process.

Book links   This website offers books, links, and resources to help you find the money you need for your education. For more information, visit www.scholarstuff.com.

Catalog of Federal Domestic Assistance (CFDA)   This is the federal government's guide to all funding programs. The catalog is a good place to start a grants search for federal funding. The CFDA number consists of two digits that identify the agency (for example, the Education Department is 84 and the Health and Human Services Department is 93). Visit its website for more information: www.cfda.gov.

College Financial Aid Handbook   This handbook is published by the American Legion and costs $3. To order, write National Emblem Sales, P.O. Box 1050, Indianapolis, IN 46206 or call 317-630-1200.

Community of Science   Federally funded research on science topics is the focus of this website. Visit it for more information: www.cos.com.

Complete College Financing Guide   This guide is published by Barron's and costs $14.95. Call 1-800-645-3476 to order.

Don't Miss Out: The Ambitious Student's Guide to Financial Aid   This guide is published by Octameron Association and costs $8. Call 703-836-5480 to order.

FinAid Newsletter   Those seeking financial assistance and other information regarding grants, scholarships, and loans for college attendance will be interested in subscribing to this free electronic newsletter (*FinAid Newsletter*). Visit its website for more information: www.finaid.org.

How to Buy a College Education   This guide is published by the Access Group and costs $14.95. Call 612-941-7103 to order.

Meeting College Costs: What You Need to Know Before Your Child and Your Money Leave Home   This guide is published by the College Board and costs $13.95. Call 1-800-323-7155 to order.

Paying for College: A Guide for Parents   This guide is published by the College Board and costs $14.95. Call 1-800-323-7155 to order.

Philanthropy Journal   Philanthropy topics and an extensive meta-index of links to other sites are presented in this website. Visit it for more information: www. philanthropyjournal.org.

Software links   This website sells books and software for searching out sources of scholarships. Visit the site for more information: www.educationpage.com.

The Student's Guide: Five Federal Financial Aid Programs   This free government publication is available from the Consumer Information Center, Dept. 511S, Pueblo, CO 81009.

Top 10 Financial Aid Questions   This is a free document published by the National Association for College Admission Counseling. Call 703-836-2222 or write NACAC, 1631 Prince St., Alexandria, VA 22314-2818.

USA Today—Financial Aid for College: A Quick Guide to Everything You Need to Know   This guide is published by Peterson and costs $8.95. Call 1-800-EDU-DATA (1-800-338-3282) to order.

Scholarships, Grants, and Fellowships

There are literally thousands of scholarships, grants, and fellowships that you can apply for if you know where to find them. Fortunately, most funding opportunities are listed in one or more of several databases that you can access over the Internet. In this section, we have identified the best sites from which to start your search.

Arts and writing awards   Information on one of the most prestigious arts recognition programs in the country is offered by Scholastic Inc. Over 1,000 awards are given annually. Visit the company's website for more information: www.scholastic.com/artandwritingawards.

Children's Scholarship Fund   This fund provides educational opportunities for low-income children. Visit its website for more information: www.scholarshipfund.org/index.asp.

College admissions scholarships   Scholarships and grants related to college admissions are offered through this website. For more information, visit collegeapps.about.com.

College Board   Free online scholarship search service includes aid programs from 3,300 sponsors and also features college and career search capabilities. Visit its website for more information: apps.collegeboard.com/cbsearch_ss/welcome.jsp.

College Scholarships   Free scholarships are added to this website every month (since 1995) for undergraduate, graduate, and international students. Visit the site for more information: www.collegescholarships.com.

CollegeNet Mach25 Scholarship Database   This website features over 500,000 scholarships from 1,500 sponsoring organizations. The site allows students to save listings and create letters requesting more information. For more information, visit www.collegenet.com/mach25.

Financial aid information   This website provides links to sources of information about student financial aid. It is maintained by Mark Kantrowitz, author of the *Prentice Hall Guide to Scholarships and Fellowships for Math and Science Students*. It includes FastWEB (which stands for Financial Aid Search Through the WEB), a searchable database of more than 180,000 private-sector scholarships, fellowships, grants, and loans. Visit the site for more information: www.finaid.org.

Florida scholarships   Statewide scholarship programs for Florida students are covered in this website. Visit the site for more information: www.floridaleader.com/soty.

Foundation Center   The Foundation Center website contains information about foundations and corporate grant makers, philanthropic news, and frequently asked questions about grants and foundations. Visit the site for more information: www. fdncenter.org.

Foundation Directory   This directory is an annual reference source for information about private and community grant-making foundations in the United States. It provides basic descriptions and current fiscal data for the nation's largest foundations. For a free catalogue, write to the Foundation Center, 79 Fifth Ave., New York, NY 10003-3076 or call 1-800-424-9836.

Free scholarship databases   In addition to searching FastWeb, you may want to search one of the other free scholarship databases. Visit this website for more information: www.finaid.org/scholarships/other.phtml.

FreeScholarships.Com   Win free scholarship money for school through this website at www.freescholarships.com.

Fresch Scholarships   This is an online database for thousands of sources of scholarships. It has tips on applying for and winning scholarships, and volunteers will answer your financial aid and scholarship questions. Visit the website for more information: www.freschinfo.com.

Grantsmanship Center   This website contains information about the center and its magazine, grant resources, and training classes. There are federal grant announcements and links to other grant sites. Visit the site for more information: www.tgci.com.

GrantsNet Scholarships   GrantsNet offers funding opportunities in the biological and medical sciences. Visit its website for more information: www.grantsnet.org.

Guide Star   This free service has information on the scholarship programs of thousands of American nonprofit organizations. The website also features news stories on philanthropy. For more information, visit www.guidestar.org.

McDonald's Scholarships   McDonald's Arching Into Education Scholarship program has more than $425,000 in scholarships available for students in the New York/New Jersey/Connecticut tri-state area who are employed by McDonald's. Visit its website for more information: www.mcdonaldsnymetro.com/html/rmhc_scholarships.html.

Financial Aid Resource Center   This is a comprehensive guide to financial aid and scholarships for college. Visit the website for more information: www.theoldschool.org.

FastWeb This is a free web version of the Scholarship Resource Network (SRN) database. The SRN database focuses on private-sector, non-need-based aid and includes numerous scholarship opportunities. To find out about contests, grants, and other aid options, visit www.studentservices.com.

Scholastic Aptitude Tests (SAT, PSAT, ACT)

Most of the country's major colleges and universities require students to take an aptitude test as part of their admissions requirement. Your score on these tests could be the determining factor as to whether or not you will be admitted. This section lists websites that will help you become familiar with the test and practice on demonstration tests.

American College Test (ACT) This test is published by American College Testing to measure a student's ability in math, verbal comprehension, and problem solving. Usually students take this test during their junior or senior year of high school. All the studying in the world won't mean a thing on test day unless you know how to take the test. Much of what you need to know on the ACT is common sense. If you want to learn more about the test, visit this website: www.petersons.com and click on the "Select a Test" option on the main menus.

Practice SAT (PSAT) tests The College Board provides a sample SAT test in its booklet "Taking the SAT by Flashpoints." Flashpoints is a comprehensive SAT study system that will familiarize you with the SAT exam format while sharpening your critical-reading and math reasoning skills. In addition, the College Board provides detailed explanations designed to improve your understanding of the exam material. By testing yourself with Flashpoints, you'll quickly be able to identify your strengths and weaknesses. This knowledge will enable you to focus on the types of questions and the subject areas you need to review most. Studying with Flashpoints will reinforce your test-taking skills and your retention of the information in an easy-to-use flashcard format. Visit this website for more information: www.nalsa.com/fpinfo.html.

SAT registration Register online for any SAT program test. New features make it faster and more convenient than ever. Visit this website for more information: www.collegeboard.com/sat/html/satform.html.

Women's Financial Aid Publications

Many excellent publications recommend funding sources for women students. In addition to the range of financial aid available to all qualifying students, many aid programs are specifically for women.

Directory of Financial Aids for Women by Dr. Gail Ann Schlachter, Reference Service Press, 1100 Industrial Rd., Suite 9, San Carlos, CA 94070.

Happier by Degrees: A College Re-Entry Guide for Women by Pam Mendelsohn, P.O. Box 4597, Arcata, CA 95518.

Higher Education Opportunities for Minorities and Women, available from the U.S. Department of Education, Superintendent of Documents, P.O. Box 37194, Pittsburgh, PA 15250-7954, call 202-512-1800, or fax 202-512-2250.

How to Get Money for Research by Mary Rubin, The Feminist Press, P.O. Box 1645, Hagerstown, MD 21741.

Professional Women's Groups, available from the American Association of University Women, 2401 Virginia Ave. NW, Washington, D.C. 20007.

Resources for Women in Science, free from the Association for Women in Science, 1346 Connecticut Ave. NW, Washington, D.C. 20036.

Women's Organizations: A National Directory, available from Garrett Park Press, P.O. Box 190, Garrett Park, MD 20896.

Women's Sports Foundation College Scholarship Guide, available from the Women's Sports Foundation, 342 Madison Ave., Suite 728, New York, NY 10173.

Work-Study and Co-Op Programs

Work-study is a need-based program in which the federal government pays 50 percent of the student's wages for private sector work and 70 percent for on-campus employment. Work-study is administered by college financial aid offices. For state-funded programs, contact your state's Department of Education, listed by state in Appendix C.

Cooperative education (co-op) programs are not based on financial need. They combine classroom work with jobs in the private sector as well as for the federal government (the largest employer of co-op students).

Work-Study

Most work-study programs are determined by a needs analysis and provide employment on campus for students who qualify. Priority will be given to students who have completed the necessary paperwork by June 1. You generally work 20 hours per week. Work-study grants of up to $5,000 per year are available to students who have a demonstrated financial need. Positions are available both on and off campus. The application process and hiring of work-study students takes place in August and September.

In addition to applying for work-study at your college's financial aid office or state Department of Education, the following website offers application instructions to students who are interested in applying for a work-study program. It also offers links to other financial aid programs. Visit it at www.ed.gov/programs/fws/index.html.

Penn State Work-Study Program   Most of the major colleges and universities offer work-study programs to their students. However, the programs vary significantly between the different institutions. Some are excellent, while others are, at best, fair. Penn State offers one of the best work-study programs in the country. Visit its website at www.psu.edu/dept/studentaid/ to learn more about the program. Then contact the financial aid office at the college(s) you're interested in attending to see what they have to offer and how it compares with this program.

Co-Op Programs

Co-op education students alternate between full-time work and full-time study, and they are paid during their work term to help offset the costs of tuition. Co-op education also provides career-related experience that extends the learning process beyond the limitations of the classroom and is valuable for entering the job market. Check with your state's financial aid office or Department of Education (listed by state in Appendix C) for information about programs in your state.

Approximately a thousand U.S. colleges and universities have co-op programs, so also check with your college's financial aid office, or contact the following:

National Commission for Cooperative Education
360 Huntington Ave., 384 CP
Boston, MA 02115-5096
617-373-3770

See if a trade association related to your field is listed under "Associations Related to Financial Aid" in this directory, and find out if any companies in your area participate in work-study programs.

Another good resource is *Gale Encyclopedia of Associations*, which lists trade associations for every field and area of business.

Eberly College of Science Co-Op Program   An example of a good resource is the Eberly College of Science Co-op Program. This program places students in government labs or industry, for pay and academic credit. Through the program, students can acquire hands-on experience in real-life situations. Co-op opportunities include, for example, astronomy research that emphasizes computer skills at government and industrial positions. Students planning to take advantage of this program should begin applying for co-op positions during their sophomore year for co-op rotations in the following summer or fall. For further information, contact:

Dr. David Burrows
Office of Cooperative Education
520 Thomas Building
University Park, PA 16802

NASA Johnson Space Center (JSC) Cooperative Education Program   The Cooperative Education Program at JSC is open to undergraduate and graduate students from around the country. As a co-op student, you alternate semesters at school with semesters at JSC working in a paid, full-time position directly related to your field of study. See JSC's website to learn more about the program: www.nasa.gov/centers/johnson/home/index.html.

State Department of Education Directory

State Department of Education agencies, colleges, and universities all play an important role in the financial aid program. They are responsible for distributing the aid money that has been collected by the federal government and passed on to them. The state agencies and educational institutions must follow strict federal guidelines and regulations as they disperse the money.

In addition to the federal financial aid program, all states and most colleges offer their own independent financial aid programs to supplement the federal programs. That's why we decided to create this separate appendix dedicated to state financial aid. Be sure you know about every financial aid program offered in your state so that you can take maximum advantage of any program that you qualify for. States are more generous than the federal government with their financial aid funds; thus, you have a better chance of qualifying for a state program. State Departments of Education are sources of information for state grants, work-study programs, and minority programs. They also administer prepaid tuition plans in states that participate in them. See the "Prepaid Tuition Plans" section of Appendix B to see if your state is one of them.

Alabama

Department of Education
Gordon Persons Building
50 N. Ripley Street
P.O. Box 302101
Montgomery, AL 36130
334-242-9700
www.alsde.edu

Alaska

Department of Education
801 W. 10th Street
Juneau, AK 99801-1894
907-465-2800
www.eed.state.ak.us

Arizona

Department of Education
United Student Aid Group
Arizona Education Loan Program
1535 W. Jefferson Street
Phoenix, AZ 85007
602-542-3186
www.ade.state.az.us

Arkansas

Department of Education
#4 Capitol Mall
State Education Building
Little Rock, AR 72201
501-682-4260
Arkedu.state.ar.us

California

Department of Education
1430 H Street
Sacramento, CA 95814
916-319-0800
www.cde.ca.gov

Colorado

Department of Education
Office of the Colorado State Board
of Education
201 E. Colfax Avenue
Denver, CO 80203
303-866-6600
www.cde.state.co.us

Connecticut

Department of Education
165 Capitol Avenue
Hartford, CT 06145
860-713-6543
www.state.ct.us/sde

Delaware

Department of Education
401 Federal Street, Suite 2
Dover, DE 19901
302-739-4654
www.doe.state.de.us

District of Columbia

U. S. Department of Education
400 Maryland Avenue, SW
Washington, D.C. 20202-0498
1-800-872-5327
www.ed.gov

Florida

Department of Education
325 W. Gaines Street
Tallahassee, FL 32399
850-245-0505
www.fldoe.org

Georgia

Department of Education
1970 Twin Towers East
Atlanta, GA 30334-5040
404-657-9954
www.public.doe.k12.ga.us

Hawaii

Department of Education
1390 Miller Street
Honolulu, HI 96804
808-586-3349
www.doe.k12.us

Idaho

Department of Education
650 W. State Street
P.O. Box 83720
Boise, ID 83720-0027
208-332-6800
www.sde.idaho.gov

Illinois

Department of Education
100 N. First Street
Springfield, IL 62777
866-262.6663
www.isbe.state.il.us

Indiana

Department of Education
State House Room 229
Indianapolis, IN 46204
317-232-0570
www.doe.state.in.us

Iowa

Department of Education
400 E. 14th Street
Des Moines, IA 50319
515-281-3575
www.state.ia.us

Kansas

Department of Education
120 SE 10th Avenue
Topeka, KS 66612-1182
785-296-3201
Ksbe.state.ks.us

Kentucky

Department of Education
500 Mero Street
Frankfort, KY 40601
502-564-4770
www.kde.state.ky.us

Louisiana

Department of Education
P.O. Box 44064
Baton Rouge, LA 70804
877-453-2721
www.doe.state.la.us

Maine

Department of Education
23 Station House Station
Augusta, ME 04333-0023
207-624-6600
www.maine.gov/education

Maryland

Department of Education
200 W. Baltimore Street
Baltimore, MD 21201
410-767-0600
www.marylandpublicschools.org

Massachusetts

Department of Education
350 Main Street
Malden, MA 02148-5023
781-338-3000
www.doe.mass.edu

Michigan

Department of Education
608 W Allegan Street
Lansing, MI 48909
517-373-3324
www.michigan.gov/mde

Minnesota

Department of Education
1500 Highway 36 West
Roseville, MN 55113
651-582-8200
www.education.state.mn.us/mde

Mississippi

Department of Education
P.O. Box 771
Jackson, MS 39205
601-359-1750
www.mde.k12.ms.us

Missouri

Department of Education
P.O. Box 480
Jefferson City, MO 65102
573-751-4212
www.dese.mo.gov

Montana

Department of Education
Office of Public Instruction
P.O. Box 200113
Helena, MT 59620-2501
406-444-2511
www.mt.gov/education.asp

Nebraska

Department of Education
301 Centennial Mall South
Lincoln, NE 68501
402-471-2295
www.nde.state.ne.us

Nevada

Department of Education
700 E. 5th Street
Carson City, NV 89701
775-687-9200
www.doe.nv.gov

New Hampshire

Department of Education
101 Pleasant Street
Concord, NH 03301
603-271-3739

New Jersey

Department of Education
4 Quakerbridge Plaza
Trenton, NJ 08625
609-292-1083
www.ed.state.nh.us/education

New Mexico

Department of Education
Special Education Office
State Education Building
Santa Fe, NM 87501
505-827-5800
www.sda.state.nm.us

New York

Department of Education
Boards of Cooperative Educational
Services
Education Building, Room 503
Albany, NY 12234
518-474-3852
www.nysed.gov

North Carolina

Department of Education
Department of Public Instruction
301 N. Wilmington Street
Raleigh, NC 27601
919-807-3300
www.dpi.state.nc.us

North Dakota

Department of Education
State Capitol
600 E. Boulevard Avenue
Bismarck, ND 58505
701-328-2260
www.dpi.state.nd.us

Ohio

Department of Education
25 S. Front Street, Room 810
Columbus, OH 43215-4183
614-644-6338
www.ode.state.oh.uss

Oklahoma

Department of Education
2500 N. Lincoln Boulevard
Oklahoma City, OK 73105-4599
405-521-3301
www.sde.state.ok.us

Oregon

Department of Education
255 Capitol Street NE
Salem, OR 97310-0203
503-378-3569
www.ode.state.or.us

Pennsylvania

Department of Education
333 Market Street
Harrisburg, PA 17126-0333
717-783-6788
www.pde.state.pa.us

Rhode Island

Department of Education
255 Westminster Street
Providence, RI 02903
401-222-4600
www.ridoe.net

South Carolina

Department of Education
1429 Senate Street
Columbia, SC 29201
803-734-8500
www.sde.state.sc.us

South Dakota

Department of Education
700 Governor's Drive
Pierre, SD 57501
605-773-3134
www.doe.sd.gov

Tennessee

Department of Education
9th Floor Andrew Johnson Tower
710 James Robertson Parkway
Nashville, TN 37243
615-741-2733
www.state.tn.us

Texas

Department of Education
1701 N Congress Avenue
Austin, TX 78701-2603
512-463-9734
www.tea.state.tx.us

Utah

Department of Education
3 Triad Center
250 E 500 Street
Salt Lake City, UT 84111
801-321-7200
www.usoe.k12.ut.us

Vermont

Department of Education
Office of the Governor
120 State Street
Montpelier, VT 05620
802-828-3333
www.education.vermont.gov

Virginia

Department of Education
James Monroe Building, 9th Floor
101 N. 14th Street
Richmond, VA 23219
804-225-2600
www.pen.k12.va.us

Washington

Department of Education
Superintendent of Public Instruction
Old Capitol Building
P.O. Box 47200
Olympia, WA 98504
360-725-6025
www.k12.wa.us

West Virginia

Department of Education

West Virginia Department of Education

1900 Kanawha Boulevard

Index